The Complete Idiot's Reference Card

Command-Key Roundup

Here's a handy-dandy table of the command-key combinations. Practice them when you have a chance—they're really time-savers.

Action	Key Combination
Open any icon	Double-click on the icon, or select the icon, and then press ⌘-↓.
Copy an icon into another folder (without moving the original)	Hold down the Option key while dragging the icon.
Clean up selected icons in a window	Hold down the Shift key while selecting Clean Up from the Special menu.
Clean up and Sort icons alphabetically	Hold down the Option key while selecting Clean Up from the Special menu.
Select an icon by name	Type the first few letters of the name.
Select the next icon, alphabetically	Press the Tab key.
Select the previous icon, alphabetically	Press the Shift and Tab keys.
Select an icon to the right or left (in Icon views)	Press → or ←.
Select icon above or below (any view)	Press ↑ or ↓.
Select multiple icons	Shift-click on the icons, or drag-select to enclose icons.
Make desktop active	Press ⌘-Shift-↑.
Close all windows	Press the Option key while selecting Close under File menu, or press the Option key while clicking on the Close Box.
Move window without making it active	Hold down the ⌘ key while dragging the window's title bar.
Display window's lineage	Hold down the ⌘ key while clicking on the window title.
Open a window's parent window	Press ⌘-↑.
Close window after opening an icon in it	Hold down the Option key while selecting Open from File menu, or hold down the Option key while double-clicking on the icon.
Zoom window to full screen size	Hold down the Option key while clicking on its Zoom Box.

Zip!

There are also shortcuts for certain commands. Use these to perform Macintosh actions in a flash.

New Folder (file)	⌘-N	Paste	⌘-V
Open	⌘-O	Select All	⌘-A
Close Window	⌘-W	Print	⌘-P
Save	⌘-S	Find	⌘-F
Cut	⌘-X	Undo	⌘-Z
Copy	⌘-C		

tear here

Mouse Movements

Point   Move the mouse pointer so that it rests on a specific screen location.

Click   Quickly press and release the left mouse button.

Double-click   Quickly press and release the left mouse button twice in succession.

Drag   Press and hold down the left mouse button, and then move the mouse.

When Things Go Flaky

If you have any trouble with your Mac, the first thing you should do is check the obvious:

- Is everything plugged in and turned on?
- Are cables connected securely to your Mac and the peripherals?
- Are the correct cables plugged into the correct peripherals?
- If it's a monitor problem (such as no picture), check the contrast and brightness controls.
- Are you using the right software for the hardware (the correct printer driver in the Chooser, the right telecommunications software for the service, and so on)?
- What's the dumbest thing you could have forgotten to do? Check that, too.

Cool Tip #1

You can manually resize any window to the exact size you'd like with the **Size Box**. It's in the lower right-hand corner of every window. Just drag the Size Box until the window is the size you want it.

Cool Tip #2

That little box in the upper left-hand corner of a window is the **Close Box**. When you click on it, the window closes.

Cool Tip #3

If you want to see every item in a window, you can quickly size the window to fit exactly around everything by clicking on the **Zoom Box**. It's in the upper right-hand corner of the window.

alpha books

The Complete IDIOT'S Guide to THE MAC

by John Pivovarnick

alpha books

A Division of Prentice Hall Computer Publishing
201 W. 103rd Street, Indianapolis, Indiana 46290 USA

International Standard Book Number:1-56761-395-0
Library of Congress Catalog Card Number: 93-71512

95 94   9 8 7 6 5 4 3

Interpretation of the printing code: the rightmost number of the first series of numbers is the year of the book's printing; the rightmost number of the second series of numbers is the number of the book's printing. For example, a printing code of 93-1 shows that the first printing of the book occurred in 1993.

Printed in the United States of America

Publisher
Marie Butler-Knight

Managing Editor
Elizabeth Keaffaber

Product Development Manager
Faithe Wempen

Acquisitions Manager
Barry Pruett

Development Editor
Kelly Oliver

Manuscript Editor
San Dee Phillips

Cover Designer
Scott Cook

Designer
Barb Webster

Indexer
Jennifer Eberhardt

Production Team
*Gary Adair, Diana Bigham-Griffin, Katy Bodenmiller, Brad Chinn,
Kim Cofer, Meshell Dinn, Terri Edwards, Mark Enochs,
Stephanie Gregory, Jenny Kucera, Beth Rago, Marc Shecter, Greg Simsic*

Special thanks to Stephen Poland for ensuring the technical accuracy of this book.

Contents at a Glance

Contents

Introduction
The Complete Idiot

The following is an excerpt from the transcript of the December 1, 1989, meeting of the CIA: *Complete Idiot's Anonymous*. The names have been changed to protect the guilty.

J: Hi. My name's John . . . no, really, it *is* . . . and I'm an idiot.

CIA: Hi, John!

J: I didn't realize until a couple of years ago how big an idiot I really am.

CIA: How many years ago was that?

J: (mutters something)

CIA: How many years?

J: Ten years, all right? Ten—are you happy?

CIA: Calm down. No one's trying to embarrass you. Admitting your idiocy is an important first step.

J: I'm sorry . . . it's just (whimpers). . . .

CIA: It's okay. What made you think you had a problem?

J: That darn computer.

CIA: Oooooooh. Computer.

J: I wouldn't read manuals. I wouldn't ask questions. I'd just try to figure things out on my own. You know, by trial and error. Mostly error.

CIA: And?

J: And, when I hit a problem I couldn't fake my way through, then I'd read the manual. It didn't help. I could barely understand them (sobbing). After ten years, I still can't get my first printer to underline or do boldface!

CIA: (nods and murmurs of agreement) So what happened?

J: I did what any self-respecting idiot would do. I bought another printer.

CIA: Tsk-tsk. You've got it bad.

J: Gosh, I feel better just admitting that.

CIA: Thanks for sharing, John.

It Takes One to Know One

I don't know how often I've said it: "I feel like such an idiot." At least a dozen times a day—more if I was heavily into some project or another. But that was before I got help, before I admitted I am an idiot and started on the road to recovery.

When a computer—even a plug-and-play Macintosh—smells the fear on you, it pushes at it and pushes at it until you're ready to snap, or until you show it who's boss.

I know. I've been there. That story about the printer was true. I had that sucker for almost six years, and I couldn't get the bloody thing to do what I wanted. If I got it to underline, I couldn't get it to stop. If I got it to do letter-quality printing, I couldn't get it to do italics. I was ready to take a baseball bat to it.

Instead, I bought a new printer, and things have gone swimmingly. But buying new equipment is not a practical solution for most problems. I learned that the hard way, too.

I've learned a lot of things on my personal road to recovery. I fell into a lot of traps and pitfalls I'd like to see you avoid.

If I could, I'd include a big picture of me from my brazen idiot days, with bags under my eyes and cowlicked hair. There would be three-inch-tall red letters stamped over my face, warning everyone: DON'T LET THIS HAPPEN TO YOU!

Instead, let me pass on the tips and tricks I've learned about dealing with computers in general, and Macs in particular. Here comes the first tip, and it's a biggie. Keep it in mind as you go through the rest of the book:

You are not the idiot. The *Macintosh* is the idiot.

Much as it pains me to say this about a machine I dearly love, Macs are stupid. *Stoo*-pid! As simple and elegant as they are, they are still only machines. They do *exactly* what they're told to do. If you tell them to do two conflicting things at once, that dopey little machine will try it's best to do both, even if it blows up in the process.

If there is any problem you or I have in dealing with our Macs, it's that we're too smart. *We* know what we want to do, and *how* we want to do it. If we happen to forget an important step, well, that's okay. We can improvise and make it up as we go along.

If you try to get a Mac to keep step with the way your mind leaps around, it goes nuts. Why? Because they can't figure things out. Macs don't think, "Oh, he must have meant this," and then just do it. They can only do exactly what you tell them to do, with the tools (software) you give them to do it. If the information or the tools aren't appropriate to the job, the Mac (or any computer) will crash.

When they crash, *we* feel like idiots. That's not the way it should be. We're just not talking down to the Mac's level. Remember:

- ☞ Macs take everything literally.
- ☞ You have to learn to think like a Mac.
- ☞ Therefore, *you* have to take everything literally.

How's that for logic? Sr. Margo (my high school geometry teacher) would be so proud.

The aim of this book, aside from enlightening and entertaining you, is to show you how your Mac works, thinks, and does things. You will learn how to tell it exactly what you want it to do, without giving it (or you) a nervous breakdown.

How to Use This Book

Okay, we've established that Macs are stupid and that you have to learn how to deal with your Mac in a way it can understand. Now that all that's taken care of, here's how to use this book.

If I were you (which I'm not), I'd read or skim the book once straight through, and then I'd put it beside my Mac where it was within easy reach for questions or problems when they crop up.

The book is organized (I hope) logically. Part I shows you how to unpack and assemble your Mac. If your Mac is already up and running, you can probably skim or skip ahead to Part II.

Part II deals exclusively with Mac basics: navigating the Finder, formatting disks, copying files and folders, moving things around, throwing junk away, and keeping things clean and safe. It also explains the ins and outs of fonts and printing. All this good stuff lays the groundwork for Part III.

Part III covers Mac *applications* (or programs). You'll find the scoop on the stuff that came with your Mac (such as Desk Accessories, TeachText, and so on), everything from starting them up and using them to shutting them down. Part III also rounds up and reviews all the major application and hardware types that *didn't* come with your Mac; the stuff that, if you want it, you have to go out and buy.

Part IV is a mixed bag. It gives you advice on where you can go with your Mac in the future, how to shop for more stuff, and how to deal with the peculiarities of PowerBooks. There's a big, fat appendix on troubleshooting some of the most common problems that crop up in Macintosh computing.

Let's move on. Everyone, stay together, and remember where you parked your car.

Convenient Conventions

The thing I like most about writing this stuff is I get to tell people what to do. To make it easier for you to follow what I want you to do, there are several conventions used throughout the book. (You thought I was going to take a cheap shot at the Shriners or something, didn't you?)

If I want you to type something, I'll say something clever, like:

Type this: **Poop Happens.**

And I'll expect you to type whatever comes after "Type this:". I'll put it in **boldface** so it's easy to spot. In this example, for some reason, I want you to type "Poop Happens." I don't know *why* I'd want you to type that, it's just an example.

If I want you to press a couple of keys on your keyboard at the same time, I'll say:

Press: ⌘-**W**

That means press and hold down the ⌘ key (also known as the Command key, or as the key with the little squiggle that looks like a four-petaled flower on it—it all depends on what keyboard you have). While you're holding that key down, press the second key. In this example, it's the **W**.

These key-combinations are *very* handy. The ⌘-W combination will close a window in almost *any* Mac application. You'll be hearing more about them later.

You should know that the first key of most key combinations will invariably be one of three: either the ⌘/Command/ Flower-thingy key, the Control key, or the Option key. They're usually located at the right or left of the Spacebar. Find them now; I'll wait.

When it comes to mousing around, I'll ask you to click, double-click, or even triple-click on things. That means I'll want you to move the mouse pointer to something, then click once, twice, or three times on it.

If it's an icon, I'll say, "Double-click on the System Folder (or whatever) icon." If it's a menu item, I'll say, "Click on the **File** (or whatever) menu." If it's a button in a dialog box, I'll say "Click on the **Cancel** (or whatever) button."

Notice how I cleverly made the words **File** and **Cancel** bold? That's a clue that I'm expecting you to *do* something with that menu item or button.

Finally, I may give you a list of several things to do. They'll show up in a numbered list like this:

1. Click on the **Special** menu, and hold down the mouse button.

2. With mouse button still pressed, move the pointer down the menu until the **Empty Trash** item is highlighted.

3. Release the mouse button.

If none of this pointing, clicking, and selecting means anything to you, don't worry. I'll go over every excruciating detail in Chapter 4, before you need to do any of it. Don't panic.

Geekazoid Stuff You Can Ignore

As if actually expecting you to *do* stuff wasn't bad enough, I'm also going to give you the opportunity to *learn* things that go above and beyond the call of duty.

None of it is absolutely, positively essential. The world will *not* end if you ignore it, but it can make your computing life a little easier, maybe even more fun. If you're interested, you'll find knowledge in boxes like these:

These explain some of the more technical information on the Macintosh. You'll find some behind-the-scenes information about the working of Macs and applications presented in a painless way. It may interest you, it may not. If it *does* interest you, you may be a potential propeller-head.

These define some of the more technical terms in ways a non-propeller-head can understand. If nothing else, you'll be able to work words like **propeller-head** into any conversation.

Propeller-head: An adjective used to describe someone fascinated by the technical minutiae of computing. From the famous propeller beanies kids used to wear. Also known as **toy brains**.

These contain quick tips and work-arounds that save you time and keep you from tearing your hair out. That ⌘-W key combination that closes a window would fit in well here.

These contain warnings and other helpful information for when things go worng— er . . . *wrong.*

By the Way . . .

These contain amusing asides and other tangential information that is *somehow* (however vaguely) related to the topic at hand, but doesn't quite fit in anywhere else.

On Your Marks

All right, then. Pencils on the table. Don't turn the page until I say so. Work at your own pace, and be sure to stay within the lines. Remember, this is *not* a test.

Okay. Turn the page.

Part I
Some Assembly Required

When I put my Mac together the first time, it took all of twenty minutes to get it unpacked, hooked up, and plugged in. All right, maybe half an hour, tops, including looking through the manuals. Compare that with my partner's new 486 IBM clone that's been sitting gathering dust for a week while I tried to figure out how to install the hard drives in a bay without brackets. The manual is sooo helpful. It says crystal clear things like: "install the hard drive in the bay." Duh! I know that, but like the old Sippie Wallace song says, "Oh, baby, but you got to know how."

So, I'm going to tell you how.

If your Macintosh is already together and humming on your desk, you may talk quietly among yourselves and skip to Part 2.

Chapter 1

The Top 10 Things You Should Know About Your Macintosh

10. It isn't a DOS machine. A Mac will not harm you.

Easy-to-use is easy to say (I think that's how Windows coasted by all these years), but the Mac is truly easy to use. From dealing with files and folders, to adding on hardware and software, the Mac remains the plug-and-play beauty it was when in first came out in 1984. Don't panic. You picked the right machine.

9. You can have your Macintosh up and running in very little time (see Chapter 2).

If it takes you more than 20–40 minutes to hook your Mac up, I'll be very surprised. I know people who are such complete idiots that I wonder how they find their way home at night. I've seen these people set up their Macs in 30 minutes or less.

The little pictures on the ports and plugs really help. If you can figure out what those international traffic signs mean (you know, the ones with the little stick figures on them rather than words), you can put a Mac together.

8. No matter what the DOS-heads say, the Mac is not a toy. The fact that even children can master the basics in no time just annoys them. (See Chapter 5.) Macs are serious, capable machines that can handle just about any task you can throw at them (given the right hardware and software tools). They're appropriate for personal, educational, home, business, and even personal home-business use.

While they are serious machines, they should not be taken seriously. They're designed to be easy to use and fun to use. You shouldn't get gray hair trying to type up a report or a shopping list—or anything else for that matter.

7. You have to format floppy disks before you can use them to store junk.

Chapter 9 goes over this stuff in excruciating detail—well, I hope it isn't excruciating, but it is, shall we say, complete.

The beauty of Macintosh is that since you *shouldn't* use a disk that hasn't been formatted, you *can't* use a disk that hasn't been formatted. If you happen to forget that little fact, your Mac will politely remind you.

6. You can customize the way your Mac works and looks to suit yourself.

My Mac has custom icons all over the place, custom startup screens (to replace that boring "Welcome to Macintosh"), and a fleet of funky sounds. I have other customizing doo-dads (extensions and control panels) out the wazoo. I rotate the custom features in and out of use to suit my mood—and I'll be the first one to tell you, I can be pretty moody.

My favorites include: a startup screen featuring Michelangelo's Creation of Man scene from the Sistine chapel; Ren & Stimpy disk icons, and a pile of sounds from the *Wizard of Oz*. ("Are you a good witch, or a bad witch?")

5. You can work with your Mac right out of the box: you already have some software! (See Chapter 12.)

You may not have enough software to write the Great American Novel, but you certainly have enough to tackle the Great American Memo or Thank-You Note.

If you were lucky (or smart), you bought a Mac that came bundled with some additional software to get you started (one of the integrated Works packages), in which case, you probably *can* tackle the Great American Novel. I'd like an autographed copy, please.

4. There's a full range of software available for your Mac, suitable for home, business, or educational uses. (See Chapter 13.)

3. Accessories can be added to Macs easily, such as CD-ROM drives, scanners, and other exciting equipment. (See Chapter 14.)

In addition to the software and hardware roundups in Chapters 12, 13, and 14, Chapter 19 will give you some pointers on how to shop.

For the terminally curious, there's even parts of Chapter 19 devoted to the hardware and software I own, and what I'd spring for if someone else was footing the bill (like that would happen).

When it comes to shopping, I've been lucky. I've never actually out-and-out hated something I paid good money for—even though I tend to buy things against the recommendations of the so-called gurus.

There is software and hardware that I hate, but I don't own it. Why would I pay for something I know I don't like?

2. Once you learn a standard command in one application, you'll know it for all Mac applications. (See Chapter 6.)

1. Lighten up! This is Macintosh. It's supposed to be the fun one.

Computing *can* be a scary and very serious business; especially if your livelihood or sanity depends upon it. That's a given. But you shouldn't have to fight with your computer to get your very important work done.

You'll find a lot of space and words in this book devoted to what to do when things go wrong. It doesn't mean that because I spend a lot of time talking about bad things that can happen, you'll be spending a lot of time dealing with them, too.

Call it an ounce of prevention, and stop worrying. This stuff is easy, once you get the hang of it.

Chapter 2
Mac-in-the-Box

In This Chapter

- ☛ Deciding where to put the darn thing
- ☛ Power considerations
- ☛ Planning for future expansion

There you stand in a pile of Apple's environmentally correct, natural, brown cardboard boxes. The credit card in your wallet is still tingling from paying for your Mac, and now you are confronted with putting this puppy together.

Before you do anything else, walk away from the boxes. Don't even look at them. Don't cut the packing tape, don't jiggle the funny little box to see what's inside.

Instead, go to the room where you're going to set up your computer, and check it out.

Where to Set Up

Ideally, and I do mean *ideally*, as "in the best of all possible worlds," which we all know this is, the room you set your Mac up in should be an official-type office. A place where you and all those who have access to your Mac can work or play in peace and quiet. A room with a door that closes firmly and a window that opens fully and looks out on an idyllic scene.

But, because that's not always possible, there are some simple guidelines for figuring out where to set up.

First, be sure your little corner of the world is out of a high-traffic area. A bedroom would be ideal if no one shares your bedroom or your Mac. Someone might have a hard time sleeping with the constant clickety-clack of keys in the middle of the night. A dining room table would be good, too, if you never actually use it for dining.

This discussion brings us to the second consideration: be sure it's a space where the Mac can stay put—unless you bought a Classic or one of the other compact models (like the Color Classic, or a real classic like the SE/30) that are easily moved. Constant assembling and reassembling causes wear and tear on your connectors and cables. Plus, the more often you *move* something heavy, the more chances you have to *drop* something heavy.

Third: the whole table issue. You just spent a largish chunk of change on a Macintosh; why would you want to set it up on a $15 card table? It isn't the price of the card table, but the design. The legs fold up. The top is thick cardboard.

Card tables are made to stand up to such vigorous use as holding 52 playing cards, maybe a pile of chips (poker and/or potato), some beverages, some dips (usually something like sour cream and chive, but often the players are dips, too, at least in my house), and that's about it. The average Macintosh monitor weighs more than 50–100 decks of playing cards, and a 12-inch monitor weighs about 25 pounds. Add to that a CPU, keyboard, printer—well, you get the idea. Don't trust your expensive techno-toys to pressed cardboard and folding legs. Use a real table.

You don't have to spend a bazillion dollars on a computer table. If *you* can sit on the table or desk without making it wobble, it is probably sturdy enough to hold your Mac—as long as you weigh more than 100 pounds. If you don't, I hate you. Go eat something.

> **By the Way . . .**
>
> Any table or desk that you can sit at comfortably—meaning your knees don't get banged up and the tabletop isn't so high you look like Lilly Tomlin doing her Edith Anne schtick— you can probably work at comfortably. The only way to be sure is to try.

If you're thinking of using a sturdy table or desk that you already own, go for it. Set up the space with a chair, even unpack the Mac's keyboard and set it on top, and try typing for a while. If it's comfortable for twenty minutes or more (even up to an hour if you're a workaholic, like me) you're probably safe setting your Mac up for keeps.

If you're going out to buy a table or desk, be sure you try them all on for size. Nothing, but nothing, can kill your productivity like uncomfortable or downright painful work conditions.

Good Light, Comfy Chair

While we're on the subject of comfort, you'll need good light (especially if you need to work at night) and a comfy chair.

Work light is a very personal issue, like how you make peanut butter and jelly sandwiches. Fights have broken out over it. Some folks I know like to work under the glare of a fluorescent desk lamp suitable for sweating confessions out of suspects. Others can work with a naked ten-watt bulb. Both of these give me headaches. I prefer a nice, bright halogen lamp, far enough away that the light doesn't glare off of my monitor, but close enough that it lights up all the things I need to see.

> ### By the Way . . .
> Pundits and office designers, have written volumes about the kind and placement of lights in a work space (ways to light your work to avoid eyestrain and headaches). If you're creating an office from the ground up, you might want to consult one of their books. Get thee to a library!

If you're cobbling together an office or work area from stuff you already have, you might want to consult the experts, but remember, your comfort is the final consideration.

SPEAK LIKE A GEEK

Ergonomics is the science of designing things to accommodate the natural shape and motion of the human body. The bridge of the Starship Enterprise is very ergonomically designed. From the Greek word "erg," ergonomics denotes a unit of work. Or, it's a cross between "ergo" and "economics" because any product that boasts "sleek, ergonomic styling" will cost 50% more than it's non-ergonomic competitor.

The same goes for comfy chairs. The experts (and I am by no means an expert on office furniture) suggest lower back support, arm rests, and adjustability, among other things, that fall under the heading ergonomics. Me, I slouch. I spin. I don't keep my feet flat on the floor. I am often forced to work with a cat in my lap. I take frequent breaks to crack my knuckles and do other things the experts don't approve of, like smoke and drink lots of coffee.

Comfort is always the final consideration. Your behind will be in that chair, not some ergonomics specialist's.

Reliable Power and the Urge to Surge

There are a few other things you need to have handy in order to run a Mac, or any computer for that matter. One of them is a convenient electrical outlet. Convenient as in close to your Mac, so you don't have to snake dangerous extension cords all over the place. Convenient as in an outlet with good wiring and reliable power, also.

Urban areas tend to have a couple of common power problems, the most common of which is *spiking*. Spiking (also called a surge) happens when the flow of electricity is uneven, sometimes a little less than normal, and then (suddenly) more than normal. If you've ever seen a light bulb dim for no good reason, then suddenly flare up brighter than ever, you have actually seen a power spike, or surge. If you've also seen that same bulb die suddenly after a spike, you've seen the damage.

One of the technological goodies invented to protect expensive electronics from the perils of power surges is called (oddly enough) *a surge protector*. Surge protectors are handy for two reasons. The obvious one is that they protect your equipment from surges and spikes. There's a small fuse inside designed to blow out before a dangerous amount of power can zap your Mac (or whatever you have plugged into it).

The second reason is a special added bonus: surge protectors come in multiple-outlet designs; I've seen them with as many as ten outlets. You can plug in all of your high-tech toys and turn them all on with the flip of the surge protector's on-switch. Very convenient.

Being able to turn on all of your Mac's peripherals (the monitor, printer, CPU, and so on) is the overriding reason for buying a surge protector. Fact is, your Mac already has a built-in surge protector, so buying another one is really not mandatory. Another fact is that I've heard of Macs with extra surge protection getting fried by power surges anyhow. Granted, they were caused by lightning striking transformers, but still, it happened. I've also heard of Macs without surge protection weathering surges very nicely, thank you. So, like life, the decision to surge protect or not is really a crap shoot.

Surge protectors range in price from about $10 to $100. The $100 jobbies have all the bells and whistles; they even have an outlet for a phone line to pass through the protector to keep your modem from being fried. But I haven't talked about modems yet, so forget I mentioned that.

Another problem is that electricity can be completely unreliable. If you live in a big metropolitan area that's subject to brown-outs—especially during air conditioner season—or in a rural area where storms and other hazards knock out your power regularly, you could be traumatized by the sudden loss of unsaved work.

There you are in the middle of writing the great American novel (or you could be ready to break through to the highest level of Lemmings, a totally addictive game) when bam! the power goes out. There goes all of your unsaved work (or the password to get you to the next level of Lemmings), and THERE'S NO WAY TO GET IT BACK except to recreate it from scratch. Trust me, this is traumatic. I have emotional scars.

If you live in an area subject to frequent power losses, you might want to consider getting a UPS. I don't mean a United Parcel Service driver. They're great, but they can't help you save data during a power outage, unless he is delivering a UPS: an uninterruptible power supply.

A UPS does two things for your Mac. It filters out the irregularities of your power supply (surges and spikes) and provides your Mac with a consistent level of power. A UPS also acts as a storage battery. When the power goes out, your Mac won't notice. The UPS will keep feeding it power, giving you enough time to save whatever you're working on, exit your applications, and shut your Mac down properly.

By the Way . . .

Does everybody need one of these? No. Not unless your work is constantly in danger of loss from power problems, or your paranoia level is so high you won't be able to sleep at night unless you have one.

UPSs are reasonably priced, considering the amount of anguish you can spare yourself, but $200 to $500 is not to be spent on a whim (at least, that's what I keep telling myself). Unless your area has regular electrical problems, you'll probably be happy with a multi-outlet surge protector.

Planning Ahead

Before getting down to the nitty-gritty of
assembling your Mac, there's one last thing
to take into consideration: room to grow.

Right now, at the very least, you have a
compact Mac that takes up about one square
foot of desk space (of course, a bigger Mac
takes up more space—how's that for a keen
grasp of the obvious?). You also have a keyboard, mouse, and mouse pad fighting for
desktop real estate. You also have (or probably
will want soon) a printer of some kind.

That's just to *start*. Down the road you might want to add an external
hard drive, a CD-ROM drive, a scanner, a different printer, big disk storage
boxes, and stuff that hasn't even been invented yet. All of these additions
drive up the value of your shrinking desktop space. If you start out all
cramped, you'll have nowhere to go, unless you physically relocate everything to a new, larger desk.

Give yourself some room to grow, try to
anticipate your future needs. Set up your Mac
on a clear desk with room to breathe. Locate
your desk near a phone jack. At the very least,
you'll be able to answer the phone without
walking away from your desk. At most, you'll
be able to painlessly add a modem (which
requires a phone line) later in your computing
career without having to move your desk or
install another jack.

A modem is an electronic
device that allows your Mac
to interact with a distant
computer over phone lines.
More about modems in
Chapter 18.

The Least You Need to Know

I know, I know, if you could foretell the future, you'd be playing the stock market and making yourself a fortune. Fine. Send me a large sum of money when you do. In the meantime, try and keep these few essentials in mind when you're selecting a place to set up your new Mac:

- ☞ Choose a sturdy desk or table as your dedicated work space. Be sure it can support all the equipment you have, and the things you may purchase in the future.

- ☞ Make your work space comfortable with good lighting and a comfy chair. Decorate, grow a plant—you're going to be spending a lot of time here.

- ☞ Check out your power supply. If it's unreliable (subject to brown- or black-outs), consider getting an uninterruptible power supply (UPS). Otherwise, just think about getting a multi-outlet surge protector.

- ☞ Leave yourself some room to grow.

Now that your work space is scoped out, arranged, and comfortable, move on to the main event: putting that Macintosh bad boy together.

Chapter 3
Insert Tab A into Slot B

In This Chapter

- ☞ Unpacking the little rascal
- ☞ Getting set up and hooking everything together
- ☞ Those pesky peripherals

Let's go over generic assembly instructions for your Mac. Generic, because there's no way I can know exactly what you bought, just like there's no way you want to plow through instructions on how to assemble all the different Mac variations. *Yawn.* What a thrill.

Consider yourself warned, then. If what I'm saying here doesn't jive with the machine you have in front of your face, ignore me and go along with the *Setting Up Your Macintosh (insert your model name here)* manual that came along with your machine.

The most obvious difference I can think of is that you purchased a PowerBook—you lucky devil. Since a Powerbook comes all in one piece, you don't have to do anything more than plug it in, charge it up, and turn it on (the On/Off switch is hidden behind a flip-down panel in the back). You're good to go, literally.

First Things First

The first thing to do is unpack everything. Check all the parts for obvious damage: cracks, dents, divots, dings, and other signs of broken-ness. If you find any damage, call the place where you purchased the Mac and tell them you want a replacement. You shelled out big bucks for a new machine; you deserve the privilege of dinging it up yourself.

It will be an irritation (to put it mildly) if you have to box everything up again and send your new baby back but, hey! You deserve the best, don't you?

By the Way . . .

A word about boxes: Save them. (Okay, so that's *two* words. Sue me.) Save the foam protectors, too. Why should you save them, when they'll take up so much of your valuable storage space? Well, for a couple of reasons: if you move, you'll have protected packaging to save your Mac from the moving company (or your close, but clumsy friends); if you need to ship your Mac somewhere for service, you'll have the proper packaging; and if you have to take your Mac anywhere, you'll have safe packaging.

Next thing to do: gather up all the little plastic bags of paper (manuals, warranty, and registration cards), and put them all together in one place. Deal with them later.

A *peripheral* is an add-on piece of equipment, such as a printer, that's not essential to operate the computer— like extra options on a car. You don't *need* air conditioning to use the car, but it makes you more comfortable.

Each box should also have a packing list right on top: if you bought a modular Mac, such as an LC III, you'll have several boxes and several lists. If you bought a Performa 405, or similarly packaged model, everything will be in one big box, unless you bought a printer or other peripherals.

The packing list tells you what's supposed to be inside. Check off items as you find them, making sure you have every single thing you're supposed to have.

If everything is there, you're ready to move on. If something is missing, call the place where you bought the Mac and tell them what's missing. If you bought your Mac at a local store, you may be able to just run over and pick up the missing piece(s). Otherwise, you may have to wait until your dealer ships out the missing parts. Make them ship by overnight express at no cost to you. You deserve it; you're having a hard day.

Generic Assembly Instructions

The CPU

The *CPU* (central processing unit) is the part of your Mac that does all the work. In reality, the CPU is the main chip inside your Mac that does the work, but the term has come to mean the box that contains the CPU and all the other goodies that make computers compute.

When people refer to chips in conversation, they usually shorten the number to the last three digits: '030 ("oh-thirty") or '040 ("oh-forty"). There's plenty to know and learn about these chips, but the only things that really come in handy are these (for now):

☞ The higher the chip's number, the faster the chip.

☞ The higher the clock speed, the faster the chip.

☞ The faster the chip, the more it costs.

TECHNO NERD TEACHES

The current line of Macs are based on Motorola processor chips. Each chip in the Motorola line is identified by a number. Macs use 68000 numbered chips, either 68030 or 68040 (some older models also used 68020). Real propeller-heads also include the clock speed of the chip (how fast the chip works), by adding the clock speed to the abbreviated chip number. "I've got an '040/33." Translated, that means this particular propeller-head has a 68040-based Mac (currently, only the Quadra line) with a clock speed of 33 megahertz.

A compact Mac, like the Classics (Classic, Classic II, and Color Classic), for the most part, *is* the CPU. The box with the built-in monitor and disk drive is the CPU. A modular Mac's CPU (such as the LC III, IIfx, or Quadra) is a fairly plain-looking box with the disk drive slot in front and the connector ports (more about these later) in the back.

Set the CPU (whatever kind you have) backwards on your desk with the connector ports facing you, and the disk drive slot facing away from you. (Of course, if there's no obstacle keeping you from working on the back-side of your Mac in its final resting place, simply ignore all of this 'set it up backwards, then turn it around' junk.)

The backside of your Mac looks something like this.

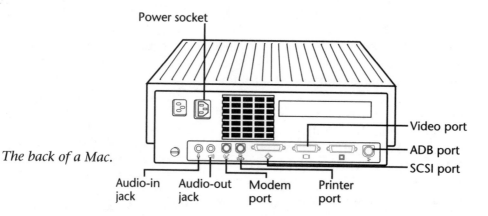

The back of a Mac.

Now go and find the Mac's power cord. It is black, with a standard grounded (three-pronged) plug on one end, and a three-prong socket on the other.

The Mac's power socket.

Plug the socket-end of the power cord into the power socket on the back of your Mac. DON'T plug the other end into a power outlet or surge protector yet. You won't be doing that until *everything* is together. Why? Just because I'm safety conscious.

Mission accomplished!

Keyboard and Mouse

The next thing you should do is grab the Mac's keyboard, keyboard cable, and the mouse (the mouse cable is part of the mouse).

You should never connect anything to your Mac while there's power running through it. You can short out both the Mac and whatever you're plugging into it. You can also give yourself a nasty shock. Always install stuff with the Mac off and unplugged. It's safer that way.

The Mac's ADB port.

Take the keyboard cable, and plug it into the ADB port on the back of your Mac. It doesn't matter which end of the cable you plug into the ADB, both ends are the same.

Notice that the ADB icon below the ADB port is also stamped on the flat side of both ends of the keyboard cable and the plug end of the mouse cable. That's so you can easily figure out which cable gets plugged into which port, and it's true for all the cables that Apple supplies. Other manufacturers aren't so kind.

ADB stands for Apple
Desktop Bus and is pro-
nounced by saying each
letter ("A-D-B"). The Apple
Desktop Bus is the standard
way of connecting mice,
keyboards, and a few other
peripherals, to the Mac.

The Desktop Bus has been
standard since Apple
introduced the Macintosh
SE. (Before the SE, they
used connectors that looked
like the ones that connect
your telephone cord to the
wall jack—in case the
question ever comes up in
Trivial Pursuit or some-
thing.)

The ADB icon also appears on your keyboard, at
the upper-right and upper-left corners. That's
because the other end of the keyboard cable plugs
into one of these ports, and the mouse into the
other.

Which cable plugs *where* is completely up to you.
If you're right-handed, you'll probably want to plug
the mouse into the ADB port on the right side of
your keyboard. If you're left-handed, you'll probably want the mouse to be left of the keyboard. If
you're ambimouse-rous, plug it wherever you want.

You will plug the keyboard cable into the port
you didn't use for the mouse, but don't do it yet. If
you attach your keyboard now, you'll just have one
more thing to juggle when you turn your Mac to
face front. Set the keyboard and mouse aside, and
let the keyboard cable attached to the back of your
Mac dangle. We'll do a grand plug-in in a couple of
minutes.

If you have a compact Mac, like a Classic, you
can skip the monitor section. Your monitor is
permanently installed, and you don't have to
bother with it.

The Monitor

Just like you can't tell the players without a scorecard, you can't tell what
you're doing on your Mac without a monitor. If the eyes are the windows
of the soul, the monitor is the window on your Mac's soul—*hmmm*, any
other clichés I can throw in here?

If you bought a Mac model other than a compact (with a built-in
monitor) or a PowerBook (also with a built-in monitor), you have to add a
monitor. Depending on the model, you may also need a video card. The
video card is a circuit board that processes all of the video information that
goes to the monitor.

Some Macs, such as the LC, Performas, and Quadras, have built-in video; no extra video card is required, unless you want to use a monitor larger than the built-in hardware supports.

Other Macs, such as the IIfx, don't have built-in video and need a video card installed to run the monitor. Lately, Apple has been introducing most new Macs with on-board video. Odds are, if you bought one of the current line of Macs, it probably has built-in video.

Check the manual called *Special Features of Your Macintosh (insert model name here)*, for a section called "Video display support." It will tell if you need a video card.

If you do need a video card, don't panic. If the company you purchased your Mac from is worth its salt, they told you that *before* they sold you the monitor. If they were really good, they installed the card for you, and you don't have to worry about it. If they were really, really good, you knew all of this already, so you can skip ahead to the next section.

If you think the video card has already been installed in your Mac, check the packing list from the monitor box. If the packing slip specifies a video card but there isn't one in the box, call the place where you bought your Mac to be sure the video card is installed.

If there *is* a video card in the box, then you either need to install it yourself (a potentially scary thing; be sure to follow the installation instructions very carefully), or take your CPU and the video card back to the place of purchase, and let them install it like they should have done in the first place.

Warranty Warning! If you decide to install the video card yourself, be aware that opening the Mac's case can void Apple's warranty. If something goes wrong and you damage the Mac or the card, you may be out of luck.

On the other hand, if you manage to install the card without a hitch, and you don't *tell* anyone, then your warranty should still be intact. It's all a question of how much you trust yourself.

Now that you've figured out if you do or don't need a video card installed, and you (or your Apple dealer) installed it, let's hook this sucker up.

Carefully now: pick up your monitor (it's heavy), and set it on the desk beside your Mac. Turn the monitor so the screen is facing away from you, and you're looking at the back of it.

Your monitor has two cables coming from the back of it. One is the power cord. Let that one be for a minute. The other is the cable that attaches to the video port on the back of your Mac.

The video port is labeled with an icon that looks like a TV's, or monitor's, picture tube. The end of the monitor's cable has the same icon if you have an *Apple* monitor (if you bought another brand, it is probably blank).

Plug the video cable into the video port. Don't plug the monitor's power cord into anything yet. Save that for the grand plug-in.

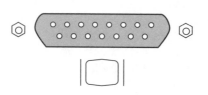

The video port on the back of a Mac.

At this point, you can set the monitor on top of the CPU or wherever you're going to place it. If you're putting your monitor on top of the CPU, keep the screen facing away from you (toward the disk drive end of your Mac). That way, when you're ready to turn it around, the monitor and CPU turn at once.

Peripheral Vision

We're almost at the end now, be brave. This is the point where you can plug in any of the other doodads you may have acquired when you bought your Mac. Let's get the little stuff out of the way first.

Microphone

You may have a microphone, you may not. You may have one and not even realize it. If you have one, you either bought a Mac that was packaged before Apple decided to sell these little darlings as accessories, or you paid extra money (under $20) for it. Or, you bought one of the *really* new Macs that have the microphone built into the monitor (like the Color Classic).

> ## By the Way . . .
> **Attention K-Mart Shoppers!** If you think you'd like a microphone but don't want to shell out $20, *any* microphone with a standard, small jack will fit the audio port and work just swell.

If your microphone is built-in, you don't have to do anything with it—just use it. If it came as a separate piece, you have to do two things. First, mount the little bracket on the side of your monitor. This involves pulling a piece of waxy paper off of the sticky part and (steady yourself) sticking it on the side of the monitor. Did you work up a sweat?

Next, you have to plug the microphone jack (which looks suspiciously like the jack you'll find on a set of Walkman headphones) into the audio-in port on the back of your Mac. It's the one with the microphone icon under it.

Now you know why consultants make hundreds of dollars an hour for doing this stuff.

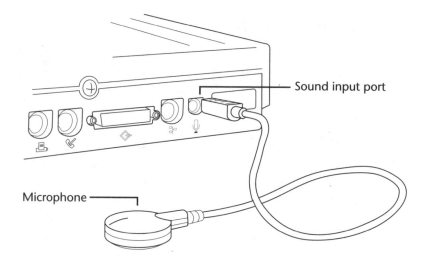

Installing a microphone.

Speakers

If your Mac came with a built-in CD-ROM drive, you're a lucky bugger. It also came with either separate speakers for dazzling stereophonic sound or speakers built into the CPU or the monitor (also for dazzling stereophonic sound).

You have built-in speakers? You're wired for sound and don't have to do much of anything. If you have separate speakers, plug their jack into the audio-out port on the back of your Mac. It's right next to the audio-in jack and looks exactly like it, except there is an icon of (*duh*) a speaker under it.

You may want to wait to plug in your speakers until you turn your Mac around; the speakers might be a little awkward to drag around as you turn the CPU. Since the plug is small, simple to insert, and easy to find (being right next to the microphone jack), this task is not too difficult.

Printer

A printer is probably the last thing you'll have to hook up right now (unless you were inspired or bullied by a salesman and you purchased a modem). Printers, except for those cute little StyleWriters and other tiny inkjet printers, tend to be large, chunky-looking things, not unlike myself.

Set the printer on (or near) your desk, close enough to your Mac that the cable reaches both with enough slack in the cable so you can plug in both ends. Turn the printer so you can easily reach the port on its back.

Take the cable and plug the small, round end (it should look like the end of your keyboard cable) into the port on the back of your Mac with the little printer icon under it. Leave the other end of the printer cable unplugged.

Find the printer's power cord (if it's not built-in to the printer), and plug the socket end of the cord into the power outlet on the back of the printer. Like every other power cord you've touched, don't plug the business end (the prong end) into your outlet or surge protector yet. That's coming up soon, but not yet.

The Grand Finale!

You survived! Congratulations! All that's left is so simple; just use this checklist:

1. Carefully lift and turn your Mac so the front is facing you again.

2. Position your Mac where you want it to stay, leaving room at the front for the keyboard and at the side for the mouse.

3. Plug the loose end of the keyboard cable into the right or left ADB port on the keyboard.

4. If you haven't already, plug the mouse cable into the *other* ADB port on the keyboard (the one you didn't use for the keyboard cable).

5. Now would be a good time to plug in your speakers, if you have them. Your microphone should already be plugged in (if you have one), and the speakers get plugged into the little port right beside the microphone.

6. Plug the loose end of your printer cable into the printer's port, and reposition the printer.

7. Take all the plug-ends of your power cords (the Mac's, the monitor's, the printer's), and plug them into the outlet or surge protector of your choice.

8. Take a break, because you're done.

You'll fire this puppy up in the next chapter. While you take a break, it might be a good time to sort through all of those packs of paper that came with your Mac. Dig them out, sort them out (separate the manuals, the disks, and the warranty and registration cards), and fill them out (whatever needs filling out).

Filling out and returning your registration cards is important. First, because Apple and the other hardware manufacturers need to know you bought their product. Second, it gives the manufacturers your address so they can let you know about cool stuff, such as new Mac models, upgrades (improvements made to stuff you already bought), or if there's ever a recall or repair (heaven forbid!) that needs to be done on a particular model. Third, with Apple's registration cards, at least, you can get **free stuff!**

When I registered my Mac, I had the choice of a free mouse pad, a very cool and necessary accessory, or a free six-month subscription to *Macworld* magazine, a very cool and necessary magazine. Take your pick, it's free!

Finally, you should fill out your registration cards because then you'll be in the company's computers, and you'll be able to get technical support over the phone. That means you can call them up if there's a problem you can't solve, and they'll help you solve it. (Before you call, though, read the "Okay, Now You Can Panic" section of the appendix, because like all things, there's a right way and a wrong way to get technical support.)

The Least You Need to Know

While you're taking your break and filling out registration cards, here are some essentials from this chapter for you to mull over:

- ☞ Never connect anything to your Mac while there's power running through it. At least make sure the Mac is shut down and turned off. For an extra measure of safety, unplug it, too.

- ☞ Remember your port icons: they make your life easy in so many ways:

  Power cord socket: To connect the power cord.

  Video port: To connect your monitor.

  Printer port: For connecting your printer cable.

  Modem port: For connecting a modem.

  SCSI port: We'll talk more about this one later.

  ADB port: For connecting your keyboard to the Mac, and a mouse to the keyboard.

  Audio-out jack: For connecting speakers.

  Audio-in jack: For connecting your microphone.

- ☞ Whenever you buy new stuff, remember to fill out and mail your product registration cards. Let manufacturers know you dropped money on their product, and they should be nice to you.

Get it? Got it. Good! Going on.

This page unintentionally left blank.

Chapter 4
Why Don't You Start Me Up?

In This Chapter

> ☛ Turning everything on in order
>
> ☛ What to do if it looks weird
>
> ☛ Shutting down

Okay! You've come very far very fast, and here comes the payoff: now you get to fire up your Mac and enter the wonderful world of computing. In this chapter, we'll go over all of the basics of starting up and shutting down your Mac, and take the briefest of peeks at some of the magic of the Macintosh.

This little taste is like the first taste of a new bottle of wine they give you in a restaurant, except you don't have to sniff the cork. Right after this little snip of a chapter, we'll jump into your new Mac with both feet—try doing that with a glass of Chateau Marmoset.

Power On!

Before you turn *anything* on, make sure that everything is plugged in, either into a live wall outlet, or into a multi-outlet power strip or surge protector that's been plugged into a wall outlet. If you're using a power strip or surge protector, make sure it's turned off, too.

Next, find all of the appropriate On/Off switches, both on your equipment and on your surge protector (if you have one). Your typical On/Off switch looks something like the one in the figure. The side of the switch with the circle is the Off position. The side with the line is the On position. Why? I haven't a clue.

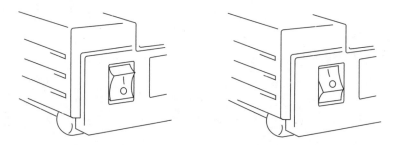

Your typical On/Off switch for the 90's.

If everything is plugged in and ready to go, let's do it. Here's the order you should turn things on. Turn them on one at a time, and (if you're using a surge protector) realize that nothing happens until you turn on the surge protector.

Peripherals First!

1. External hard drive (if you have one) to get it up to speed before the Mac comes looking for it.

2. Printer, if you need it on.

3. External modem, if you have one and want it on.

Mac Parts Next!

1. The CPU.

2. The monitor.

> **By the Way . . .**
>
> If you have a Macintosh II-something (fx, ci, and so on), Centris or Quadra, you can turn your Mac on from the keyboard. There's a button that floats all by its lonesome on the keyboard that has a little left-pointing arrow on it. That's your power switch. Press that, and your Mac should fire right up.
>
> If you have any *other* model Mac, you'll *still* have that key, and you can punch it until you're red in the finger, but it won't do anything. Sorry.

> **By the Way . . .**
>
> Some models of Macintosh monitors will turn themselves on automatically when you fire up the CPU. Don't panic. It means to do that. Your Mac isn't possessed. Naturally, you'll know which kind you have the first time you power on the CPU.

Turn on the power strip/surge protector *last*.

What Happens Next

When the power reaches your Mac, you'll hear a variety of noises. Macs are like people in the morning—it takes a little grunting and groaning to get them out of bed.

First you'll hear a little whine. That's your hard drive spinning up to speed, and the Mac's internal fan starting up. Then you'll hear some ticka-ticka kind of noises; that's the startup information being read from the hard drive. Finally, you'll hear a musical tone. The sound varies from Mac model to Mac model. On mine, it's a baritone bong. Yours may be something different.

Put on a Happy Mac

If everything goes smoothly, a smiling Mac appears briefly on your screen, as shown in the figure. A few seconds later, it disappears and is replaced with a screen welcoming you to the wonderful world of Macintosh. What a polite little machine!

The happy Mac.

After a few more seconds, you may or may not see some small icons appear at the bottom of your screen—either way, they're nothing to be alarmed about. They only appear if certain tiny programs (called *Extensions*) are being loaded. If there aren't any installed on your Mac, you won't see them. I'll talk about Extensions in more detail in Chapter 11.

After a few more seconds, the startup screen and the tiny icons (if any) disappear, and you're at (ta-da!) the desktop.

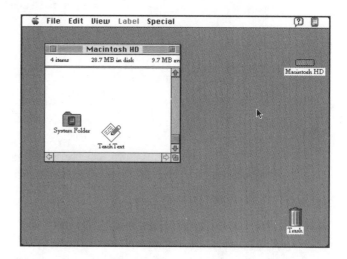

The desktop.

Questionable Disk

When you powered up, if you were greeted by the icon shown in the next figure (the disk with a question mark, instead of a smiling Mac), you've gotten your hands on a Mac without its System software installed.

It's not a big deal.

Disk with question mark icon.

Turn your Mac off, either just the CPU with the switch on the back, or the whole system with the switch on the surge protector. Then, locate your System Disks. They'll be in one of the bags of paperwork and junk from the Mac's box. With the disks in one hand, flip to Chapter 21 for the lowdown on installing System software.

If anything else (other than the two scenarios described above) happens when you power up your Mac, run, do not walk, to the "Before You Panic" section of the appendix. It explains, in gory detail, all of the bad things that can happen at startup, and what you can do to fix them.

Shutting Down

Well. I think that's quite enough excitement for one chapter. Let's shut this puppy down—but don't reach for those power switches yet. Because of the way Macs work, you should shut down everything the machine is doing before you actually shut off the machine.

This is important because shutting down what your Mac is doing saves the state of your Mac. Remember the picture of the Desktop back in an earlier figure? Well, when the Mac saves its state, that means all that stuff you see on the Desktop (the Trash, the hard drive icon, plus funky stuff, such as windows, that we haven't talked about yet) is saved just the way it appears. The next time you turn your Mac on, everything will be exactly the way you left it. How many other things can you say that about?

Just cutting off the power can do bad things to whatever programs you're running—especially the System software. The program information can become corrupt.

If your software is corrupt, that doesn't mean you will find it taking bribes or trying to lure school kids into the back seat of your car with candy. It means that the program information can become unreadable. If the Mac can't read the information, the Mac can't use the information, and that's a bad thing.

However, just like grammar, there are always exceptions. This doesn't mean that you can never turn off your Mac without shutting it down properly. You'll find examples in the troubleshooting appendix, where just turning it off is *all* you can do. However, let's learn the rules before I show you how to break them.

Details, Details

Okay. This is a very brief introduction to the mouse and cursor. We'll really put them through their paces in the next chapter. For now, here's enough information to get you started . . . well, stopped. Shut down, even.

The *cursor* is a mouse-controlled pointer (that can take many shapes). It indicates where you are on your Mac's screen. We'll talk about the cursor a *lot* more in the next chapter.

Start by moving your mouse around randomly on your desk or tabletop, while watching the monitor. See how the arrow moves around the desktop the same way you move the mouse? Practice for a minute or two, until you can get the arrow cursor to point where you want. This is one of the few circumstances where it *is* polite to point.

When you feel comfortable moving the mouse and arrow cursor around, move the mouse so the arrow cursor points at the word **Special** in the menu bar at the top of your screen. With the cursor still touching the word **Special**, press and hold down the mouse button. Voilà! A menu drops down.

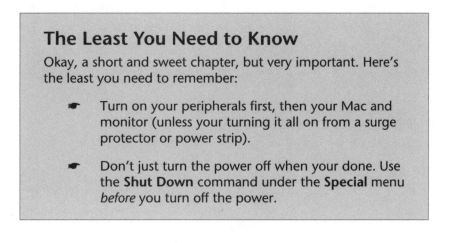

The extremely Special menu.

Still holding down the mouse button—don't worry, this gets easier with practice—slide the arrow cursor down the center of the menu. That's called *dragging*. As the cursor touches each word, you'll see them turn white on a black bar. That word is *selected*.

Move the arrow cursor down until the phrase **Shut Down** is selected, then release the mouse button. The black bar blinks a few times, and your Mac shuts itself down. If it doesn't, your hand probably slipped and you missed the words **Shut Down**. Try, try again.

Now it's safe for you to turn off the power.

The Least You Need to Know

Okay, a short and sweet chapter, but very important. Here's the least you need to remember:

☞ Turn on your peripherals first, then your Mac and monitor (unless your turning it all on from a surge protector or power strip).

☞ Don't just turn the power off when your done. Use the **Shut Down** command under the **Special** menu *before* you turn off the power.

This page unintentionally left blank.

Part II
Getting Down to Brass Macs

I bought my Mac through very roundabout, but strictly legal, means. I won't bore you with the details, but suffice it to say that sometimes the idiocy of others can work in your favor.

Anyhow, the long and short of it is that, though I got a real bargain on my Mac, I didn't have much money left for other stuff. I was so poor, I couldn't pay attention. For the space of two weeks (until the next paycheck rolled through the door), I didn't have anything to use on my Mac except the stuff that came bundled with it.

With the clarity of 20/20 hindsight, I think it was the best thing I could have done. People, generally, are usually in such a rush to get to the application side of computing—using a word processor or drawing program—that they neglect the basic system side, and miss out on a lot of great tips and tricks.

Since it worked so well for me, I thought I'd inflict the same learning experience on you. IF YOU TRY AND SKIP AHEAD, THE PAGES OF THIS BOOK COULD VERY WELL EXPLODE. DON'T SAY I DIDN'T WARN YOU.

Just kidding. Maybe. Anyhow, this part (Part 2) of the book is devoted to covering the essential things you really need to know to work your way around your Mac. It's basic stuff that you'll use day in and day out, every time you power up your Mac.

Fasten your seatbelts. The captain has turned on the no skimming sign.

Chapter 5
All Systems Go

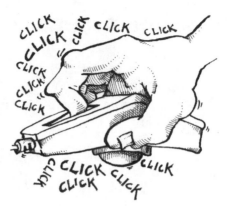

In This Chapter

- ☞ The nickel tour of the desktop
- ☞ It's so nice to have a mouse around the house
- ☞ When is a window not a window?

This is all basic System information. You should read it, and where appropriate, follow along on your very own Mac. Pictures of my Mac's screen won't help much if you can't reproduce them on your own screen.

If the writing gets dense (meaning if *I* get dense) and stops making sense to you, stop. Go back and reread it, and retry it until you get it. I can't stress enough that this stuff will come in handy every time you turn on your Mac.

In this chapter and the next, we'll lay down the very basic concepts of the Macintosh, the ones that make Macs Macs. We'll start with the desktop, add the mouse, and then go over the windows. In Chapter 6, we'll talk about menus, icons, and other stuff you'll find littered all over the desktop.

Mousing Around: A Tour of the Desktop

If your Mac is turned off, fire it up (unless you're, like, reading this standing on a bus or in the bathtub, or something). We'll start at the desktop. If you've forgotten what it looks like, here's a little refresher I like to call the desktop figure. (Actually, I like to call it "Nude Descending a Staircase," but that's just me.)

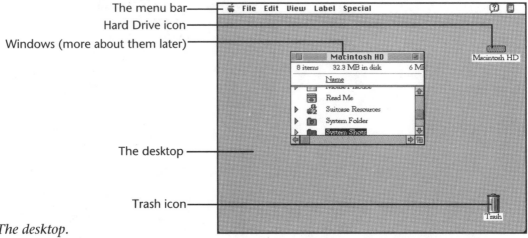

The menu bar ⎯
Hard Drive icon ⎯
Windows (more about them later) ⎯
The desktop ⎯
Trash icon ⎯

The desktop.

This Looks *Nothing* Like My Desktop

The Mac's desktop never fools anyone. It doesn't look or work like any desktop I've ever seen. Who keeps their garbage can on their desk? The Mac's desktop is a metaphor.

So what's that mean? Well, it means that folks who named the desktop never intended for you to think of it as a *real* desktop. They called it the desktop to give you the idea that it's your home base, the place where you begin, tinker with, and complete all of your work on your Mac. A desktop is familiar—every desk you ever worked at had one. It's a known quantity, and the known is always more comfortable than the unknown.

> ### By the Way . . .
> The dreaded **C:>** prompt of the DOS world is not familiar, and is an unknown quantity. In fact, some folks I know find it vicious and intimidating—me for one—but don't get me started on *that* subject.

To carry the idea of a real desktop through the whole Mac environment, you'll use folders that work like file folders, and throw stuff you don't want or need any more in the trash. That's about as far as the metaphor goes, though. (Unless you have a really funky desk that has windows you can open.)

You'll spend a lot of time flitting back and forth between the desktop and all the other things you do on your Mac. The secret little ways around and through the desktop can make your computing life very simple and satisfying. Some of the more fundamental ways around the desktop are coming right up.

SPEAK LIKE A GEEK

In computerese, the *environment* is much like the environment of the world at large, or your work environment. It's the atmosphere, surroundings, even the decor of your computer. The Macintosh environment is graphical (sometimes called a graphical user interface or GUI, pronounced "GOO-ey") because it uses pictures (icons) to represent functions and operations.

Click a Little, Drag a Little

Raise your right hand and repeat after me:
"The mouse is my friend, I shall not fling it across the room in fits of irritation."

Think of your mouse as a digital index finger. You'll use it to point at and select all kinds of doo-doo (I mean doo-doo in the kindest possible sense of the word) around the desktop—just like you did in the last chapter when you shut down your Mac.

TECHNO NERD TEACHES

If you actually pick up your mouse and turn it over, you'll see that the mouse moves the cursor (right now, the cursor is an arrow) by means of a small, hard rubber ball in the bottom. When you move the mouse, the ball rolls with the motion, and the mouse translates that motion and sends it to your Mac. Your Mac then moves the cursor accordingly. It all happens so quickly that you don't even notice the time it takes to relay the movement to the screen.

Click!

When I (or anyone) tell you to *click on* something, that's a shorthand way of saying move the mouse until the tip of the arrow cursor is touching the icon (or menu, or folder, or whatever), and then press the mouse button once. *Click!*

Whatever you were pointing at is now *selected*. When you select something on the desktop the Mac lets you know it's been selected by changing how it looks. Because it's easier to show you than to explain how things look when they are selected, let's select something.

Move your mouse so the arrow pointer is pointing at your Hard Drive icon. The tip of the arrow should be touching either the picture of the hard drive, or the name below the picture. When it is, click once.

If you point and click accurately, your Hard Drive icon is now selected. To give you a comparison, there's a before-and after-clicking picture shown in the following figure. You'll notice how the picture of the hard drive darkens, while the name of the drive goes from black-on-white to white-on-black.

The Hard Drive icon before and after selecting.

Not selected   Selected

Macintosh HD   Macintosh HD

OOPS!

If you accidentally select something you *don't* want selected, just click once somewhere else (preferably on the thing you *do* want to select).

To unselect (or deselect) the icon, just click anywhere else on the desktop. That works in most circumstances.

This is *such* a difficult concept (SARCASM ALERT! SARCASM ALERT!), I expect you to be wrapped up in its tacky rococo intricacies for all of five seconds. Once you feel comfortable selecting and deselecting the Hard Drive icon, why don't you try clicking once on some of the other things littered around the desktop. Just for laughs.

Click and Hold

In the course of your clicking experiments, if you happened to click on one of the words (menu names) or icons in the menu bar (shown in the following figure), you may have seen a menu drop down briefly and disappear. Getting the menu to stay around (so you can read it and do something with it) requires another step added to the basic click.

|  File Edit View Label Special ◙◙ | ⑦ ▣ | *The menu bar.* |

When you click on a menu heading in the menu bar, you need to click and hold; that is, don't release the mouse button. As long as you hold the mouse button down, the menu stays open, and you can select something from it (like you selected **Shut Down** from the **Special** menu in the last chapter).

We'll be doing a complete menu roundup in the next chapter. For the moment, just get used to clicking and holding open the menus without trying to select anything.

What a Drag!

Okay, so we've clicked and we've held. Next on our list of things to do is *drag*.

Now, don't go running to your closet to pull out your stash of the opposite sex's clothing. It's not that kind of drag. We're talking about drag as in "Look what the cat dragged in," only in this case, it's the mouse that does the dragging.

The principle is simple, and it proceeds from the mouse maneuvers you've already mastered. First you click on something (let's say the Trash) to select it. When it's selected (that is, turned dark like the Hard Drive icon did earlier), click and hold on it. While you're holding down the mouse button, move the mouse around. The pointer drags the Trash can around the desktop—actually, just an outline of the Trash, as shown here —until you release the mouse button. When you release the button, the Trash drops wherever it is.

The Trash does drag.

The same thing happens with any icon on the desktop, or in a window. Menus and windows themselves behave differently, but you'll learn all you need to know about them in later parts of this chapter and in the next chapter. Let's proceed with this click thing.

Fortunately, the Mac's designers knew that everybody wouldn't double-click at the same speed. I guess that's why they make the big bucks. There is a way to adjust how your Mac receives and interprets your clicks (we'll cover that in Chapter 11 when we talk about your customizing options). For now, it will do you good to learn double-clicking at the preset speed; later, you'll know whether you want to change the mouse's response speed.

Click-Click!

Since we've pretty much exhausted the clicking, holding, and dragging options on the bare desktop, let's dig up some more stuff to fool around with. To do that, you're going to double-click on your Hard Drive icon to get at the goodies within.

A double-click (if you haven't guessed) is just two clicks in click—er, quick succession. Click, click.

For some folks, double-clicking can take a little practice. If you click too slowly, the Mac treats your double-click as two single clicks. If you double-click too quickly, it treats it as just one single click.

> **Put It to Work**
>
> Move your mouse so that the tip of the arrow pointer is touching the Hard Drive icon, just like you did when you first learned how to click. This time, instead of a single click, hit it with a double-click and watch what happens.

Windows and Icons and Bears (*Oh, My!*)

When you double-clicked on your Hard Drive icon, you should have seen the icon go very dark (darker than when only selected), and a little animation should have happened as the hard drive window opened.

If an icon is a picture that represents something else, like a hard drive, then the window is the way you get at the stuff inside the icon. In this case, the window holds the stuff that's stored on the hard drive.

With the window to your hard drive open, it should look something like the one shown back at the first figure in this chapter. It will look only *something* like it because, while the window itself (the box or frame) will be the same, I probably have more junk stored on my hard drive than you do on yours.

To level the playing field a little bit, let's take a look at a window full of completely made up stuff, just so you get the parts of the window before you start to worry about what's inside.

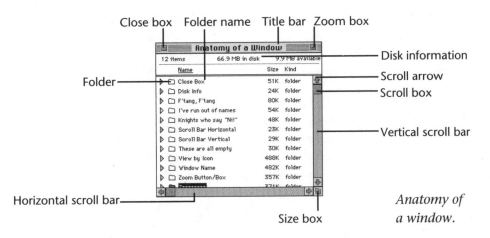

Anatomy of a window.

TECHNO NERD TEACHES

That stuff below the title bar in the figure is all *disk information*. Specifically, it tells you how many items (folders, applications, and so on) you have on that disk or in that folder, how much storage space you've used (in this figure, 66.9 megabytes, or MB), and how much space is left (9.9 MB). It also puts headings above the information, so you know what you're looking at in each column. All of these are important bits of information and will be covered in detail later.

Breaking Windows

As long as you are staring at a window, let's break it down into its component parts. You can refer to the one in the preceding figure, or you can look at one on your own Mac. It don't make me no nevermind. (That's hillbilly for "I don't care.")

Close Box

In the upper left hand corner of the window, you'll see a small box. That's the *Close box*. When you click on it, the window closes. If you're at your Mac, try it with your hard drive window, and then just double-click on the Hard Drive icon to reopen it.

Title Bar

That striped bar that the Close box sits on is called the title bar because it contains the title of the window (which is the same as the name of the hard drive or folder the window belongs to).

The title bar can do a couple of cool things. First, it acts as a handle to make moving windows around easier. If you click and hold on the window name (in the last figure, that would be **Anatomy of a Window**), you can drag the window around the desktop. Try it, you'll like it.

If you press and hold the ⌘ key (a.k.a. the **Command Key** beside the Spacebar on your keyboard) *before* you click on the name in the title bar, and then click and hold on the name, you'll see a pop-up list of the window's lineage. We talk about the lineage (especially of several windows) as parents and children. Continuing with the example, my

Anatomy of a Window window is the child of **Macintosh HD** because the **Anatomy of a Window** folder is on the **Macintosh HD**. I have to open the **Macintosh HD** window to get to its child, the **Anatomy of a Window** window.

If I opened a folder (say the one called **Knights who say "Ni!"**) from the **Anatomy of a Window** window, and held the ⌘ key while clicking on its name, the pop-up list would show:

1. The folder **Knights who say "Ni!"**

2. Its parent folder, **Anatomy of a Window**.

3. Its *grandparent* (the parent of the parent of the child) folder, **Macintosh HD**.

I'll talk about this feature in more detail later because its one of those truly helpful features that many folks seem to forget about (me included). I thought a little extra exposure to it would help you remember it.

Zoom Box

In the right hand corner of the window is a small box with a smaller box inside. That's the *Zoom box*. It's called that because when you click on it, the window zooms out to a larger size, or (if it's already large) zooms down to a smaller size.

Try it now. Try it twice.

This kind of function is called a *toggle*. Think of a toggle like an On/Off switch. If you hit the switch, it does one thing (in this case, zooms the window to a larger size). When you hit the switch again, it does the opposite (zooms the window small again).

By the Way . . .

You'll run into a lot of toggles, not only on the desktop, but in other applications: to turn features on and off, to do and undo certain actions, and so on. They're handy because you can do two functions by remembering just one action.

Hey, Scroll Me Over

On the right and bottom sides of the window are what I call the "scroll assemblies." I call them that because I haven't heard an official term for them. They are generally talked about by their component parts. *Scrolling* is another important concept that you'll use all the time.

Your Mac's screen is only so large (only nine inches diagonally on a compact Mac). Any window you open is always somewhat smaller than the monitor. What you're looking at, or working on, in the window is usually longer or wider than the window displaying it.

With a real window, the kind built into walls, if you need to see something outside, you can mash your nose against the glass to look, or just open the window and stick your head out. That doesn't work on a computer. Scrolling lets you look at everything that's hiding beyond the edges of the windows.

With the scroll box, you can drag the box to the exact position you want. The window's contents move accordingly.

Clicking once on one of the scroll arrows scrolls the window's contents one line in the direction the arrow is pointing. Clicking once in the scroll bar scrolls the window's contents several lines towards the side of the scroll bar where you clicked.

You know what I'm going to say now: try it. So what am I saying it for? If the window's scroll bar (either, horizontal or vertical) is completely gray (as shown in the next figure), that means there's nowhere to scroll—everything there is to see has been displayed.

Does Size Count?

Yeah, size counts. If it didn't, why would your Mac windows have a second sizing option built into it? It's right down there at the lower right hand corner of the window: a box with overlapping boxes inside. It's cleverly called the *Size box*. You use it to manually resize the window to the exact size you'd like.

To use the Size box, click-hold on it, and drag the corner down and/or to the right to enlarge the window, or up and/or to the left to make it smaller.

The window won't resize as you drag the Size box, instead you'll see an outline of the window moving as you resize. When you release the mouse button, the window itself changes size.

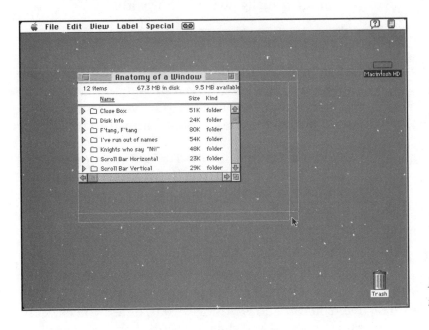

Resizing a window manually.

Try it on for size. (Ouch! Sorry.)

Window Management Tips

Don't waste your money buying expensive window cleaners and paper towels. Instead, use a little vinegar in warm water and old newspapers to clean your windows. Oh, wait. This is a computer book, not a *Hints from Heloise* column. But, seriously, just like there are tips to make cleaning the windows in your home easier, there are tips to make managing windows on your Mac easier. Here are a few of them.

With windows (and applications), *active* and *inactive* mean pretty much what you'd expect. An active window is the one that is foremost on your screen. All of its details, such as the stripes in the title bar and the dot pattern in the scroll bars, are right where they should be. You can work in or with this window. All of the windows that are behind the active window will be stripeless and dotless. These windows are *inactive*. You can't do anything with them unless you click on them to bring them to the front.

Which Window Is Which

That's not as silly a question as it sounds. Not that you wouldn't be able to tell which window is which by name, because the name is right up there in the title bar. The annoying question is which window is the active one; that is, which is the one you can actually do something with.

To figure this out, you'll need more than one window open on your desktop, so double-click on the **Trash** icon. Unless you threw something away when I wasn't looking, you should now have an empty window named **Trash** on your desktop, in addition to the one called **Macintosh HD**.

You'll notice when the Trash window opened, it opened on top of the one called **Macintosh HD**. The one called **Macintosh HD** also kind of faded into obscurity: the stripes disappeared from the title bar; the scroll bars turned white and lost all detail.

That's a visual clue to tell you that the one in the background that's turned white is inactive. You can't do anything with it, unless you click on it to make it active again. Go ahead and click on its title bar or any portion of it that's showing.

Click on the desktop, not any open window, and *all* of the open windows become inactive.

You'll notice that the two windows have traded places: the Trash window has moved behind the Macintosh HD window; the Trash window also lost all of its details, while the Macintosh HD window has earned back its stripes. The Macintosh HD window is now the active one, the one you can work with, and the Trash is inactive.

You can click on each of them in turn, switching them from active to inactive until you're bored senseless, which takes about 10 seconds.

Multiple Windows

Window management gets a little complicated when you have a pile of overlapping windows open on the desktop. Usually, some are completely hidden so you can't even find a corner to click on. That can get ugly.

There are two ways to avoid that. The first is annoying: keep all of your windows small and arrange them so the title bars are all showing so you can click right on the one you want to bring to the front as the active window. How anal-retentive is that? I've never been able to orchestrate it without losing track of what I was really trying to do. That brings us to way number two.

Remember when I told you about holding down the ⌘ key when clicking on the window's name? That list of the window's parents and grandparents that popped up can cut through a lot of the confusion surrounding a lot of open windows.

Many of the windows and folders you'll work with on a single project (if you're organized) will be parents, grandparents, or children of the same folder or two. So, if you need to pull a related window to the front, you can select it from this pop-up list, rather than clicking and dragging a bazillion windows around on your desktop.

> ## By the Way . . .
> You select the name of the window you want from the list by dragging the pointer down the list of names until the one you want is selected. Select the same way you selected the **Shut Down** option from the **Special** menu back in Chapter 4. Pretty cool!

We'll talk about organizational strategies in Chapter 10. Be warned that organizing your hard drive, and therefore your work, is a highly personal thing. If you're sloppy away from your desk, you'll probably be a slob at your desk (I know I am).

With time, your Mac skills will develop, and you'll grow your own computing style. Managing your windows will become second nature to you, and your management style will reflect your personality. I'm all for personality and style, so while I'll give advice and tips, I don't expect you to swallow it all hook, line, and sinker. I expect you to develop your own style. My feelings won't be hurt if you try my advice and then chuck it in the Trash—hey, I won't even know that you did it.

Closing Windows

That's about it for windows, for now. Let's clean up your desktop so we can move on. You'll recall from the section on the anatomy of windows that you can close a window by clicking on the **Close box** in the upper left hand corner. That works.

You can also (if you remember how from the Introduction) use the key combination ⌘-**W**. That means that you press the **Command** (⌘) key and hold it down. While still holding that down, press the **W** key. The active window closes.

Or you can hold down the **Option** key while you click on the **Close box** (or press ⌘-**W**), and *all* of the open windows on your desktop close.

You'll find that many things you want to do on the Mac can be done about three different ways: via the mouse, clicking or double-clicking on a box or something; via the keyboard, using a command-key combination; or via a menu, selecting a command from a list of related functions.

The Least You Need to Know

- ☞ The Mac's desktop is a metaphor to make it easier for you to get a handle on what it does. File folders are for putting junk in, the trash is for throwing stuff away.

- ☞ Your mouse makes manipulating things on the desktop easy. You'll use it to click, double-click, click-hold, and drag various things, and to select commands from menus.

☞   You access all of your files and folders via windows that you can make bigger or smaller, or scroll through to view everything inside.

☞   You can only work in the active (foremost) window on the desktop. To work in any inactive window, click on it to make it the active one.

This page unintentionally left blank.

Chapter 6
Menus in the Macintosh Cafe

In This Chapter

- ☞ What's on the menu?
- ☞ Chopping up the menu bar
- ☞ Throwing it away

Why don't we take a quick spin through the menus: see what they are, what they do, and why they don't do everything all of the time.

The Menus

If you look at the menu bar, you'll notice that there are two kinds of menus on your Mac. The first kind is an *icon* or *picture* menu. Instead of a descriptive word heading, there's a picture of Apple's seven-color apple logo. At the other end of the menu bar, there's the Balloon Help menu (the one with the comic strip speech balloon with a question mark inside), and the Application menu (the one with the little picture of a Mac). These *icon menus* let you do specific things all the time, regardless of what application you are using.

Between the icons on the menu bar are five menus with word headings. Unlike the icon menus, the word menus do specific things only under certain conditions.

Working with the word menus on your Mac is like ordering from a menu in any restaurant. Because I love it, and because I'm craving some, let's say it's like ordering food in your favorite Chinese restaurant.

Let's be even more specific and say that you're ordering from the family special page. You know the page I mean, the one where you choose a soup for everyone, an appetizer (I'll have the Pu-Pu platter, thank you), and then two or more entrées: one from column A and one from column B.

With the Mac's menus (with the exception of the icon menus), you need to choose two things. The first is the thing (a folder, document, line of text, or whatever) you'd like something to do something to; the second is the thing you want done.

Because many of the operations chosen through the word menus depend on you selecting something for them to work on, the menus, or items in the menu, are sometimes unavailable. They won't become available until you select something they can work with. When they're unavailable, the word heading or menu item turns from black to gray.

If you don't have any open windows, your **View** and **Label** menus will be gray because they both require an open window on the desktop to be active. The **Label** menu also requires an icon in that window (a folder, document, or application) be selected before it will become active.

Okay, if you're not totally confused, let's look at the menus one at a time (in order of appearance). I'll try to refresh you on the difference between menus with icon headings and those with word headings.

The Apple Menu

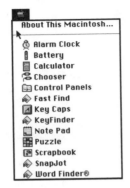

The Apple ⬤ Menu.

The ⬤ Menu, since it is an icon-headed menu, does only specific things, but it does them all the time, no matter what application you're using.

It is the home of your Desk Accessories (DAs) that we'll go over in Chapter 12. For now, you should know that a Desk Accessory on your Mac, such as the Alarm Clock or the Calculator, are available to you whenever you're at your Mac.

They work just like the assortment of desk accessories (such as a stapler, letter opener, alarm clock, or calculator) you may have on your real desk. You can use them whenever you are at your desk, too.

The most flexible item in the ⬤ menu is the first one. Right now, and whenever you're at the desktop, it's called **About This Macintosh. . .**, and it gives you information about your Macintosh. Go figure.

Desk Accessories (DAs) are mini-applications that let you do a variety of things. Why call them desk accessories instead of little applications? Because you can call them up and use them no matter where you are or what you're doing on your Mac. Instead of being full-featured applications, most desk accessories will help you do one or two little things (jot a note, add a couple of numbers, and so on) to supplement whatever big application you're using.

Just for the heck of it, click-hold on the menu, and drag the mouse pointer down a little bit, until **About This Macintosh. . .** is selected. Release the mouse button. After your Mac churns for a second, you'll see a simpler version of the window like this.

Macintosh model ⎯⎯⎯⎯
Memory allotted ⎯⎯⎯⎯

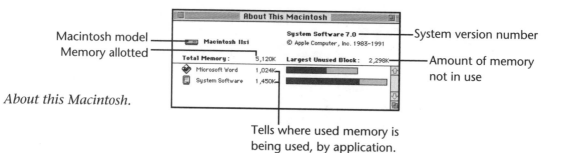

System version number
Amount of memory not in use

About this Macintosh.

Tells where used memory is being used, by application.

The About This Macintosh window shows you how much random-access memory (or *RAM*) is installed in your Mac. You can think about RAM like your own memory: all the things you can remember off the top of your head. RAM is volatile. No, it doesn't have a temper, but any information in your Mac's RAM disappears when you turn your Mac off. We'll talk more about memory in detail a little later. For right now, you should know that the About This Macintosh item in the menu can display how much RAM you have, and how it's being used.

The About This Macintosh window is just chock full of useful information. It tells you the model of Mac you're looking at (in case you don't know), and the version of the System Software installed (which is good if you're looking at an unfamiliar Mac). And the rest of the information is devoted to how much memory is installed and in use on the Mac.

The lower half of the window shows you all of the applications you have running (including your System Software) and how much RAM each is eating up. The display changes as you open and close applications.

This comes in handy if you find yourself getting a lot of **Out of Memory** messages in the middle of important projects. **Out of Memory Messages** are discussed in the "Digital Amnesia" section in the appendix.

Applications have their own menus, with their very own "About *(insert application name here)* . . ." item. You can use it to find out a little bit more about the application you're using.

Put It to Work

Computer programmers are an interesting bunch. They like to sign their work by hiding their names or funny little animations in their programs. These hidden gems are called *Easter Eggs*, because you have to hunt for them.

Usually, finding an Easter Egg involves using an extra key while clicking on something in a program. One Easter Egg is on your desktop right now. Press and hold the **Option** key before clicking on the menu. When the menu drops down, instead of About This Macintosh, you'll see **About The Finder**. (The *Finder* is the part of the System Software that gives you the desktop and the menu bar, and so on.)

When you select **About The Finder**, you'll get a black-and-white drawing of the sun rising (setting?) over a mountain range. That's what the first Mac owners saw. Wait a few seconds and a scroll of programmers names will run across the bottom of the picture. It's a real history of the Macintosh.

That's just one of the dozens of Easter Eggs salted around your Mac's System Software. Try to find others. Happy hunting!

The File Menu

File	
New Folder	⌘N
Open	⌘O
Print	⌘P
Close Window	⌘W
Get Info	⌘I
Sharing...	
Duplicate	⌘D
Make Alias	
Put Away	⌘Y
Find...	⌘F
Find Again	⌘G
Page Setup...	
Print Window...	

Command key equivalent

Grayed-out items are not available.

The File menu. Oooh. Ahh.

The **File** menu is one of those word-headed menus that usually require something to be selected or open on the desktop before you can use it.

The **File** menu has several active functions, and several that are inactive (grayed-out).

You'll find keyboard short-cuts in most menus. They're very good to know.

After some of the menu items, you'll see a command-key equivalent, or keyboard shortcut. They're used by pressing and holding down the command-key and pressing the indicated letter key (like ⌘-**W**, to close a window).

The specific functions of each menu (or even the number of menus) change in each program you use, however, the basic commands remain the same. That's a good thing. When you know how these work, you'll pretty much know how they work in almost any application you use.

To spare you any more confusion, I'll just run down the list of commands in the **File** menu, in order:

New Folder: Creates a new, empty, untitled folder on the desktop or in the active window.

Open: Opens the selected item, if appropriate.

Print: Sends a selected file to the printer for printing.

Close Window: Closes the currently active window.

Get Info: Gives you information on the item you've selected on the desktop or in a window.

Sharing: Applies only to Macs on a network. If your Mac isn't on a network, ignore it. If your Mac is on a network, then you probably have a network administrator to manage this stuff. Don't sweat it.

Duplicate: Makes a copy of the selected item.

Make Alias: Makes a little clone of the selected item. It's a handy feature we'll talk about later.

Put Away: Ejects a selected disk from the disk drive, and removes its icon from the desktop.

Find: Helps you find a misplaced file on your hard drive or a disk.

Find Again: Lets you search more, or widen the search for the thing you were trying to find with the **Find** command.

Page Setup: Tells your printer what size paper you're using, as well as other special printer commands. More on this in the section on printing.

Print Window: Prints the contents of the currently active window. If there is no window open on the desktop, this item reads **Print Desktop**.

Many of these menu items will be covered in upcoming sections, but it never hurts to see them before you're called on to use them.

The Edit Menu

The Edit menu.

The **Edit** menu deals almost exclusively with text and graphic information. On the desktop, you'll use the **Edit** menu mainly for changing the names of folders and icons.

Again, I'll briefly describe the functions, but we'll explore them in detail in an upcoming section.

Undo: Restores the very last thing you did to the way it was before you did it. If you accidentally delete a paragraph of text, Undo will bring it back.

Cut: Removes the selected text or graphic from wherever it is and places it in the Clipboard for later use, or until you cut or copy (see below) something else.

Copy: Similar to **Cut**, except that it leaves the selected text or graphic in its original position and places a copy (*duh*) in the Clipboard.

Paste: Takes whatever is stored in the

Warning! Undo is a great command, but some things cannot be undone. Undo only works on the very last action you took. Selecting Undo won't fix what you did three commands ago, and it won't recover a file you accidentally deleted. Don't get the idea that you can do no wrong as long as the Undo item exists. You can, so be careful.

The *Clipboard* is a bit of reserved memory that holds a limited amount of information, both text and graphics. It's handy to cut or copy stuff from what you are doing, and then paste it back in at one or more locations. What you store there stays put until you cut or copy something else, or until you turn off your Mac.

The striking, yet handsome, View menu.

Clipboard and places it where the insertion point (or cursor) is placed.

Clear: Works like **Cut**, except the selected text or graphic is *not* placed in the Clipboard.

Select All: Selects anything and everything that can be selected in the currently active window.

Show Clipboard: Displays the contents of the Clipboard, in case you forgot what's in there.

The View Menu

The **View** menu lets you control how information

```
View
  by Small Icon
  by Icon
✓ by Name
  by Size
  by Kind
  by Label
  by Date
  by Version
```

is displayed in your windows on the desktop. How you want to look at stuff is strictly up to you and your eyesight.

View by Small Icon: Gives you the smallest icons for your folders and so on, with no other information to get in your way.

View by Icon: Gives you the largest icons for your folders and so on, also with no other information to get in your way.

View by Name: The display option I personally prefer. It gives you a tiny icon for folders and so on, in alphabetical order by name, but follows each up with more information. *Kind* tells you if it's a folder, application, or document. *Size* tells you how much room it takes up.

By the Way . . .

The arrows in front of the folders let you look at what each folder contains without opening another window. Just click on an arrow, and the folder's contents will drop down from the folder, (indented a few spaces). Clicking on the same arrow will hide the folder's contents again. It's a great feature that spares you from a lot of window-clutter.

View by Size: Only works when you display by Name. If you select **View by Size** while displaying any of the icon views, the display will automatically switch to the list, or Name view. Instead of alphabetical order by name, View by Size sorts from the largest to the smallest items in your window.

View by Kind: Like View by Size, View by Kind only works when you display by Name. If you select **View by Kind** while displaying any of the icon views, the display will automatically switch to the list, or Name view. Instead of alphabetical order, it sorts your window putting applications first, then documents, and then folders.

The **View** menu only affects the active window. You can, and you may want to, have different windows show different views. Only time and experience will tell you what works best for you.

With the window of your hard drive open, why don't you try each option and see which you like best. I'll wait.

The Label Menu

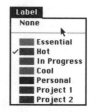

The Label menu.

The **Label** menu is a handy way of color coding the stuff on your Mac. Simply select an icon, then click-drag on the **Label** menu until the label you want is selected. When you release the mouse button, the selected icon turns the color of the label you choose. The label word (like *Essential* or *Hot*) appears in the Label column when you view by Name, Size, or Kind.

When you view by name, and have labels applied to stuff in a window, you can also sort the window by labels by clicking on the word **Label** beneath the title bar as described in the E-Z sidebar. It's convenient for pulling related files (for a project like this book) together without having to hurt yourself coming up with an alphabetical naming scheme for each project.

You can also sort a window that is displayed by Name by simply clicking on the word (Size or Kind) below the title bar. The window contents sorts by the word you click, and that word appears <u>underlined</u> to remind you of how you sorted things.

If you don't have any labels applied, then there's nothing to sort by, so nothing happens.

The labels shown in the last figure can be customized to suit your needs. I'll show you how later, when we go through the Control Panels in Chapter 11. Be patient.

The Special Menu

```
Special
Clean Up Desktop
Empty Trash...

Eject Disk      ⌘E
Erase Disk...

Restart
Shut Down
```

The Special menu. Isn't that special.

We already looked at the **Special** menu back in Part I when I showed you how to shut down your Mac. Of course, it does other things, or it wouldn't be special, now would it?

Clean Up Window: Sometimes, the icons in a window just get to be a mess. They fall all over each other so you can't read their names, or folders pile up on each other. Select **Clean Up Window** to make your Mac straighten things out for you.

Empty Trash: Empties the Trash after you've chucked something into it. We'll do an exercise with this one at the end of the chapter.

Eject Disk: Gets your Mac to spit out the floppy disk in your disk drive. A diskette icon must be selected for this option to work. Unlike **Put Away** (under the **File** menu), the disk's icon remains on the desktop. This is good for copying disks, or working with files from several disks at one time.

Erase Disk: Completely erases the contents of the selected disk, even on your hard drive. Don't use it unless you really, really mean it.

If you like to view your files by icon in your windows (like we discussed when we talked about the **View** menu), but you like the convenience of having them in alphabetical order, do this:

With the window you want to alphabetized active (open it, or click on it to make it active), hold down the **Option** key while you select the **Special** menu. When the **Special** menu drops down, the **Clean Up Window** option will have changed to **Clean Up By Name**. Select **Clean Up By Name**, and watch as your window throws itself into alphabetical order.

Luckily, the ellipsis (. . .) after the name means that selecting this menu item (or any menu item with ". . ." after it) will bring up a *dialog box* before it actually does anything. It gives you a chance to chicken out if you've selected it accidentally. Erasing disks and all sorts of other disk tips will be covered in Chapter 9. It's required reading. No excuses.

Restart: Puts your Mac through its startup routine without having to turn the power off. When you install software, you are sometimes required to restart your Mac before you can actually use it.

Shut Down: Shuts off all the applications (even the System Software) running on your Mac before you turn the power off. On some Mac models (like the Quadras), it even turns the power off, too. Check your manual if you're not sure.

Balloon Help

The Balloon
Help menu.

Balloon Help marks the return to those icon-headed menus that perform specific functions all of the time. You'll probably find Balloon Help really cool—for about a hot minute.

Balloon Help displays little speech balloons with short explanations when you point at various things around the desktop and in applications written to include help balloons (not all have them).

It *is* handy for folks just starting out with Macs, there's no denying it. There is, however, also no denying that it slows you down: every time the arrow cursor touches something that has a help balloon attached, you get to see it whether you want to or not.

Once you have the basics down, you'll probably want to keep it turned off until you have a new program to learn or need a refresher on basics.

About Balloon Help: Tells you about Balloon Help (duh.).

Show Balloons: Turns Balloon Help on. If Balloon Help is already on, this item becomes Hide Balloons, and selecting it turns Balloon Help off. (This is known as a, what class? A *toggle*, like we talked about in the last chapter)

With Balloon Help turned on, pointing the arrow cursor at your Hard Drive icon brings up the Help balloon.

Finder Shortcuts: Brings up a set of five cards that summarize almost 30 keyboard shortcuts that you can use at the desktop. After a while, you'll find this feature more helpful than the actual help balloons.

When you're using an application that includes full Balloon Help, this item turns into that application's access to help (in Microsoft Word, for instance, it reads "Microsoft Word Help").

And that's all she wrote about Balloon Help. You'll have to decide if it's helpful for you. My opinion shouldn't dissuade you from using it if you like it.

Did you ever accidentally (or on purpose) stick your finger into an electrical socket? (If you were ever a three-year-old, you must have.) It wasn't very pleasant, was it?

Well, something similar happens to your Mac every time you turn the power on. Some compare it to pouring hot water into a cold glass, or constantly revving the engine on your car. It isn't necessarily a bad thing to do; you have to turn your Mac on to use it. However, over-using it can put unnecessary strain on the electronic components. That's why there's a **Restart** option in the **Special** menu. Using **Restart** puts your Mac through its startup sequence without applying a shock (literally) to its System.

Words of Wisdom: It is better for your machine if you leave it running, rather than turning it on and off two or three times a day. If you need to restart it because of a problem, or because of new software you've installed, use **Restart**. Your Mac will be much happier.

The Application Menu

Right now, with no applications open, your **Application** menu will look just like this. Not a lot of help.

This is the Application menu.

> Hide Finder
> Hide Others
> Show All
> ✓ 🖥 Finder

The **Application** menu comes in handy when you have one or more applications running at once (that's called *multitasking*). As you open applications, their names get added to the list at the bottom of the menu.

The Application menu with stuff in it.

> **Hide Finder**
> **Hide Others**
> Show All
>
> ✓ 🖥 Finder
> ◆ Microsoft Word

SPEAK LIKE A GEEK

Multitasking is a geeky way of saying "doing more than one thing at a time." In computing, it generally means running more than one program simultaneously.

I'm going to run through the menu based on the preceding figure, the one with an application showing, because the menu really only works when you have other stuff running. When you use it yourself later, just substitute your own application name for the one shown here, okay?

The Menu Icon: While it isn't really a selectable menu item, the menu icon lets you know what application is active in the foreground. Like an active window, an active application is the one up front on the desktop, the one you can actually do stuff with.

In the last figure, the active application is the Finder (the desktop). You can tell, first, by the little Mac icon that heads the menu, and second, because there is a check mark next to the Finder in the bottom half of the menu.

If, in the figure, Microsoft Word was the active application, it would be checked in the bottom half of the menu, and its icon (to the left of its name) would be the one that appeared in the menu bar.

Hide Finder: Hides all of the windows on the desktop associated with the Finder. If Microsoft Word were the active application, this item would read **Hide Microsoft Word**.

Hide Others: Hides all of the windows associated with the applications other than the active application. This is very handy for reducing desktop clutter when working on a complicated project.

Show All: Shows all the windows associated with all of the open applications. This is handy if you're lost and don't know where you want to go, or what you want to do. Needless to say, I use this feature a lot. **Show All** only becomes an active (not grayed-out) choice when you've used **Hide Others** to hide other windows and applications.

The Applications List: You can select the name of any application in this list to make it the active application (that is, the one in the front that you can do something with).

I think it is easier to select it from this list than to **Show All** of your application windows and then click on a window associated with the project you want. Both ways work, though, and you may find it easier the other way.

The benefits of the **Application** menu and System 7's ability for multitasking are only truly apparent if you've ever worked on an involved project and only been able to use one application at a time. You can really burn up the desktop, and as Ray Bradbury says, "It was a pleasure to burn."

A Pause for the Cause

That was certainly a lot of stuff to go over. I think you should probably take a break right about now—unless you snuck out while I was babbling away.

Before you run off for a cup of coffee or some other beverage, let's run through a quick exercise to pull some of the huge amount of boring, yet factual, information together so it sticks a little better.

If you're not at your Mac, get to it. If it isn't turned on, fire it up. You'll need your hard drive window open on the desktop, so if it isn't there, double-click on your Hard Drive icon to get it there. Ready? Begin.

Taking Out the Trash: An Exorcise

That's not a typographical error, it's a joke, and we haven't quite gotten to the punch line yet. (I hope it'll still be funny.) Okay. With your hard drive window open and active on the desktop, we're going to create and dispose of a little trash. That way, you can use some of the menu and window features we've been talking about without running the risk of accidentally throwing out something you need.

If the folder name doesn't get highlighted (it should, but just in case), hit the **Enter** key. That should do it.

Your Mac wants to show you when you've selected an item. Icons go dark. Text, including the names of files and folders, gets washed with a color (I'll show you how to change the highlight color when we talk about Control Panels in Chapter 11).

To remember the *highlighting* term, think of the colored highlighting markers you buy to highlight important phrases in a text book.

1. Select **New Folder** under the **File** menu. That creates an untitled folder in your hard drive's window.

2. When the untitled folder appears, its name is first black (new folders are automatically selected) and then turns a different color (probably gray, unless you've been playing with the Color Control Panel behind my back). That's the highlight color, and the name is highlighted. That means you can change the folder's name.

3. While the folder name is still highlighted, type in its new name. For the sake of my pathetic joke, type: **Demon Folder** (if you don't want to play along, call it anything— up to 27 characters, numbers, and spaces). The first character you type replaces the old name. Press **Enter** again. The folder is renamed, re-alphabetized by its new name, and still selected.

4. Now, while the renamed folder is still selected, pull down the **File** menu again, and select **Duplicate**.

5. A folder called **Demon Folder copy** (if you called it Demon Folder like I asked you to) appears in the window after the original. It's a carbon copy of the original, except for the name *You can't have two files with exactly the same name in any window or folder*—your Mac won't let you, so don't even try.

6. Rename the copy as you did the original. Name it **Beelzububba**.

7. Drag the folder Beelzububba until it is on top of the original Demon Folder. The Demon Folder turns dark, as if selected, when the arrow pointer touches it. See what I mean?

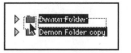

8. The folder Beelzububba is now inside the Demon Folder (you can double-click on the Demon Folder icon and see, if you don't believe me).

9. If you care to, you can repeat the process (creating new or duplicate folders, renaming them, and dropping them into the Demon Folder) to your heart's content, or at least until you run out of demon names. Or you can just move on to the next step.

10. With a folder with something inside of it now, drag and drop the **Demon Folder** on the **Trash** icon. The Trash behaves like any other folder, so when the pointer dragging the folder touches the Trash, the Trash turns dark.

11. When you drop the Demon Folder into the Trash, the Trash icon changes to show you there's something inside. Neat, huh?

12. Now that the Trash is full, you may as empty it. Select **Empty Trash** from the **Special** menu.

13. You'll receive a warning that you're about to throw away something that might be important. Since we want to get rid of these Demons (exorcise them, as it were), click in the circle that says **OK**. That's called a *button*, and they work like, buttons that you push (as opposed to buttons on clothes).

By the Way . . .

If you find that warning annoying each and every time you want to throw something away, you can turn it off. Here's how:

1. Click on the **Trash** icon to select it.
2. Select **Get Info** from the **File** menu. You'll see the Info window.
3. Click on the check mark in front of **Warn Before Emptying** so the check mark goes away.

Congratulations, your Trash Warning is disabled. Now, be careful that you don't throw anything important away.

That wasn't too difficult, was it? And you even picked up a few bonus bits of information along the way.

The Least You Need to Know

I don't expect all of this menu stuff to stick. It gets easier with practice and patience. The essential thing to remember is the location of this chapter. Use it for easy reference as you explore your new Mac.

If you *must* have something to remember from this chapter, remember:

- ☞ The menu bar is your friend. It gives you speedy access to nearly every single function your Mac can perform.

- ☞ You'll also find keyboard shortcuts for the most frequently used commands right after their menu entries (like ⌘-S for Save). They give you even speedier access to often-used commands.

- ☞ The View and Label menus offer great organizational tools, if you're inclined to use them.

- ☞ The icon-headed menus (the and Application menus) give your Mac an incredible amount of flexibility: the menu for letting you use DAs any time, and the Application menu for letting you switch between any and all open applications without having to quit or restart any of them.

Okay, take your break, you've earned it.

Chapter 7
Programs, Aliases, and Other Hocus-Pocus

In This Chapter

- ☞ 3, 2, 1 . . . We have lift-off!
- ☞ The alias relocation program

Welcome to Chapter 7. In this chapter, we'll look at all the different ways there are to launch (that is, *start*) applications, and how to simplify that process with spiffy little things called *aliases*.

There's a method to my madness (actually, people don't usually question the madness part, just the method). What I'm trying to do is build up your Mac skills gradually, layer upon layer, so that by the time we're done, you'll be ready to take on any application or problem the Mac throws at you. You may not learn exactly what you need for every situation, but I hope to give you the power to know where to look and how to look for solutions on your own.

The Face That Launched 1,000 Applications

That may be stretching the truth a bit. I don't think Helen of Troy owned a Mac. But if she had, she would have launched millions of applications by now.

When you start an application, you *launch* it (also called *starting* or *opening* an application or program).

Launching, or starting, an application is something you're going to do often. As cool as the desktop is, there aren't a lot of productive things you can do with it. You have to start up another program. So, let's see how to do it.

As I mentioned earlier, there are usually several ways to accomplish the same task on a Mac. Launching an application is no different. Here are five methods you can use to directly launch a program. (I stress *directly* because there is a way to launch a program indirectly. We'll be talking about that later on.) Let me count the ways:

☞ Click on an application's icon to select it, and then use the **File** menu's **Open** command to open it.

☞ Use the shortcut key ⌘-**O**.

☞ Double-click on the application's icon.

☞ Double-click on a document icon.

☞ Drag a document icon onto an application icon.

We'll go over each of these ways in the next few sections.

Click on an Icon and Use a Menu

A common way to launch a program is to select the program's icon and then use the **Open** command. To select an icon, simply click on it. When it's highlighted, pull down the **File** menu and choose the **Open** command.

For example, look in your hard drive's window for the **TeachText** icon. It should be right out there in the open. When you find it, click on it to select it. While it's selected, go to the **File** menu, and select **Open**. Then, jump back. (James Brown noises are optional.)

Click on an Icon and Use a Shortcut Key

A careful observer might have noticed that the **Open** command on the **File** menu has a keyboard shortcut: ⌘-**O**. Surprisingly enough, that shortcut key is the second way to launch a program. To use it, you select the program's icon, and then press the ⌘ and O keys simultaneously.

Simon Says Click Twice

Here is an excruciatingly simple way to start a program: just double-click on the application's icon. This is probably the fastest way to launch an application. Just point right at the program's icon with the mouse pointer, and click twice on it. It'll start right up, easy as pie.

Just about any file you produce with an application is called a *document*. Your Mac calls these files *documents* to easily distinguish them from applications and folders. (You can see what your Mac calls each type of file by reading down the **Kind** column when you view a window by name.)

The Sneaky Back-Door Method: Double-Clicking on a Document

Did you notice that in the preceding sections I kept telling you to select a program's icon, or an application's icon? I had to be specific because there are different types of files. There are also *document* files, which are the files you create when you use a program.

You can launch a program through one of its documents just by double-clicking on the document's icon. For example, if you double-clicked on a Read Me file, the TeachText program would start, and the Read Me document would immediately appear on-screen.

So, you've just learned another way to launch a program. Believe it or not, there is still another way. Keep reading.

Drag 'N Drop

The last way you can open an application directly is by dragging a document icon and

Every document you produce with a program is tagged with *File Type* and *Creator* information. The File Type tells whether a file is a word processing document, picture file, or something else entirely. The Creator is a coded version of the name of the program that produced the file. Both are stored in a little snip of information called a *File Header*, the first place your Mac looks when you double-click on a document.

dropping it right on the application you want to use to open it. I say the application you *want* to use, because sometimes, you have a mystery file and you don't know (or don't own) the program that created it. You can *try* to open it with an application you do own by dragging and dropping the document on that application. Sometimes it works and sometimes it doesn't, but it doesn't hurt to try.

You drag and drop a document onto an application the same way you dragged and dropped a folder onto the Trash.

Get Me Outta Here!

Now that you've launched the program, you're going to need to know how to get out of it. That's called *quitting*. Quitting an application is just a fancy-schmancy way of saying "shutting it off." To quit, select **Quit** from the program's **File** menu. Or you can use the key combination ⌘-**Q** to quit.

Put It to Work

Try the drag and drop method now, using the Read Me file we talked about earlier. If TeachText is still open, you need to **Quit** it. Then, locate a Read Me file, and drag and drop it right on top of the TeachText icon. Bada-bing, Bada-boom: TeachText launches, opening the file in the process.

Now, **Quit** TeachText again. You'll notice that the Read Me file didn't move when you dragged it onto TeachText. It stayed right where you left it. That's so you don't end up moving your document files every time you drag and drop them. You'd really have a hard time keeping track of them if that happened.

So, you've learned how to launch a program, and you've learned how to quit a program. And you think you've got this whole launching business under control. Well, think again. There's an indirect, yet very cool, way you can start a program. You can use an alias.

Alias Smith and Jones

I mentioned *aliases* earlier when we looked at the **Make Alias** command in the **File** menu. You were probably scratching your head over that one. Rest assured, they have nothing to do with the Witness Relocation Program.

Aliases are so cool. They are little clones of anything you care to clone: applications, documents, file folders, even your hard drive or the Trash. They take up very little disk space—only 1–3K each, which is gobs less than if you dropped actual copies of things all over.

Aliases act like a trail of bread crumbs leading back to the original application (or whatever). When you double-click on an alias, the double-click follows the trail back to the original application (or whatever), and reacts as if you'd double-clicked on it. It's like you're creating little brothers Karamazov: poke one, the other says "ouch!"

You leave your frequently used items (applications or folders, and so on) wherever they are on your hard drive, and scatter their aliases where you can get at them easily (on the desktop, in the menu, anywhere convenient for you). The next section will tell you how to make one.

OOPS!

Aliases are a smart idea. Your Mac, however, is still an idiot. If you move (or remove) the original application (or whatever), the alias' trail of bread crumbs won't follow along. The double-click follows the trail back to where the application *used* to be, and you get a cranky screen message about being unable to locate the original. When you move an original, you have to delete the old alias and make a new one. If you delete an original, delete the alias.

Alias *This*!

Let's make an alias. In this example, you'll make an alias of TeachText and put it on the desktop, and then move it into the menu. While this example uses TeachText, keep in mind that the procedure is the same for everything you want an alias of.

Start by clicking on the **TeachText** icon to select it. While TeachText is selected, click on the **File** menu, and select the **Make Alias** option. When you see the TeachText icon again, you'll be surprised to find its alias lying right beside it in the window. That's all there is to it.

*TeachText and
its alias.*

You'll notice two things about the alias. First, your Mac added the word *alias* to the end of the file's name. This is partially to identify it as the alias, but mostly because you can't have two files with exactly the same name in the same place. Second, you'll notice that an alias' name appears in *italics*; even if you change the alias' name (and we will), it will always be in italics.

The Alias Relocation Program

One of the handier places to put an alias of a frequently used item is right on the desktop. As long as it doesn't get buried behind a dozen windows, it's always right there where you can see it and get to it. Another good place to put an alias is on the menu, so you have access to it from any application.

To the Desktop

To put your TeachText alias on the desktop, just drag it from your hard drive's window, and drop it wherever you like on your desktop. You can form a conga-line of aliases across the bottom or down the left side of your screen—whatever works for you.

Now that it's out of the same window as its original, you can rename the TeachText alias, if you care to. Personally, I just delete the word "alias" and shorten the name: I shortened my *Microsoft Word alias* to just *Word*.

With the alias settled in its new home on the desktop, you can use it to open TeachText without having to root around for the original. The TeachText alias responds exactly the same way the original TeachText icon responds to any of the launching techniques you've already learned. Try some now.

When you've finished amusing yourself with opening the alias, let's move it into the menu.

If you don't remember how to rename a file, look back in the last section of Chapter 6, where you renamed the untitled folders for the Trash exercise.

To the Menu

Putting an alias into the menu is easier than you think. To begin, look for the folder named **System Folder** in your hard drive's window. Double-click on it when you've found it. This is the grand-daddy of all folders.

Look around inside the System Folder for the folder named **Apple Menu Items**, and double-click on that, too. You'll recognize it by the Apple logo on the folder. When the Apple Menu Items window opens, you'll find everything that shows up in your menu (except **About This Macintosh . . .**).

If you look closely, you'll see you already have an alias in there: the *Control Panels* folder. You can tell it's an alias because its name is in *italics*, even though the word "alias" was edited out.

Drag the TeachText alias from the desktop, and drop it in the Apple Menu Items window. Your Mac will churn for a second or two (you'll know it's working because the pointer icon will turn briefly into an animated ticking watch).

Now, select the menu, and scroll down the list. You'll see your TeachText alias listed there, right after the Scrapbook DA. To launch TeachText from the alias in the menu, just select it like you would any other menu item. TeachText will launch.

Sorting Aliases in the Menu

Things in the menu are sorted alphabetically. If I'm remembering the alphabet correctly (Q, R, S, T . . .), that's why TeachText shows up after Scrapbook. You can't change how the menu sorts things, so if you want menu items to show up in a different order, you have to change their names so they fall where you'd like alphabetically. The easiest way to do that is to add a space in front of the name(s) you want at the top of your list, because blank spaces come before everything else in the alphabet.

To add a space, click on the **TeachText alias** icon to select it. When the name is highlighted, position the I-beam cursor over the beginning of the name, and click so that the insertion point appears before the **T** in **Teach**.

Editing an alias'
name.

Press the **Spacebar** once, and then press **Enter**.

If you want to get fancy, you can use two spaces for some menu items, and they'll float to the very top of the list. Use one space for the ones you want below those. Leave the names of the ones you want below those alone—don't add anything. You now have three levels of importance in the menu. Slick?

TeachText alias
*on top of the *
menu.

If you want to add another level to your menu, you can add a special character called a *bullet* (•) to the beginning of the alias' name by pressing the **Option-8** key combination instead of the Spacebar. Special characters, like the bullet, sink to the bottom of the list alphabetically.

As you get more experience, and come to rely heavily on more programs and folders on your Mac, you may wind up with a very full menu. Mine's crammed full of stuff (if you don't believe me, look at the next figure), so much so, you can't even look at all of it at once. The little downward arrow at the bottom of the menu means that there's more stuff down there, and you have to scroll down there to see it.

That's true of all long menus. A downward pointing arrow means there's more to come. A sideways pointing arrow means there's a sub-menu that pops out when you select that menu item. In the figure, the QuicKeys menu is a sub-menu.

Special characters, such as the bullet (•), are part of the character sets of most of the *fonts* (typefaces, such as Times and Helvetica) on your Mac. Special characters are accessed by using the Option key plus a character key (like the Option-8 combination for the bullet), or the Option key plus the Shift key plus a character key (Option-Shift-8 gives you the symbol for degrees Fahrenheit, as in 451°).

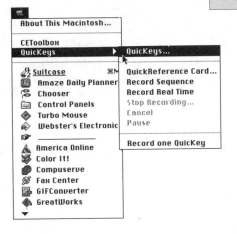

A stuffed menu.

I'll talk more about customizing the (the symbol is made by pressing **Option-Shift-K**, by the way) when we talk about customizing options on your Mac in Chapter 12.

The Least You Need to Know

Now that you know how to launch applications, you're probably going to want to actually do something with them once you start them up. Before you skip to the next chapter and start learning, refresh your memory by perusing these important concepts:

☞ There are usually a few different ways to accomplish the same task on a Mac: through a menu, with the mouse, or with a command-key combination.

☞ You can launch (*start*) an application with its icon, or with a document's icon, by selecting it and choosing **Open** from the **File** menu, or pressing ⌘-**O**. Double-clicking on either kind of icon also works.

☞ Aliases are simple to make: click on an application (or whatever) icon, and select **Make Alias** from the **File** menu. They simplify your life.

☞ You can add aliases (and most anything you like) to the menu, just by dragging it into the Apple Menu Items folder inside the System Folder.

Chapter 8
Your Basic, Everyday Mac Duties

In This Chapter

- ☛ Chatting with dialog boxes
- ☛ Opening, saving, and closing files
- ☛ S.C.R.A.P.: selecting, copying, replacing, and pasting

I *have* to share this with you.

I walked into the living room this morning just in time to hear Geraldo Rivera say to an unusually unusual-looking guest, "So your parents never smelled the gasoline on your breath?" I didn't know what they were talking about, and I didn't *want* to know. I was so scared, I had to change the channel. Now, for some reason, I can't get it out of my head.

Thanks for letting me get that off my chest.

Let that highly unusual (at least to my way of thinking) episode lead us into a *very* usual discussion of three of the most commonly used commands on a Mac: Open (⌘-O), Save (⌘-S), and Close (⌘-W).

The big three are all located in your File menu. How *big* are they? Well, try not using at least one of them in any session on your Mac—it can't be done. You'll wind up just sitting there, staring at your desktop. That's how common and important these little beauties are.

Open Sez-Me

Say you're using the TeachText program, and you want to *open* a file (that is, load it into memory so you can tinker with it). When you select **Open** from the **File** menu, TeachText presents the Open dialog box shown in the next figure. This dialog box is necessary because the Mac needs to know which file you'd like to open.

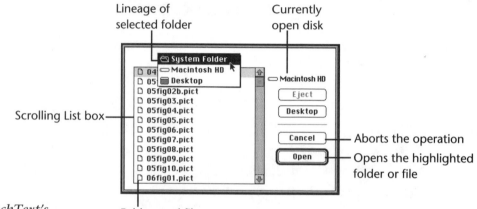

Lineage of
selected folder

Currently
open disk

Scrolling List box

Aborts the operation

Opens the highlighted
folder or file

*TeachText's
Open dialog box.*

Folders and files
to choose from

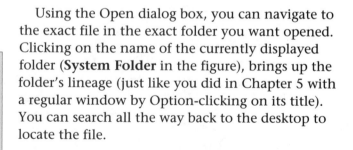

Use the shortcut key ⌘-O to open a file. It will work on any Mac application worth its salt . . . in short, it's a standard.

Using the Open dialog box, you can navigate to the exact file in the exact folder you want opened. Clicking on the name of the currently displayed folder (**System Folder** in the figure), brings up the folder's lineage (just like you did in Chapter 5 with a regular window by Option-clicking on its title). You can search all the way back to the desktop to locate the file.

To the right, the little picture of a hard drive (named **Macintosh HD** in the figure) shows the name of the currently open disk or drive. If it is a disk you're looking at, the picture of the hard drive is replaced by a little picture of a diskette. Also, if you're looking for a file on a disk, and the disk doesn't contain the file you want, clicking once on the **Eject** button (duh) ejects that disk from the drive.

Clicking on the **Desktop** button changes the file display to show all of the items, such as hard drives, disks, or files (like the Trash), actually stored on the desktop.

This is a speedy way of digging yourself out of a folder buried deep within other folders.

The **Cancel** button lets you stop the process (if you clicked **Open** by mistake or change your mind). Your Mac always gives you a chance to change your mind, especially before you do something destructive, like erase a disk. I'll talk about destructive things in detail in Chapter 10. Just call me Uncle Fester.

The **Open** button opens the selected file or folder in the List box. Imagine that.

SPEAK LIKE A GEEK

Sometimes, when you give your Mac a command (like to open or save a file), your Mac requests more information to complete the task. Macs get this information by using *d*ialog boxes. They're called dialog boxes because the Mac asks you a question and you answer it. That's a dialog—short and sweet.

By the Way . . .

If you don't have an existing document to open, you can create a brand-spankin'-new one by selecting the **New** command from TeachText's **File** menu. You can also use the ⌘-N key combination.

Any application that lets you create a document (of any kind) will respond to the New command.

Save Me!

Do you remember reading about *RAM* (random-access memory) in Chapter 6? Whenever you are working with a document in an application, the document is held in your Mac's RAM. It's the kind of memory that goes away when you switch off your Mac. As you add stuff or remove stuff from the document, the changes are also stored only in RAM.

If you switch off your Mac, the document goes away forever unless you first save it to your hard drive or a diskette. You save a document by selecting **Save** from the **File** menu. When you use the Save command in TeachText, you'll see the Save dialog box shown here. Other programs use variations of this dialog box. Some are more complicated, others are less complicated. Through them all, these features remain standard.

List box   Currently open disk

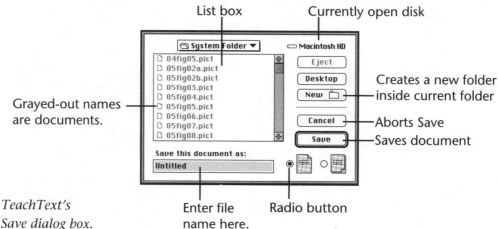

Grayed-out names
are documents.

Creates a new folder
inside current folder

Aborts Save

Saves document

TeachText's
Save dialog box.

Enter file   Radio button
name here.

To quickly save a file, use
the key combination ⌘-**S**.
This shortcut works in any
Mac application.

Related to the Open dialog box, a kissing-cousin, as it were, is the Save dialog box, like the one shown in the figure. Let's take a brief tour through the Save dialog box.

The folder name (which pops up with the folder's lineage), the Current disk name, Eject, and Desktop buttons function exactly the same way as they do in the Open dialog box (or any dialog box, for that matter). You can use them to navigate to the exact folder where you want to save your file.

The New Folder button creates a new folder inside the currently open disk or folder. If you click on the **New Folder** button, you are presented with a small dialog box asking you to enter a name for the new folder.

The Cancel button aborts the Save operation and returns you to the application.

The Save button saves your document in the currently open folder or disk. Because it has that thick, black border, you can simply press your **Enter** key, rather than clicking on it to save. You can click on it, too.

By the Way . . .

If you select a folder in the list box, the Save button changes to Open, so you can open that folder. You may also open a folder by double-clicking on its name in the list box.

Below the Save button, you see two document icons with *radio buttons* beside them. The filled (selected) radio button indicates that the current document will be saved as a regular document. The document icon beside it, with the bottom right corner folded up, when selected (just click on the radio button to select) will save the current document as a *Stationery Pad.*

Finally, below *Save this document as:* is an edit box where you can enter a name for the file you are saving. The name should be something obvious, and under 32 characters. A letter to your parole board might be named ParoleBoard Memo (or ParoleBoard Memo10, if you write to them frequently). When you have the List box displaying the folder you want to save the file in, and you've entered the file's name, just click on the **Save** button (or press **Enter**), and the file will be saved with that name in that folder.

A *Stationery Pad* behaves like its real-world counter-part. A document saved as stationery, when opened in an application, appears as a *new, untitled* document, so the original Stationery Pad is never altered.

This format is ideal for letterheads, or form letters, or any other kind of file of information you use frequently with only minor changes.

Closing Time

So, your file is saved, and you're ready to work on something else. Before you open another file, you should close the one you're working on. You can leave it open if you want to, but if you left all your files open, you'd have a bunch of open windows scattered all over. They would hog your system resources and slow down your Mac. Bad news. It's best to close documents when you're done with them.

All you have to do is open the **File** menu, and choose **Close**. Talk about easy. If you've saved your document, the window closes, and you'll be able to open another file or create a new one. If you have made changes in your file since the last time you saved it, a dialog box will ask if you want to save the latest changes. I suggest saving your changes. When the Mac is finished updating the file, the window closes.

Now that you know how to get in and out of documents, let's move on to something meatier.

Selecting Stuff

Probably the most-used operations on the Mac are copying, replacing, and pasting. In order to do those actions, you have to first learn how to select the things that you want to copy, replace, or paste. You've already done some selecting when you clicked on an icon to select it, but there are many other ways to select things. Let's go over a few.

Icons, Icons Everywhere

You know how to select a single icon, but if you have a few you want to do something to (like make a pile of aliases all at once), it's easiest to select them altogether. If you selected them singly (clicking on one, making an alias, clicking on the next, and so on), it can get pretty tedious. Don't worry, you're covered.

Try these handy selecting methods:

If you select an icon in the group that you *don't* want selected, you can hold down the **Shift** key and click on the selected icon to deselect it.

☞ If you hold down the **Shift** key, you can click on several icons, and they'll all be selected. Strangely enough, this maneuver is called a *shift-click*.

☞ You can also select a whole passel of icons: click in the window near the first icon, and drag the mouse towards the other icons you want to select. You see a dotted-line box start at the point where you clicked. When you drag, as the box touches icons, they will be selected (as shown in the figure). That's a *drag-select*.

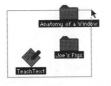

Drag-selecting icons.

☛ If you want to select *everything* in a window you can use the key combination ⌘-A (A is for All), and everything in the active window will be selected. ⌘-A is one of the key combinations that works in most applications.

If you get carried away, you can always go back and shift-click on icons you didn't mean to select.

Text Selection

You have a few more options when you select text, depending on the complexity of the word processor you are using. TeachText, which we'll use for the examples here, has very few text selecting options. Microsoft Word, on the other hand, has *gazillions* of them.

We'll look at the basic ones that are available in TeachText. When you move up to a more comprehensive word processor, make sure you check out your text selecting options in the manual.

To start, launch TeachText by whatever method you prefer. When it's opened, you'll have an *untitled* text window. In order to select some text, you're going to need some text to select. Type in a paragraph or so of anything you care to enter. I'll be working with the text shown in the figure.

```
▬▬▬▬▬▬▬▬▬▬▬ Untitled ▬▬▬▬▬▬▬▬▬▬▬
This morning, I walked into the living room and heard Geraldo say, "Didn't your parents
ever smell the gasoline on your breath?"  I had to change the channel.  He scared me.
```

Here's a text window.

Put It to Work

After you've entered text, you may as well save it, just for the practice. Select **Save** from the **File** Menu, or press ⌘-**S**. When you see the Save dialog box, type in an appropriate name, and press **Enter**, or click on the **Save** button. After your text is saved, the "Untitled" in the title bar changes to whatever you've named your document.

Just for practice, move the cursor around your screen. When the cursor is over the text window, it's the I-beam cursor. When it strays to the scroll, title, or menu bars, it turns back into the arrow cursor. That's because your Mac only lets you do what's appropriate at the point the cursor is touching. It's not appropriate to enter text directly on the title bar, so you don't even have that option.

Position the I-beam cursor so it's touching one word, and double-click. Boom, that word is highlighted.

To select more than one word, position the I-beam cursor at the beginning of the first word you want to select, and then drag until all the words you want selected are highlighted. In this manner, you can select two words, a sentence, a whole paragraph, or even more.

To select *all* of your sample text, you can drag over the whole paragraph. Or you can simply use the **Select All** command under the **Edit** menu, or press the ⌘-**A** combination.

By the Way . . .

Some more advanced word processors have additional ways of selecting text. For example, triple-clicking selects a whole line of text in Microsoft Word and other word processors. Check the manual that came with your program for more information.

Since a whole bunch of text is selected, let's play around with it.

Copy, Cut, and Paste

Sister Mary Mayonnaise was a terror when it came to her students' copying. I guess this is the best revenge: teaching a lot of people how to copy all at once. I'll try not to be smug.

Copy

Copying text comes in handy when you find yourself typing the same word or phrase over and over in a document. Say you were writing a paper about Joseph Conrad's *Heart of Darkness*. You'd get pretty tired of typing "Belgian Congo" and "whited sepulchers" over and over (especially "sepulchers" because it's hard to spell).

By using the **Copy** command, you can copy the ticklish word or phrase to the Clipboard (discussed back in Chapter 6), and then just **Paste** it into your document wherever you need it. Here's how.

Pick a word, any word, from your sample text. Double-click on it to select it. While the word is highlighted, select **Copy** from the **Edit** menu (or press the ⌘-C combination). That word is now in your Clipboard. If you don't believe me, you can select the **Show Clipboard** command, also under the **Edit** menu.

Paste

Now that the tricky word (or phrase, or paragraph) is right where you want it, you can Paste it anywhere you care to. To Paste *anything* from the Clipboard, simply move the I-beam cursor to the spot where you want to paste, and click once to put the insertion point in that spot. Select **Paste** from the **Edit** menu (or press ⌘-**V**). Your Mac drops the word (or words) from the Clipboard at the insertion point.

Remember that the Clipboard can only hold *one thing at a time*. If you copy another word or phrase to the Clipboard, it replaces whatever was in there before. If there's something you want available for pasting all of the time (like your name and address), you might want to add it to your Scrapbook. I'll show you how in Chapter 12 in the " Night of the Living DAs" section.

Cut and Paste

Cut and Paste is a similar operation to Copy and Paste, except for one big difference. When you copy text, the original word or phrase you selected stays right where it was in your document. When you cut text, the original word or phrase is *removed* from the document.

Cut and Paste comes in handy if you find yourself juggling paragraphs. If you find a paragraph at the end of your *Heart of Darkness* report that should have been at the beginning, you can drag to select it, and choose **Cut** from the **Edit** menu (or press the ⌘-X combination). Then, **Paste** it where it belongs. Cut and Paste can save you a lot of needless retyping.

Replacing Text

Sometimes, when you're writing (at least when *I'm* writing), you find that a word or phrase is completely wrong. You want to replace it with something else—preferably something better.

If you accidentally start to type while a word or phrase is selected, stop. Select **Undo** from the **Edit** menu, and cross your fingers. That should restore the text you accidentally replaced.

There are several ways to do that.

☞ You can position the insertion point after the offending word or phrase, and use the **Delete** key to delete it one letter at a time, then type in a new word or phrase.

☞ You can select the offending word or phrase and **Cut** it, and then type in the new one.

☞ You can select the word or phrase, and then just start to type. Whenever you select a letter, word, line, or paragraph of text, it is replaced by *whatever you type next*. Take this as a warning as well as a hint: Whenever you select a letter, word, line, or paragraph of text, it is replaced by whatever you type next.

By the Way . . .

There's a fabulous program called QuicKeys from CE Software that is a comprehensive set of utilities that let you automate a lot of the tedious and repetitive tasks on your Mac. QuicKeys lets you build *macros*, which are complex sets of maneuvers (like opening an application and a set of documents) reduced to one or two keystrokes. It does this by recording all of the moves you make (either with the mouse or the keyboard), and then replaying them back when you press a certain key combination. QuicKeys also comes with some predefined macros, so you don't have to build them all from scratch.

More germane (isn't he one of those Jackson brothers?) to the discussion at hand is the fact that it comes with little mini-utilities, such as Grab Ease and Paste Ease. Grab Ease lets you select and "grab" frequently used text and store it (permanently). Paste Ease lets you select from a menu of stored text clips you've "grabbed" and paste them into any document anytime. It beats the heck out of cutting, copying, and pasting with the Clipboard.

The Least You Need to Know

Whew! That was quite a chapter. And, as usual, it was jam-packed with absolutely essential information. Let's review:

☞ Use the File menu to do things like Open, Save, and Close documents. Of course, you can also use the command-key shortcuts, too.

☞ It's important to save your work often. If your power accidentally goes out or your Mac crashes, you'll lose everything you haven't saved. Save early, and save often.

☞ Your Mac hits you with a dialog box when it needs more information from you to do its job.

☞ Before you can copy, replace, or paste anything, you have to select it.

☞ The Clipboard is the temporary holding area for all the things you cut and copy. Just remember—it can only hold *one* thing at a time.

Chapter 9
Floppies Don't Flop & Other Floppy Facts

In This Chapter

- ☞ Floppy flavors
- ☞ Inserting and formatting disks
- ☞ Care and feeding of your floppies

Once upon a time, there was a boy who didn't believe in floppy disks. He was a diskless wonder. Sure, he'd use his original disks to install programs, but then never touched them again. He just saved all the work he did to his hard drive and thought it was good enough. Even though the Village Geek had warned him that not keeping backup copies of his programs and data was a big, BIG mistake, nothing can sway this diskless wonder. He was a *very* foolish boy.

Then one day, from out of the silicon jungle, a troll appeared. Not just any old troll, but a Technical Troll, wielding the awful power of magnets, dust, and other assorted airborne crap. The Troll saw the boy's hard drive and thought it a tasty-looking morsel. He let loose all his might upon it: magnetic fields to scramble the data; a fistful of poisonous dust and goat hair shoved right into the computer's case; and he even gave it a severe thwacking to jiggle the heads until they cracked and crashed.

The diskless wonder begged for mercy. "No, please, Sir Troll!" he cried, "My life is on that thing. How will I survive?" The Troll finally went away, and the boy saw the state of his hard drive. He went wildly insane and disappeared in the silicon jungle. He was never heard from again. The end.

You may now hiss the villains: dust, magnetic fields, and other assorted *schmootz*. They're *real* bad guys. This chapter is your number one defense against these creeping horrors. In it, you'll learn all you need to know about floppy disks, and how they can save you and your valuable data from Techno Trolls and their nasty bags of tricks.

Floppies Are Your Friends

Next to your Mac, your best friend is your floppy drive—okay, people come first, *then* your Mac, *then* your floppy drive. In addition to being a way to get junk onto your Mac's hard drive, your floppy drive is a way to get your valuable data and programs out of your Mac onto disks that can be kept somewhere safe in the event some disaster strikes your hard drive or disk files. Remember my motto: poop happens.

Diskettes are storage (like your hard drive). They hold data that can be read and loaded into your Mac's RAM, worked with, and then saved again to the storage disk. Storage, like RAM, is measured in bytes. Standard floppies hold either kilobytes (K or KB) or megabytes (M or MB) of information.

The *capacity* is how much something holds. In this case, capacity means how much crap you can cram onto a diskette.

If you bought any model from the current Mac line (or a Mac made in the last couple of years), your Mac has a *SuperDrive*. It doesn't have a big S on its chest, but it *is* able to read and write to just about any *capacity* Mac-formatted 3.5-inch disk. With the proper software (I'll talk about that later), it can even read and write to (oh, ack!) DOS format-ted disks.(Maybe it *should* have a big S on its chest.)

> ## By the Way . . .
> The first floppies were big, 8-inch monsters made of a soft plastic that sort of flopped—well, they *moved*, anyhow. Then came those 5.25-inch disks you see a lot of DOS users using. When 3.5-inch disks were introduced (since they're so small and cute), they called them *diskettes*. But you can call them disks if you want.

Did that all read like a treatise on the laws of supply-side economics? Don't sweat it: here come the details.

Anatomy of a Floppy

From the outside, all 3.5-inch disks look kind of the same (if you scrunch up your eyes and ignore the little details). From the front, they're 3.5-inch X 3.5-inch squares of colored plastic with a shallow area for a label. A sliding metal shutter protects the disk's innards while it's out of a disk drive.

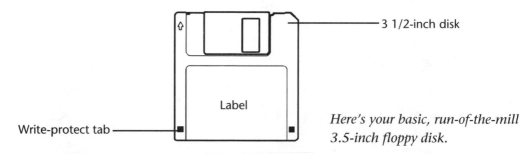

Here's your basic, run-of-the-mill 3.5-inch floppy disk.

A couple of holes and notches let your Mac know what kind of disk it is, and, usually, some writing helps *you* identify the manufacturer and the disk's capacity.

On the backside of the disk, there's the back of the protective shutter, a metal circle that lets your drive spin the disk of magnetic media inside the plastic shell, and a couple more holes and notches.

The magnetic disk is kind of shiny, and it's the same sort of stuff that video and audio cassettes are made of. You can look at it by *carefully* sliding the metal shutter back. The magnetic media is easily scratched by dust and grit, and easily clogged by the natural oils from your skin. So you can *look*, but you better not touch.

On the back, in the upper left corner (with the shutter at the bottom), is a hole with a sliding tab. That's the *write-protect tab*, and it lets you *lock* the disk. When the disk is locked, you can't accidentally write to or erase anything from the disk.

When the plastic tab covers the hole, the disk is un-locked (you save to, and erase from the disk). When you can see through the hole (the tab is up) the disk is locked, and you can't do anything except read data from the disk. If you forget which is which (I *always* have to look), the kinder diskette manufacturers put a little diagram on their labels to remind you how to lock and unlock the disk.

Floppy Flavors

While 3.5-inch disks all *look* kind of the same, they aren't: the main difference is how much stuff they hold. Right now, 3.5-inch floppy disks come in three different capacities: 1.4 megabytes (*DSHD*), 800 kilobytes (*DSDD*), and 400 kilobytes (*SSDD*). Sound like more gibberish? Wait a sec, I'll explain everything.

Floppy disks by format-ted capacity.

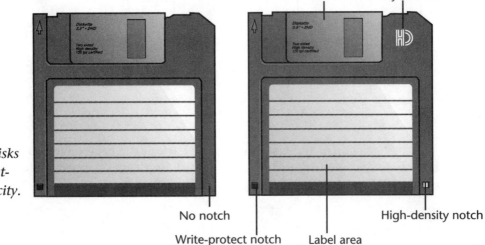

SSDD: Single-Sided, Double-Density

Originally, 3.5-inch disks held about 400K of data written on only one-sided magnetic media. The "double-density" refers to how tightly spaced information can be written on the disk, not its stupidity.

Since "Single-sided, double-density disks" is a mouthful, the name is abbreviated to SSDD, or even 1S2D. (Don't you just *love* how easy that makes it to remember things?)

> ### By the Way . . .
> SSDD disks are pretty much obsolete. You can use them (if you can *find* them), but they don't hold much data. It's more economical (that is, cheaper) to use higher capacity disks.

DSDD: Double-Sided, Double-Density

Double-sided, double-density disks (also called DSDD, or 2S2D) have double the capacity of the older disks, about 800K. They added extra storage space by putting magnetic media on *both* sides of the disk (double-sided—get it?).

These are the best disks to use for exchanging data with your fellow computer users, especially if you aren't sure the recipient has a high-density disk drive.

DSHD: Double-Sided, High-Density

Double-sided, high-density disks (DSHD, or 2SHD) hold twice again the amount of data that DSDD disks hold, which is about 1.4 megabytes. The capacity was increased by

When you buy a box of DSDD diskettes, don't be shocked to see that the box claims that each disk holds 1.0 MB. A DSHD disk holds 2.0 MB of data. Brand new, right-out-of-the-box, they *do* hold that much, but you can't use it all.

Here's the catch: you have to *format* or *initialize* a disk before you can use it. I'll tell you what that is and how to do it in a minute. For now, just remember that formatting a disk uses up some of the available space.

decreasing the amount of space data takes up: data can be written smaller, fitting more information in the same amount of space.

A *backup* is a spare, or emergency, copy of something. You can backup your hard drive, make a backup copy of a program or data disk, and even backup a single file.

While everybody should back up their data on a regular basis, the only folks who actually do it are the ones who have been traumatized by the loss of an important file. I have been traumatized by severe data losses. I backup regularly, because *poop happens.* I'll explain how to make a backup shortly.

High-density disks are workhorses: you can cram a lot of data on them. They're great for big data files and *backup* copies of your important data, and for programs from your hard drive. You do, however, need a drive designed to use them, like the SuperDrive.

You can spot a high-density 3.5-inch diskette by two easy means:

☞ Where 800 K (DSDD) disks only have one hole (the write-protect notch), high-density disks have *two*, one on the right and left sides of the label.

☞ While not all DSDD disks have any writing on them to identify them as DSDD disks, *all* high-density disks have a stylized HD near the shutter (it looks like a *CH* if you look at it upside down).

Inserting, Formatting and Other ING Words

Your disk drive is pretty smart. You *can't* insert a disk incorrectly (unless you take a hammer and force it), but just so we can say we've been thorough, here's how disks go into your drive:

Holding your disk, label side up, between thumb and forefinger (the extended pinkie is optional), insert the shutter-end of the disk into the drive. It's like inserting a cassette into a VCR, after a certain point, you can feel the mechanism catch on and take the disk the rest of the way.

When you insert a disk, the drive whirs for a second trying to read whatever is on the disk. If it's a brand-spanking-new one, just out of the box, your Mac won't know what to make of it. Disks are meaningless to your Mac until they've been *formatted* (or *initialized*).

When you insert a disk that hasn't been formatted, your Mac tries to read it, but can't. You'll get a message on your screen saying **This disk is unreadable: Do you want to initialize it?** with three buttons beneath it: **Eject**, **One-Sided**, or **Two-Sided**.

If you *don't* want to initialize the disk, click on **Eject**. If you want to initialize the disk, click on **One-Sided** or **Two-Sided**, as appropriate to the disk. When you tell it to initialize the disk, your Mac (kind and concerned as always) reminds you that formatting the disk erases any data that may be on it—are you *sure* you want to do this?

If you suspect that there's information on the disk that may have been damaged somehow (it *can* happen), you can click on the **Cancel** button and abort the operation. Formatting a disk destroys any files on it forever. Think before you click!

If you decide you want to proceed, click on **Erase**, or press the **Enter** key. Your Mac then asks you to name the disk. Type in a name (something obvious, so you can remember what's on it), and click on the **OK** button. Your disk drive churns away, formatting it. When it's done, the disk is ready to store your valuable data and program files.

Ejecting a Disk

If you want to eject the disk (because you're formatting a whole box of disks for later use), you can drag the disk's icon onto the **Trash** icon to eject it, or click on the disk to select it, and choose **Put Away** from the **File** menu. Or you can press ⌘-Y instead of using the menu.

Formatting a disk is like cutting up a pizza into easy to manage, easy to eat slices. A whole blank disk is just too hard for a Mac to eat in one quick sitting, so it cuts it up into smaller, easier-to-read sections. It then writes a map of the different areas so it can keep track of where it put things (this map is the *Desktop file*). That makes it easy for the Mac to find things quickly when you ask for them.

When I get a new box of disks, I format them all at once. I call them all *untitled* (which is the name your Mac automatically gives a disk if you don't type in a name) if I'm too lazy to type the word *blank* ten times. I slap a blank label on the formatted disks, so I know they're formatted. When I use them, I give them real names. When all my labeled, blank disks are gone, I know it's time to buy or format more.

The **Put Away** command (⌘-Y) under the **File** menu does the same thing: it ejects the disk and removes its icon from the desktop. That's called *dis-* or *unmounting* a disk. It's the opposite of when you insert a disk and its icon appears on the desktop: that's called *mounting* a disk.

The **Eject Disk** command (⌘-E) under the **Special** menu ejects the disk but leaves its icon on the desktop. You'll see why in a minute.

Storing Diskettes

The best way to store disks for easy access is in a disk-file that you keep near your Mac. The 3.5-inch disks aren't really *fragile*, but you can ruin them. Moisture, dust, too much heat, and too much cold aren't good for disks. Moisture mucks them up, dust (including cigarette smoke, pet hairs, food crumbs) clog them up and scratch the media, and heat and cold melts or cracks them.

Magnets are a major no-no. Data is stored magnetically on the disk. If another magnetic field (like a magnet's) gets near a disk, the disk's magnetic charges (your data) can get all scrambled. Bad, *bad* news.

By the Way . . .

All the things that are bad for your disks are also bad for your disk drive and computer. Go figure.

Important disks (original System disks, expensive applications, important documents) should be duplicated, even *before* you use them. Keep the copies around to actually use, but put the originals somewhere safe.

Some people go so far as to put their backup copies in a safe, or a safe-deposit box, even a fireproof box (but plastic melts before paper burns, so it really isn't that much protection). Other people put a rubber band around them and stack them on a shelf in the closet. Other people don't do diddly.

It's hard to say *do this, don't do that*. It all depends on you and what you're like. How safety-conscious are you? How important is your data to you? How many earthquakes, fires, or floods did you have last year? How good is your homeowner's or renter's insurance? Let your paranoia be your guide.

Stuff to Store

Once you have a stack of formatted disks, you can use them to hold anything you'd normally throw on your hard drive. You can save your work to them directly, or copy files from your hard drive to a disk.

To copy data files from your hard drive, just drag the file's icon from your hard drive's window onto the disk's icon (or into its open window). Your Mac copies the file onto the disk. For multiple files, repeat the process for each, or just shift-click to select all of the files you want to move, and drag them onto the disk's icon. To copy files from a disk to your hard drive, just reverse the process.

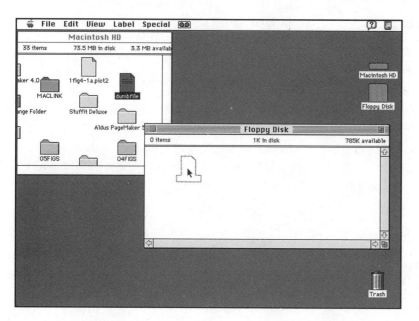

Copying a single file to a floppy disk.

When you copy applications, you can also drag the application's icon onto the disk's icon. Be warned, though, most applications these days take up more than 1.4 megabytes of disk space. If something won't fit on your disk, you'll get a warning that says: **There is not enough room on the disk *Name* to copy *File Name* (an additional 00 KB is needed).**

SPEAK LIKE A GEEK

A file that's been mashed down with a *file compression utility* to take up less disk space is *compressed*. Files get "mashed down" by replacing repetitive data in a file (like all the E's and I's in a text document) with teeny-tiny place-holders that take up less space than the original data. Compressed files have to be *decompressed* before you can work with them.

You may be better off copying the original disk(s) the application came on (which are probably *compressed*) rather than the full-sized version from your hard drive.

You can copy an entire disk for backup purposes, or to share files with a friend or coworker. Follow these instructions (this is where the **Eject Disk** command comes in):

1. Insert the *original* disk you want to copy into your disk drive.

2. When its icon appears on the desktop, select **Eject Disk** from the **Special** menu (or press ⌘-**E**). The disk ejects, but its grayed-out icon stays on the desktop.

3. Insert the disk you want to copy to.

4. When its icon appears on the desktop, drag the grayed-out icon of the *original disk*, and drop it on the new disk's icon.

5. Your Mac churns. It ejects the blank disk, and asks you to insert the original disk. Do what it says—it does that for what feels like forever. Keep swapping disks until the deed is done.

6. Pat yourself on the back. You've made yourself a backup copy.

By the Way . . .

If you have a Mac (like a Performa) that had all the System software and (maybe) some applications already installed on the hard drive and *no actual disks included*, you should *run*, not walk, to the nearest computer store. Buy a couple of boxes of disks, and copy *everything* on your hard drive for safekeeping, even if it means dragging each file individually onto the disk.

If something nasty happens to that software while you're learning your way around, you're out of luck. Back it up *now*.

The Least You Need to Know

As I said at the top of the chapter: floppy disks are your friends. They give you virtually unlimited storage capacity (as long as *you* have the space to store all those floppies), and they act as a safety net (when you back up your files) to keep you from losing your valuable data and applications should anything untoward happen.

- ☞ 3.5-inch floppy disks come in different capacities: 400 K, 800 K, and 1.4 M. The 400 K disks are pretty much obsolete. 800 K disks are good. 1.4 M disks are real workhorses.

- ☞ Disks have to be *formatted,* or *initialized,* before you can use them.

- ☞ You should make *backup copies* of *all* your important data and application files just in case poop happens.

- ☞ Disks of important data can be *locked* with the sliding tab on the back of every disk. If the tab is *open*, the disk is locked. When the tab is *closed*, the disk is unlocked.

- ☞ Disks should be stored carefully, *away from moisture, dust, heat, and extreme cold.* Be especially careful to keep disks away from magnets.

This page unintentionally left blank.

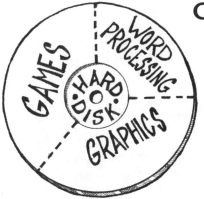

Chapter 10
Hard Drive Facts

In This Chapter

- ☛ Formatting and partitioning
- ☛ Making backups
- ☛ In case of emergency . . .

This chapter is all about intentionally destroying and preventing unintentional destruction of your hard drive's data.

Now, I'm not a violent person by nature (and I'll beat the crap out of anyone who disagrees—*just kidding*), but I do get a certain grim satisfaction out of destroying things when it becomes necessary. I also feel smarter than all get-out when I accidentally trash some data but have a spare copy of it lying around—at least I don't feel like an idiot, anyhow.

WARNING: DON'T do anything I talk about in this chapter while you're reading it. I don't want you accidentally erasing your hard drive. When you've read it all, you may want to try some of it, you may not. This chapter is mainly for future reference.

Formatting and Partitioning

The big truth about hard drives is that they're just like really big floppy disks to your Mac: they have to be formatted before your Mac can do anything with them.

By the Way . . .

Don't panic! The hard drive that came installed with your Mac was already formatted. You don't have to do it. Later, if you get a new one, or you decide to reorganize your old one, you may have to format or reformat.

Using the Erase Disk command under the Special menu is kind of slow for a 1.4 MB floppy. It would take 40, 80, or more times as long to format a hard drive, so there's special software for it. One hard drive formatting software came with your Mac, called *Apple HD SC Setup.* You'll find it on the Disk Tools disk from your set of original System disks. You'd launch it like any Mac application. When it starts up, you'll see the screen shown here.

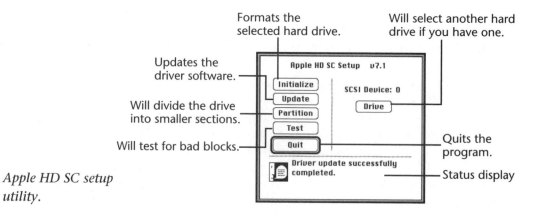

Apple HD SC setup utility.

By clicking on the **Initialize** button, you format your hard disk (and erase everything you had stored on it). Clicking on the **Update** button updates the software your Mac uses to control and reads the hard drive. You use this if your drive starts behaving badly (the driver software might have developed a problem) or if you upgrade your System software (from 7.0 to 7.1, perhaps) and want to be sure the driver software is compatible.

Clicking on the **Partition** button brings up a new dialog box. The Partitions dialog box lets you drag the existing partitions on your hard drive to make them bigger or smaller, or add new ones.

Clicking on the **Test** button causes the utility to check your hard drive for *bad blocks* (tiny segments that can't be used because they are somehow damaged).

Clicking on the **Drive** button won't do anything unless you have more than one hard drive connected to your Mac. If you do have two or more hard drives, it lets you select which one you want to mess around with.

Look Out, I'm Backing Up

Unlike floppy disks, you can't just drag your hard drive's icon onto the icon of a blank disk. All that stuff that's built up (or will build up) on your hard drive just won't fit on a floppy. You can, if you have a free day or two, just sit there dragging icon after icon onto disk after disk and backup the files manually. Talk about tedious!

There are such beasties as *backup utilities* (such as Central Point MacTools or The Norton Utilities for Macintosh). In addition to other stuff, they'll take care of the annoying

A *partition* on a hard drive is like a partition in a house. It's a wall that divides one section of your hard drive from another. Creating a partition is destructive: you'll erase everything from your hard drive. You need to copy everything onto floppies before you try this, so you can copy it all back when you're done.

Why would you want to partition your hard drive? Well, for a couple of reasons:

- ☞ It can speed up your Mac. If you have a big hard drive (80 megabytes or bigger) that isn't partitioned, your Mac has to look through *every* file on the drive until it finds what you're looking for.

- ☞ It can give you privacy, if you password-protect it (more on passwords later).

- ☞ It can help keep you organized (more on that later, too).

TECHNO NERD TEACHES

There are less painful ways to back up your hard drive, but they require more hardware. You can (with the same backup utility) back up onto another hard drive, a *removable-media drive* (like a SyQuest or Bernoulli drive, where the hard drive media pops out like a video tape), or a *tape drive* that uses data cassettes to record huge amounts of data.

Adding hardware to make backups isn't really practical unless you have a huge hard drive, chock full o' data, or if you're backing up a lot of hard drives. I'll talk more about these hardware add-ons in Chapter 13.

task of figuring out how much junk fits on how many disks. All you really have to do, besides remembering to do it, is sit there and feed disks into the floppy drive. It's still kind of tedious, but much less so than doing it all yourself.

Keeping House

You can keep your backup and maintenance chores down to a minimum if you start out with some good habits. The first way to keep your computing life simple is to start out organized—because it's easier to *stay* organized than it is to *get* organized.

I know Mac users whose hard drives are a mess: everything is everywhere and all higgeldy-piggeldy. There isn't a folder on the drive that doesn't have at least one more folder inside it. There's stuff buried so deep on their drives that it squints when they call it up into the light of day. That's not good. It's really easy to lose stuff that way. You don't have to be as picky as I am about this stuff, but there are some easy things you can do to keep your act together.

MacStyles of the Poor, but Anal-Retentive

☞ **Keep application-related stuff in one folder.** Most programs, when you install them, neatly put all the junk they need (and lots more) into one folder on your hard drive. Leave it there. If you want to move the application around, do it with aliases.

> ### By the Way . . .
> If you want to be really obsessive, you can group related applications, like those for word processing, into one folder, graphics into another, and games into another.

☞ **Keep project folders.** Letters, business, accounting, and home-work folders—whatever is appropriate for whatever you do.

While writing this book, I had one **Complete Idiot** folder with everything I needed inside: folders for letters, chapters, screen shots, notes, and sample files. The screen shot folder had a folder for each chapter inside.

That way, the project never went more than three folders deep: The Idiot folder, the component folders, and chapter folders inside those. I didn't have to search for anything.

☞ **Throw out old crap.** If you're done with a project, throw it away. If you think you might have need of it again, move it onto a floppy (or floppies) and file them somewhere safe, then trash the originals from your hard drive. It keeps you from building up too much folder fodder and from running out of space.

☞ **Make up your own mind, make your own style.** If this isn't your style, cross out this section with a thick magic marker and ignore it. I've been told I'm just the tiniest bit compulsive. My way might not be your way.

Save Early, Save Often

Whether you save your work to a hard drive or to a diskette, one of the best (and safest) habits you can develop is to save often. When you work on a file, it only exists as electronic impulses stored in your Mac's RAM until you save it.

RAM is *not* permanent. If you turn off your Mac, the file goes away. If the power goes out, the file goes away. When you save a file, your Mac copies those electronic impulses in RAM and transcribes them to the disk of your choice. The file, written to a *storage* medium, stays exactly the way you saved it, until you save it again.

You save a file, in any application, by selecting the **Save** command from the **File** menu. For a new file, one you haven't saved before, your Mac asks you to enter a name for a file, and tells it where to store it, just like it did back in Chapter 8 when you saved the sample TeachText file.

After you save a file for the first time, you can simply use the **Save** command, and the new copy of the file replaces the old one. If you want to save another copy of the file while you're working on it, you can use the **Save As** command, also under the **File** menu. Save As creates a whole new file on your disk. Your Mac asks you to give this new file a name (it can't be the same as the original; no two files can have exactly the same name in the same folder). You can add a number to the original name: save your file **Mom.letter** as **Mom.letter2**. Or add **copy** or **backup** to the original name (**Mom.letter copy**).

By the Way . . .

If you're saving the copy to a different folder, or to another disk, you can leave the name the same (as long as that won't confuse you).

Saving often costs you only a little effort and can save you some heartache. Here's a couple of good times to stop and save the file you're working with:

- ☛ Save your work before you walk away from your Mac.

- ☛ Save your work whenever you reach a point where you wouldn't want to go back and recreate it: after a page or two of text, a couple rows of a spreadsheet. Save it, and then continue working.

- ☛ Save your work whenever you stop to make changes. That way, if you don't like the changes, you have the file on disk exactly the way it was before you changed anything.

- ☛ Save your work whenever you stop to answer the phone, the door, the kids, the dog—in other words, whenever you stop working.

Some programs give you the option of setting *automatic saves*. My copy of Microsoft Word is set to prompt me to save what I'm working on every

15 minutes. All I have to do is press **Enter** when it beeps, and a copy of my current document is saved. If I don't want to save it, I just click on the **Cancel** button.

This is a great feature. More programs should offer it. I mean, I know how stupid I can be. That's why one of my mottoes is this: "Save early, save often."

Safety First!

While saving your work often and backing up your hard drive regularly go a long way toward protecting your valuable work from disaster, there's more you can do. If you're the only one who uses (or is *supposed* to use) your Mac, you can install security software (like NightWatch II)that requires a password before allowing access to the desktop. Theoretically, only you should be able to use your Mac. However, if you have to share your Mac with others, you can still protect your files.

Goof-Proof Your Mac

You can (insert appropriate adjective here)-proof your Mac: If you have children using it, kid-proof it; Co-workers, geek-proof it; and if your mom uses it, Mom-proof your Mac.

There are a couple of ways you can do it. Start by doing a safety check: power up your Mac and look at everything that's accessible at startup. If there's anything there that you can't live without, or that you don't want just anyone looking at, protect it.

You can protect your data files simply by copying them onto disks and deleting the originals from your hard drive. Put the disks with your sensitive files into a file box that locks. Keep the key with you. No one but you can get at the disks (unless they *really* want to, and then they can break the lock). If it's just a question of keeping the file safe (you don't care if someone looks at it), you can leave them on your hard drive and lock them.

To lock a file, click on its icon to select it. Choose **Get Info** from the **File** menu (or press ⌘-**I**). You'll get a dialog box like the one shown in the next figure.

```
╔═══════════════════════════╗
║ ▣ ▤▤▤▤▤ dumbfile Info ▤▤▤▤▤ ║
╟───────────────────────────╢
║   ▢  dumbfile              ║
║                           ║
║   Kind: TeachText document ║
║   Size: 2K on disk (8 bytes used) ║
║                           ║
║  Where: Macintosh HD :     ║
║                           ║
║ Created: Fri, Oct 29, 1993, 2:29 PM ║
║ Modified: Fri, Oct 29, 1993, 2:29 PM ║
║  Version: n/a             ║
║                           ║
║ Comments:                 ║
║ ┌───────────────────────┐ ║
║ │                       │ ║
║ │                       │ ║
║ └───────────────────────┘ ║
║ □ Locked      □ Stationery pad ║
╚═══════════════════════════╝
```

*The File Info
window.*

You can use the **Get Info** command to get some general information about the file. You can click inside the **Comments** box and write yourself a note to remember things about the file. Most important, you can click in the check box at the bottom of the dialog box to lock the file. A locked file, like a locked disk, cannot be altered or deleted without being un-locked.

Naturally, this is no protection if the tampering person knows how to unlock a file. It should, however, prevent the file from being accidentally deleted or altered.

You can add file protection software, like FolderBolt, which password protects certain folders and locks everything inside so it cannot be altered or deleted without the password. If you feel you need even more security for your data files and applications, you can create a separate partition on your hard drive (as discussed in a previous section) and password protect it with security software like NightWatch II.

Keep everything that's personal and confidential in that partition. Your Mac starts normally, and unprotected files are fully accessible to average users, but the things in that partition are unavailable unless the user knows the password. Some security programs even make that partition *invisible* (literally) so average users won't even know it's there.

Atten-*shun*! *AtEase*!

If the main concern is keeping kids from accessing or deleting your impor-tant files, you can use a Finder replacement, such as Apple's AtEase 1.0 to restrict the child's access.

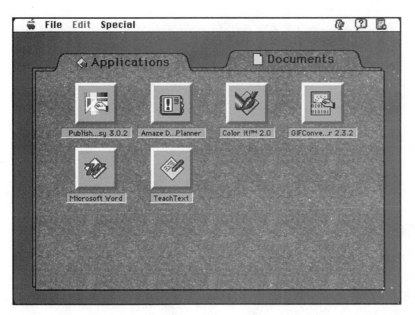

The AtEase 1.0 screen.

As you can see in the figure, AtEase 1.0 allows limited access to the functions of the Finder. Instead of the desktop you're used to seeing, when you start up your Mac with AtEase 1.0 installed, you get a different, simpler desktop. You can look at it as a restrictive security measure, or a simplification for youngsters and other Mac novices. You can only use the applications and documents set from the AtEase Control Panel, or documents created while AtEase 1.0 is running.

You can also specify that files created in the AtEase 1.0 environment must be saved to a floppy disk, instead of to your hard drive. If your child tries to save a file with the same name as one of your files, making him or her save the file to a disk will keep your file from being destroyed.

There are other Finder substitutes (like KidDesk) that eliminate the application loophole. If you're looking for real protection for your files, AtEase 1.0 isn't it, at least not without one of the other protection ideas mentioned here.

The simplified menus let you quit to the Finder or open other applications, but you can password protect the options. You can also enter a clue to the password (in case you forget things easily).

The advantages of AtEase 1.0 are simpler interface, easier for kids and Mac novices of any age; password protection for the Finder and more powerful applications; and the *save only to disk* option.

The drawback of AtEase 1.0: it doesn't offer any real security. Applications aren't AtEase savvy. If your child can access an application, that application can be used to open any compatible document on your hard drive. What does an application know?

That means your kid can *still* destroy your files, given the chance.

Rescue Me

Okay, we've formatted disks and backed up everything on your hard drive. We've gone to lengths worthy of the CIA to protect your data, and still something goes wrong with your hard drive. What are you gonna do?

A Rescue Disk

If your hard drive goes ker-flooey, you still start your Mac with a System disk in the floppy drive. Ideally, that System disk (sometimes known as a *bootable* disk) will have some utilities on it to help you fix whatever went wrong with your hard drive.

Fortunately for you, you already have one: the Disk Tools disk from your original set of System disks. It contains a stripped down version of the Mac's System software, the HD SC Utility we talked about earlier, and a spiffy little program called Disk First Aid.

In the computer-geek business, we call this a *Rescue Disk* because it can save your butt.

> ## By the Way . . .
> Later on, if, or when, you buy a set of disk utilities, such as Norton Utilities for Macintosh, or Central Point's MacTools, you can create a similar rescue disk with their utilities.

Disk First Aid is a disk-fixing application. It checks all of the things a Mac needs from a disk to operate, and if it finds something wrong, tries to fix it. You can use it on any disk, hard drive, or floppy. In fact, you should keep a copy on your hard drive, too, for fixing flaky floppy disks.

If you're trying to fix a flaky hard disk, you'd pop the Disk Tools disk in your floppy drive just after turning on your Mac. Your Mac will run from the System software on the disk, instead of from your hard drive. When you get to the desktop, open the **Disk Tools** disk's icon, and launch **Disk First Aid**.

Click on the **Drive** button until the name of your hard drive appears in the top half of the dialog box. Clicking on the **Open** button opens the hard drive and brings up the Disk First Aid test screen shown here.

Disk First Aid test screen.

Click on the **Start** button, and Disk First Aid begins examining your disk for problems. If it can fix something, it tries (or it asks you if it *should* try). If it can't, it tells you. If your hard drive is toast, it tells you that, too.

To use Disk First Aid to fix a disk in your floppy drive, launch a copy of the application from your hard drive. When it starts, use the **Disk** button to locate the disk you want to repair, and click on the **Open** button. It

When you throw a file into the Trash and empty it, your Mac marks that file as deleted, saying that bit of hard drive real estate is back on the market (available for use). The file isn't actually destroyed until your Mac writes another file on top of it. Only then is the deleted file officially kaput.

If you act quickly (like, before you save another file), your deleted file is still there and can be recovered with the proper utility.

works the same for disks as hard drives; hard drives just take longer to test. Disk First Aid can fix a lot of the common problems that plague disks and hard drives, but it can't fix everything.

Undelete Utilities

When your hard disk was finally repaired with the rescue disk, you discovered that your kid (or your co-worker) deleted a couple of important files that you didn't back up (shame on you). Now what?

Well, if you don't already have a set of hard drive utilities like The Norton Utilities or MacTools, you need to get some—especially if young kids have access to your Mac. They *love* to throw things out and empty the Trash.

Most utility packages come with an *undelete utility* that tries to recover accidentally deleted files. It will scan your disks or hard drive, looking for intact files that have been marked as "deleted." When it finds one, you can tell it to remove the "deleted" marker, and the file will "exist" once more.

The Least You Need to Know

In my opinion (and you may feel free to disagree), we have gone over some very important stuff. I'd like to see you remember most of it, because you can't be too safe. However, times being what they are, here are the *really* essential things for you to walk away with:

- ☛ If you don't want to back up your important files individually, you can use a backup utility to make a copy of your entire hard drive for storage. You should do one or the other. Doing both is best.

- ☛ Hard drives can be formatted like disks. They can also be partitioned into smaller sections to speed up your Mac and improve your file security. *Always back up your hard drive before formatting or partitioning it.*

☞ Save your file frequently as you work, using the **Save** (⌘-S) or the **Save As** commands under the **File** menu.

☞ Play it safe when other people have access to your Mac: protect the files you cannot live without. Lock them with the Get Info (⌘-I) dialog box, or use security software to password-protect files, folders, or hard drive partitions.

☞ Don't rely on AtEase 1.0 to protect your files unless you are using an additional security measure.

☞ Expect the best, but plan for the worst from your Mac: keep an emergency rescue disk handy, like a copy of the Disk Tools Disk from you original System disks. Or create your own rescue disk with utilities from a commercial utility package.

In computing, as in life, bad things happen when you haven't provided for them. If you take precautionary steps, you might never have a problem. Even if you do have a problem, who cares? You're ready for it.

This page unintentionally left blank.

Part III
Growing a Macintosh

Your Mac, out of the box, is full of potential, but you have to work with your Mac to realize that potential. You'll both grow as your skills increase and your needs get more specific and demanding; you'll do more complicated work as you learn about the more complex tools you can add to your Mac.

In Part 3, we'll look at the stuff that comes with your Mac as the place where that potential begins to be realized. We'll also look at some of the software and hardware you can buy to turn that potential Mac into the actual Mac you need and want.

*It's about growth. It's about needs. Most important, it's about **shopping**.*

Chapter 11
A Peek Inside the System Folder

In This Chapter

☛ The System Folder demystified

☛ Extensions explained

☛ Control panels condensed

☛ Items you can toss (if you don't need them)

It's time to let loose with all of those voyeuristic tendencies you've been hiding from the world. Here's an opportunity to take a peek into the heart of your Macintosh: the System Folder.

The System Folder, more than any other folder on your hard drive, is like a Stephen King hotel: every folder is a room. Some of the rooms are used just for storage, some are haunted by creatures that work invisibly, others are a hotbed of activity. Put on some sneaky shoes and glasses that are good for peeking; we're about to get nosy.

Do Not Disturb

Some of the things stored in the System Folder (shown in the following figure) are there only for the convenience of the System software. You can't do anything much with them except move them around, throw them out (we'll talk about unwanted baggage you can throw out at the end of this chapter), or just stare at them and wait for a cosmic revelation.

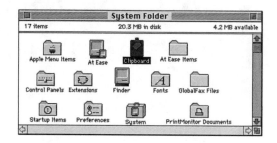

The System Folder.

They aren't dead weight, by any stretch of the imagination. They're things that the System itself (or other applications) use. If you double-click on them, you'll get an error message saying something to the effect of: "Leave me alone, I don't work for you." How rude.

Right now, you probably have these things lying around:

☛ *At Ease*: If you have it (and you may not), At Ease is the application that creates the simplified Finder we talked about in the last chapter. You don't do anything with the application, you control it with the At Ease Control Panel in the Control Panels folder.

☛ *Clipboard*: The file where all the items you copy and cut hang out until you paste them into a document, or cut or copy something else. You can see what's in a file by using the **Show Clipboard** command on the **Edit** menu.

☛ *Finder*: The application that puts up the desktop, menus, and so on for you. It's always active. You make changes to the Finder through your Control Panels and Extensions, not directly through the application.

☛ *Scrapbook File*: Like the Clipboard, it holds whatever you have stored in your Scrapbook. You can only alter its contents by using the Scrapbook DA (on the ⌘ menu).

Cold Storage

Other folders in the System Folder just hold stuff and keep it all together for safekeeping and easy access by you, the System, and any applications that might care to use them.

☞ *Apple Menu Items folder*: Holds all of the DAs (and whatever else you care to throw in) that appear in your menu. We talked about adding aliases and other things back in Chapter 7.

☞ *At Ease Items folder*: This is where all the aliases landed if you selected applications to be accessible to At Ease.

☞ *Startup Items folder*: Contains anything you want to launch every time you start your Mac. The easiest way to use this is to throw an alias of an application, sound, or document in there (rather than the original or a copy). When you start your Mac, the application launches, the sound plays, or the document opens with the application that created it. It's great for programs and documents you use every day.

☞ *Preferences folder*: Most programs allow you to customize them to some degree. Whenever you tell an application that you always want it to do something a certain way (the way you prefer) the program writes itself a note (a *preferences file*) and chucks it in this folder. That way, it'll do things your way, each and every time.

☞ *PrintMonitor Documents folder*: If you have a laser printer and you use background printing, this is where the *spooled files* go until print monitor prints them for you. Chapter 15 has the scoop on printing and PrintMonitor.

If you ever delete, upgrade, or reinstall an application, make sure you trash its preferences file, too. Otherwise, you can wind up with many preference files taking up space, and no application to use them.

If you're reinstalling a program because it started getting flaky on you, you should definitely trash the preferences file. It could be part of your problem, and if you don't delete it, it could pass the problem along to the fresh copy of the application.

Neither Fish nor Fowl

Two things in the System Folder don't fall nicely into either category: the *System file* and the *Fonts folder*. Depending on what kinds of things you do with your Mac, you often may be poking around inside them, or not at all. They deserve some special attention.

The System File

Once upon a time (before System 7), just about all the cool things you added to your Mac were dumped into the *System file*: fonts, sounds, and Desk Accessories. In theory, it was like my grandmother's attic: full of all kinds of fascinating junk that you only dragged out once or twice a year, and then put back for safekeeping.

The *keyboard layout* tells your Mac what letter or symbol you mean when you press a key on the keyboard. If you only use a standard QWERTY-style keyboard (like a typewriter's), you don't have to worry about it.

If you work in a foreign language, like Japanese, or with an alternate keyboard layout (like Dvorak), you can drop the appropriate keyboard layout in your System file and select it with the *Keyboard Control Panel*. (More about what Control Panels are, and do, in a minute.)

With System 7.1, all you'll see in the System file is your assortment of installed sounds and any funky *keyboard layouts* you might have. Fonts are in the Fonts folder, and DAs are in the Apple Menu Items folder, or wherever you dropped them. Got that?

The Font Folder

The *Font folder* is strictly a System 7.1 enhancement. Before System 7.1, your fonts were stored in the System file. Now, they just go in the Font folder.

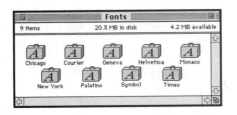

Inside the Font folder.

Those little suitcase icons you see in the figure are, well, *suitcases*. Your Mac uses them to pack related fonts together in one place. You open a font suitcase by double-clicking on it. Inside you'll find a bunch of font files, all variations of the font in the suitcase name (such as Chicago or Courier).

If you are the adventurous, creative type I think you are, you'll be in here a lot, tinkering and adding fonts all the time. All of Chapter 16 is dedicated to fun, fabulous, fantastic font facts.

Custom Mac Options

The two remaining folders inside your System Folder contain all the things that make your Mac *your* Mac. They're the little snips and snails that let you customize the way you and your Mac work together.

You can add extra capabilities by adding *Extensions* and *Control Panels* to the appropriate folders.

Extensions

Extensions expand the capabilities of your Mac. In pre-System 7 days, Extensions were called *INITs*, which is a shortened form of *Initialization Program*. INITs or extensions load when you start up your Mac (they're those little icons popping up across the bottom of your screen) so their capabilities are available to you all the time.

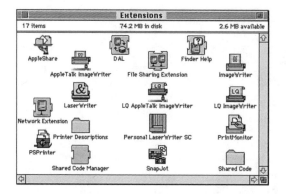

Inside the Extensions folder.

The AppleShare, File Sharing, and Network Extensions give your Mac the capability to interact with other Macs on a *network* (two or more Macs linked together by cables that allow them to communicate).

All of the X-Writer Extensions (StyleWriter, ImageWriter, LaserWriter, and so on) are Chooser Extensions that give your Mac the capability to send data to an Apple printer for printing.

The PrintMonitor Extension lets your Mac print while you continue working on other things. (All of Chapter 15 is devoted to the paraphernalia of printing. Check it out.)

The Control Panel Handler Extension allows your Mac to better deal with your Control Panels (we'll talk about them next).

The Finder Help Extension gives you access to your help balloons all the time.

The QuickTime Extension gives your Mac (if it can handle it) the capability to display what the technoids like to call "dynamic data," but which you and I call "moving pictures." QuickTime is the coolest Extension that comes with your Mac; it allows you to show little movies in a window on your screen. However, unless you do multimedia presentation work, it probably won't do more than amuse you for a while. It is cool, though.

By the Way . . .

There are many applications that come with Extensions: calendar programs that flash a message when you're scheduled to do something; backup programs that warn you it's time to backup your hard drive; and many other different things.

There are even Extensions that come by themselves and make your Mac do entertaining things, such as shut down to a little glowing dot like an old-fashioned TV set, make a vomiting sound when you empty the Trash, scream, and so on.

The best thing about Extensions is that you don't have to do anything except drop them in the Extensions folder and forget about them.

The worst thing about them is that they (and your Control Panels) take up RAM, and are the source of many of the problems you may experience with your Mac. Extensions sometimes squabble like spoiled children, resulting in a conflict that crashes your Mac. Also like spoiled children, the more you have, the more chances there are for such squabbles.

For just that reason, there's a whole section devoted to resolving Extension conflicts in the appendix.

Control Panels

Control Panels are more flexible than Extensions. Most of them include a set of options you can set to your liking. You access your Control Panels folder one of two ways: either by selecting the **Control Panels** item in your menu, or by double-clicking on the folder itself, which is inside your System Folder.

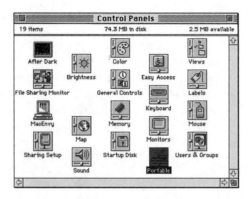

*Inside the Control
Panels folder.*

For descriptions of the Control Panel features (alphabetically), read on:

☛ *At Ease Setup:* Configures the Finder replacement *At Ease* for you.
   We talked about it in Chapter 7.

☛ *Color:* Lets you pick the color of highlighted text. You can choose
   from several standard colors, or pick the **Other** selection. Selecting **Other** gives you a color wheel so you can pick the perfect
   color—something that matches your eyes, perhaps.

☛ *Date & Time:* You can set the current date and time here, as well
   as specify what formats your Mac uses for each. Dates can be set
   in just about any standard date notation (Dec. 1, 1960, 1 December 60, 12/1/60), and the time can be displayed in 12- or 24-hour
   (military) format.

☛ *Easy Access:* Gives your Mac special skills to make the keyboard
   easier to use for folks who can't handle a mouse or have limited
   motor skills.

☛ *General Controls:* Lets you change the pattern on your desktop.
   You can select one that's already prepared by clicking on the
   arrows over the mini-Desktop, and then clicking on the pattern
   you want to select. You can also edit a pattern or create a new
   one.

   You can change the color set for any pattern by double-clicking
   on the color square you want to change, and selecting a new
   color with the color wheel. You can set the rate at which your
   insertion point blinks, and how many times a menu item blinks
   when it is selected. You can also mess with the time and date.

☞ *Keyboard:* Lets you set the *Key Repeat Rate* (how fast the keyboard throws rrrrepeat letters up on your screen when you press a key). You can also set the *Delay Until Repeat* (how long you can hold down a key before it repeats itself). How you set these depends on how fast a typist you are.

☞ *Labels:* Lets you set the color and word labels you can apply to any file with the **Label** menu in the **Finder** (as we discussed in Chapter 6). Double-click on the color to select a new one from the color wheel. Drag to select the word-label, and type in a new one. Choose colors and words that are significant to you, so you can tell at a glance what the file is for. (I cleverly use labels to color code different projects.)

☞ *Map:* Use this one to find different cities around the world by keying in a name. Cities are marked by flashing dots (handy for world travelers).

☞ *Memory:* (No, don't sing that song from *Cats*, please, anything but that.) The *Memory Control Panel* does different things on different Macs:

All Macs can set a *Disk Cache* of various sizes, which speeds up your Mac by holding data in the cache (a block of RAM set aside to only store data) so your Mac doesn't have to go back to read from a disk so often.

Some Macs (like the LC) have a *32-bit Addressing* option, which allows your Mac to use over 8 megabytes of installed RAM. If you have over 8 megs of RAM installed without 32-bit Addressing turned on, all the extra memory will be ignored. It's a case of use it or lose it.

TECHNO NERD TEACHES

How large a cache you set depends on the amount of RAM you have to start. If you only have 2 or 4 megabytes, a small cache (64–128K) can help without interfering too much with your ability to open other applications.

With more RAM, you can set up a larger cache. Just be warned, memory you set aside for a cache can't be used for anything else. If you start getting **Application out of memory** messages, reduce the size of your cache and try again. It's all cache as cache can, anyhow.

Virtual memory uses part of your hard drive as a substitute for RAM. The information that normally gets stored in RAM gets written to an area on your hard disk. Virtual memory can fake applications into thinking you have more RAM than you really do.

Any changes you make in the Memory Control Panel won't take effect until you restart your Mac.

Some other Macs have an option for *virtual memory*, which should only be used as a last ditch effort (in my opinion) because your Mac will slow down horribly. You'd be better off springing for more RAM and saving your hard drive for storage (Chapter 14 has information about adding more RAM to your Mac).

☞ *Monitors:* The top half of this Control Panel lets you reset your monitor to display black and white, shades of gray, or color (if your have a color monitor). How many options you get depends on the capabilities of your monitor.

The bottom half is useful only if you have more than one monitor attached to your Mac. It lets you set which monitor will show the menu bar, and which monitor is secondary. You can tell which monitor is which by clicking on the **Identify** button.

☞ *Mouse:* This Control Panel lets you set how quickly the cursor moves in relation to how far or fast you move the mouse. You can also set the speed of your double-click so your Mac knows what you mean by a double-click. (If you double-click slowly, your Mac might read it as two single clicks unless you set this to your own speed.)

☞ *Numbers:* Lets you set the decimal and thousands separators for numbers (like 2,001.367). You can also set the currency symbol ($) and whether it comes before or after the number.

☞ *Sharing Setup:* You'll only use this if you're on a network. You can identify yourself and your Mac to the network and enter a password so no one else can use the network with your name. Check with your Network Administrator if you have any questions about it.

☛ *Startup Disk:* Specifies which hard drive (or hard drive *partition,* as described in Chapter 10) you want your Mac to startup from. This is convenient for users who keep different versions of the Mac System software on different partitions or hard drives, or who want to keep their kids or strangers out of their personal files.

☛ *Sound:* Lets you set which installed sound in your System file will be used (called the *Alert Sound*) when you do something your Mac doesn't like.

You can also set the volume of your Mac's speaker (if it has one). If your Mac came with a microphone (built-in or as an accessory), you can record your own sound by clicking on the **Add** button. You'll get a dialog box that looks and acts like the controls of a tape recorder.

You can record any sound your Mac's microphone can pick up. If you like it, clicking on the **Save** button will bring up a dialog asking you to name the new sound. When you name it and click on **OK**, your Mac adds it to the sound files in your System.

☛ *Users & Groups:* For use on networks only. You can add new user and group names to the list of folks who have access to the information on your Mac. Check with your Network Administrator if you have any questions about it.

☛ *Views:* Gives you three sets of options for how your Mac presents information to you. You can select the font (and its point size) used for file and folder names. It's great for people like me, who have trouble reading teeny-tiny type all the doo-dah day.

You can also select how your icons land in your windows, or on the desktop. You can have them line up in straight, neat, little lines (straight

Whatever you do, *don't* select the Calculate folder sizes option because your Mac will slow down horribly. You'll sit there waiting while your Mac adds up the sizes of all the crap in all the folders in your window. You could go gray. Or bald. Don't do it.

If you really need the size of your folders from time to time, simply turn the feature on and off. Just use it when you need it, and leave it off the rest of the time.

grid), or you can have columns of icons offset slightly (staggered grid) so there's less chance of name overlap (I hate that). If you click on the check box next to Always snap to grid, icons always fall into the nearest grid position.

Finally, you can specify the information presented in windows when you view by name. You can select the *size* of the icon shown, as well as eight options for information displayed. Click on the check boxes in front of the information you want displayed, and turn off the rest.

By the Way . . .

There are hundreds upon hundreds of other Control Panels you can add to your Mac: Control Panels to add clocks; to blank your screen when your Mac's idle; to make random noises when you type and do other things. There are literally tons of Control Panels. I think I personally have most of them installed and running all at the same time.

Don't throw away things that directly control your Mac. Without the Mouse Control Panel, you can't mouse around. Without the Monitors Control Panel, you can't control your monitor.

Always think before you trash. Ask yourself, "Do I use this function or feature? Does my Mac need it to operate?" If you trash something vital, your Mac may not work properly, and you'll have to reinstall either the item or the whole System software. When in doubt, leave it alone.

Junk You Can Throw Away

Now that you know where everything is and what it does, here's a big secret: You don't have to keep all of it! If you don't use it, why keep it? It's only taking up space on your hard drive, and probably nibbling away at the precious little RAM you have. Ditch it.

When (or if) you discover you need these puppies, you can always reinstall them. There are step-by-step instructions for installing and reinstalling System software in Chapter 21.

Trashing Extensions

Right now your Extensions folder is choked with Chooser Extensions for every single printer that Apple makes. You own, what, one? Maybe two?

Find all the ones that aren't for the printer(s) you own and throw them in the Trash.

Are you on a network? If not, you can safely trash the AppleTalk, File Sharing, and Network Extensions. Drag them (kicking and screaming) into the Trash.

When you've thrown away everything you want, select **Empty Trash** from under the **Special** menu and kiss those bad boys good-bye.

Surrendering Control (Panels)

Like the extensions, there are some Control Panels you can trash and not miss at all. If you aren't on a network, you can easily trash the File Sharing Monitor, Sharing Setup, and Users & Groups Control Panels. If you don't like (or don't use) the Map Control Panel, throw it out. If no one using your Mac has difficulty maneuvering a mouse, trash Easy Access as well.

Miscellaneous Trash

Here's more junk you can trash:

☛ If you don't like, need, or use At Ease, you can trash it, too. Its component parts are scattered throughout your System Folder. Throw them out. The application and At Ease Items folder are just inside the System Folder. The At Ease Setup Control Panel is in the Control Panels Folder.

☛ There are probably one or two Read Me files scattered throughout your hard drive. If you've read them, throw them out.

☛ If you played around with any of the networking Control Panels, you've probably added a couple of *preference files* to your Preferences folder. When you've trashed the networking Extensions and Control Panels, be sure to trash any preference or data files that may have been added to the Preferences folder.

The Least You Need to Know

These are the few things you really need to remember about your System Folder. The rest of it might come in handy some time, but this is stuff you'll use frequently.

☛ Some of what's in your System Folder is only for use by the System software. It won't let you do anything to them (such as the Clipboard and Scrapbook files) unless it's through the appropriate application or DA.

☛ Anything you put in the Startup Items folder will launch every time you start up your Mac.

☛ The actual System file holds different things, depending on what *version* of the System you are using.

☛ Extensions (or INITs) add a wide range of capabilities to your Mac. To install them, drop them in your Extensions folder, and **Restart** your Mac.

☛ *Control Panels* customize the operation of your Mac to match your own computing style.

☛ Extraneous items may be in your Extensions and Control Panels folder (such as all of those printer drivers). Only keep the ones you need to keep your Mac up and running. The rest can be thrown away.

Chapter 12
Things You Already Have

In This Chapter

- ☛ What everything is
- ☛ What everything does
- ☛ What you can do with it
- ☛ Available replacements when you outgrow things

The future of your Macintosh is uncertain (not like the future glimpsed through one of those Magic 8-Ball toys, "Future uncertain, ask again later") because what becomes of your Mac is dependent on what becomes of you.

As you develop your computing skills, your computing needs become more refined and demanding. That's why your Mac is as flexible as it is. With hardware and software add-ons, it can grow right along with you.

The junk that came with your System software (TeachText and all those Desk Accessories) are just the beginning. Some of them you'll outgrow quickly. Others may be useful for as long as you use a Mac.

Night of the Living DAs

You heard briefly about the Desk Accessories (DAs) when I talked about the ⬢ menu in Part 2. DAs are available to you as long as you are able to select the ⬢ menu, no matter what application you're using. That makes them very handy indeed.

The Alarm Clock

The Alarm Clock DA gives you an alarm clock on your desktop. (I have a keen grasp of the obvious.) You can use it to tell the time, or set it to go off whenever you want.

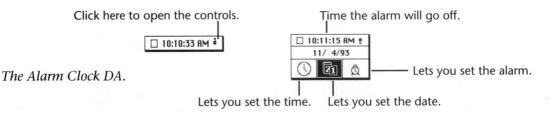

Click here to open the controls.

Time the alarm will go off.

The Alarm Clock DA.

Lets you set the alarm.

Lets you set the time.   Lets you set the date.

The first time you select the Alarm Clock from the ⬢ menu, it appears in its small version (the one on the left). To get at its controls, click on the little *handle* to the right of the time display. Two additional panes drop down.

The center pane will vary, depending on which option you select in the bottom pane. This is where you'll change the time, alarm time, and date.

To set the time, click on the **clock face** in the bottom left corner. The center pane shows the currently set time. Click on the **hour**, **minutes**, or **seconds** to select each. You can use the little up and down arrows at the right to adjust the selection up or down, or you can just type in the new numbers.

Click on the **calendar pages** to change the date, just like you changed the time.

Click on the **alarm clock** to set the alarm. You set the time the alarm will go off the same way you set the regular time.

In the center pane, to the left of the time, is a little oval with what looks like a keyhole drawn in it. Click there to turn the alarm on or off (in the figure, the alarm is off). Now, when the real time matches the alarm time, a blinking alarm clock icon appears in your menu bar until you turn the alarm off.

You can position the Alarm Clock anywhere on your desktop, but it tends to get hidden by windows. In System 7, if it gets buried, you can call it to the front by selecting **Alarm Clock** from the **Application** menu.

By the Way . . .

If you have a bad memory, or have more demanding needs, you'd do better with one of the many excellent freeware and shareware clock DAs, or a commercial clock/calendar/ reminder program. I'll talk more about getting new software, especially freeware and shareware, in the next chapter.

The Calculator

The Calculator DA gives you a basic add, subtract, multiply, and divide calculator right on your Mac's screen.

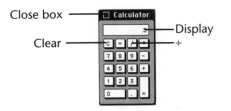

The Calculator DA.

I'm sure you know how to use a calculator. You can click on the Calculator's buttons if you want, but using the number keys on your keyboard is easier. If you have a keyboard with a numeric keypad, it's even easier. The only difference between the Calculator DA and any calculator you may have used is that some of the math symbols are different, because there isn't a symbol for them on your keyboard.

The keyboard equivalents are:

+ = add

− = subtract

* = multiply

/ = divide

You can copy any number shown in the Calculator's display with the **Copy** command (⌘-C) and **Paste** it (⌘-V) into any document.

By the Way . . .

If you need to do anything beyond these four basic functions, you'll either need to use a real calculator or replace this DA with one of the many shareware, freeware, or commercial calculator programs available. There are calculator replacements that do all sorts of zippy scientific calculations—all the ones I refused to learn in high school.

Key Caps

The Key Caps DA finally solves the mystery of where all those special characters (√, Ω, ¥) are hiding.

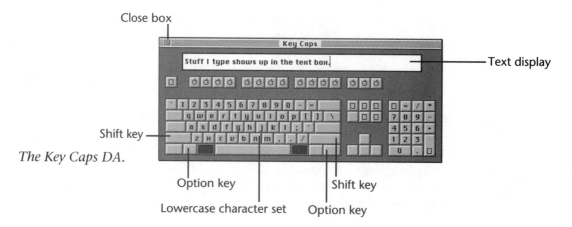

The Key Caps DA.

The Key Caps keyboard will reproduce your keyboard, key for key. You select a font by pulling down the **Key Caps** menu. It works just like any other font menu. When you select a font, Key Caps shows that font's lowercase character set, like the one shown here.

If you hold down the **Shift** key, the display changes to the uppercase character set. Release the **Shift** key, and press the **Option** key, and the display shows you what special characters are made with the Option-character key combinations. Press the **Shift** key again, while still holding down the **Option** key, and the display shows you the characters made with the Option-Shift-character key combination.

There are tons of other font utilities flying around that are variations on Key Caps, some are better, some are worse, and most of them are geared toward the special needs of designers and layout artists.

Any key in the display that shows a box doesn't have a special character assigned to it. That's okay. If you ever need a box, you know where to get one.

Instead of trying to remember the key-combination you need to produce a special character, you can just type it in Key Caps, **Copy** it from the text display, and **Paste** it into the document of your choice. Cool beans.

The Note Pad

The Note Pad is digital scratch paper (do people other than nuns say "scratch paper" any more?). When you launch it, the Note Pad looks like a blank pad of paper (there's that keen grasp of the obvious again). You can type a short note to yourself, lists of things to do, ideas for work, stuff to remember, and so on.

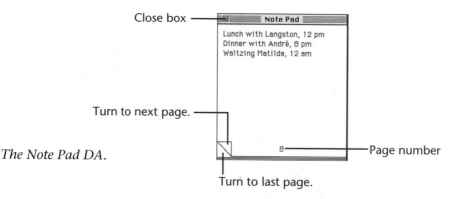

Close box ——

Lunch with Langston, 12 pm
Dinner with André, 8 pm
Waltzing Matilda, 12 am

Turn to next page. ——

The Note Pad DA.

8 —— Page number

Turn to last page.

Everything you type in the Note Pad stays there until you delete it. Not only that, but you can also copy and paste from the Note Pad into any application.

The Note Pad is limited in usefulness: it only holds eight pages of notes, with about twelve lines per page. I've written longer grocery lists.

By the Way . . .

I don't like the Note Pad. I replaced mine with an alias of TeachText. But, I know folks who can't work without it. If you don't like it, you can always trash it and just use TeachText, too.

Puzzle

The Puzzle DA is great for wasting time. It's also a blast from the past for me: I remember getting (and giving) those little plastic puzzles as birthday party favors. Ah, youth.

Close box ——

The Puzzle DA.

When you first launch the Puzzle, it's a scrambled version of the Apple logo. The apple's been cut into 10 squares, and there's one empty square. Click on the adjacent piece you want to slide into the empty square, and keep doing that until you get the apple back to its rightful configuration.

If you solve it, you get a little surprise. If you get too irritated trying to solve it, you can select **Clear** from the **Edit** menu, and the annoying apple will go away. It will be replaced by the mundane (and easier to solve) number puzzle.

By the Way . . .

If you get tired of both versions of the Puzzle, you can copy and paste just about any small (about 1-inch square) picture into it. Using your favorite paint or draw program, select a graphic (or part of a larger one) with the appropriate selecting tool. **Copy** it to the Clipboard, and then **Paste** it into the Puzzle DA. A scrambled version of the graphic appears in the puzzle, ready for you to try and put back together. To remove a custom puzzle, select **Clear** from the **Edit** menu while the Puzzle DA is active.

The Scrapbook

The Scrapbook DA is highly underrated and underused, in my opinion. Like a regular scrapbook or photo album, you can stick things in your Mac's Scrapbook for future use: pictures, logos, QuickTime movies (if you have QuickTime), and just about anything you can copy and paste.

Close box ————

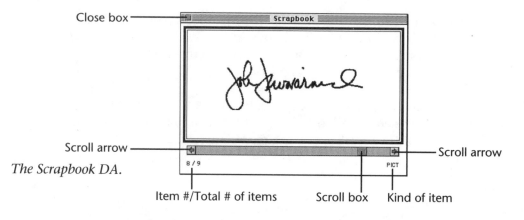

Scroll arrow ————

The Scrapbook DA.

———— Scroll arrow

Item #/Total # of items   Scroll box   Kind of item

Scan(ned, -ner): A scanner is a piece of hardware that converts text, photographs, or line drawings into digital information that can be used on a computer. I'll talk about scanners and other hardware add-ons in Chapter 14.

As the figure shows, I keep a scanned copy of my signature in here so I can slap it into documents I'm too lazy to sign.

When you open the Scrapbook DA, you can skim through its contents by sliding the scroll box or clicking on either scroll arrow. Apple thoughtfully added some things you might like, but you can't use all of it: there's a sound you can only listen to; and (if you have QuickTime) two little movies. You can copy and paste the QuickTime movies into an application if it can cope with them.

If you'd like to use something in the Scrapbook, here's how:

1. Scroll to it, and select **Copy** from the **Edit** menu.

2. **Close** or **Hide** the Scrapbook.

3. Open the document (or whatever) you want to paste into, and select **Paste** from the **Edit** menu. Voilà!

To paste something into the Scrapbook, reverse the process:

1. Select the text or graphic you want to paste into the Scrapbook, and copy it to the Clipboard.

2. Open the **Scrapbook**, and scroll to the item after where you want your new one to land.

3. Select **Paste** from the **Edit** menu, and the Scrapbook adds a new page in front of the current page to hold your new scrap.

You can permanently remove an item from the Scrapbook by scrolling to it and selecting **Cut** (⌘-X) from the **Edit** menu.

There are some more advanced Scrapbook replacements available if you find yourself outgrowing the original Scrapbook: SmartScrap and ClickPaste are both more flexible and powerful.

In addition to this nifty assortment of Desk Accessories, you Mac also came with a few basic applications. Along with TeachText, Disk First Aid, and the Apple HD SC Utility (which we've talked about in previous chapters), you get two other important applications: HyperCard (or the HyperCard Player) and Apple File Exchange.

HyperCard

HyperCard is the software equivalent of an index card file. If you were using index cards for a research paper, you could write information about one topic on each card and refer to the information on other cards with little notes to yourself.

You can have several different Scrapbooks, if you care to. You can find the Scrapbook file in the System file. You have to rename the original Scrapbook file (call it Original Scraps, perhaps). With the file renamed, the next time you open the Scrapbook, it will be empty. If you want another Scrapbook, repeat the process, giving the new file a new name (something to remind you what its contents are).

Here's why it works: The Scrapbook only opens the file named **Scrapbook file**. To access any of your other Scrapbooks, you'll have to change the name of the current Scrapbook file to something else, then rename the file you want to use **Scrapbook file**. Sound confusing?

HyperCard lets you do the same kind of thing, only with more flexibility. It's basic unit of information is a card. A collection of cards is called a *stack*. You can sort through these cards one at a time, or (if the stack is written that way) click on a word, phrase, or picture on one card, to automatically bring up a card of information related to that word, phrase, or picture.

It's also a programming tool, because its *scripting language* (way to write commands for it) lets you create stacks that are actual applications.

Playing HyperCard Stacks

The HyperCard Player is basically just something to play stacks. You can tinker with them a little, but not much—nor can you create your own stacks. You can launch the Player one of three ways: double-click on the **HyperCard Player** icon, the **Home** icon, or the icon of the stack you want to play.

Your Mac churns a little as it reads the information. If you clicked on the **HyperCard Player**, or **Home** icons, you'll get the Player's Home Stack as shown in the figure. If you clicked on a stack's icon, you'll see that stack—and it'll look like whatever it looks like.

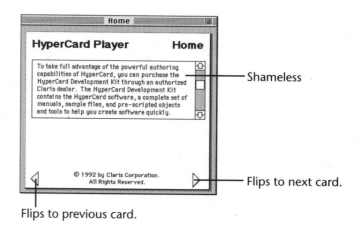

HyperCard Player Home.

Shameless

Flips to next card.

Flips to previous card.

You can use the right and left pointing arrows at the bottom of the card to flip through the rest of the Home stack. There isn't much to it. The last card of the stack is your *Preferences Card* (shown here). It lets you set the level of stuff you can do with the Player. Adjust the User Level by clicking on the level you want to set, or by sliding the white arrow to that level.

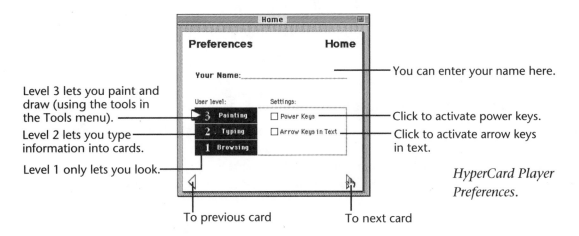

Level 3 lets you paint and draw (using the tools in the Tools menu).

Level 2 lets you type information into cards.

Level 1 only lets you look.

You can enter your name here.

Click to activate power keys.

Click to activate arrow keys in text.

HyperCard Player Preferences.

To previous card   To next card

From the Player's Home stack, you can launch another stack by selecting the **Open Stack** command from the **File** menu. It gives you a standard Open dialog box to navigate to the stack you want to open.

HyperCard's Painting and Drawing Tools

HyperCard and the HyperCard Player's palette of tools are closely associated with the menu bar: when you select a particular tool, the menu bar will have additional menu items added.

By the Way . . .

HyperCard's palette of tools is similar to most of the tool palettes you'll run into in other painting and drawing programs. Other programs may give you more tools, but most of these will turn up in just about any program you can draw with. Once you've learned how to use them with HyperCard, you'll know how to use them anywhere. That's one of the beauties of Macintosh.

Painting tools (such as the paint brush and the spray can) bring up a menu of *patterns* you can use. The text tool adds the **Font** menu. The *shape tools* can be modified by pressing the **Option** or ⌘ key while you use the tool to draw a shape.

You don't really want to be reading about tools: you want to be playing with them. That's okay. Learning by playing is much more fun than learning by reading. Launch the HyperCard Tour stack. Go play. I understand.

Apple File Exchange (AFE)

Maybe you were suckered in by those commercials that said Macs will let you use DOS applications, documents, and disks. It wasn't a lie exactly, but it did stretch the truth a little. You need to buy special software to run DOS on a Mac (such as *SoftPC*), or to format and open DOS disks like they were Mac disks (such as Apple's *Macintosh PC Exchange*).

You do have the ability to turn DOS files into Mac files, and vice versa. *Apple File Exchange (AFE)* is the utility that lets you translate DOS-format documents into Mac-format documents. You'll find it in the *Apple Utilities folder* on your original *Tidbits* disk. It's easier to use if you copy the AFE folder to your hard drive (you'll need your disk drive for a DOS-formatted disk).

AFE launches like any other application. When it's fired up, you can insert a DOS-formatted disk in your disk drive (if you put the disk in before you start AFE, your Mac will say the disk is unreadable). The DOS disk's contents appears in one of the scroll boxes in the AFE dialog box (shown on the next page).

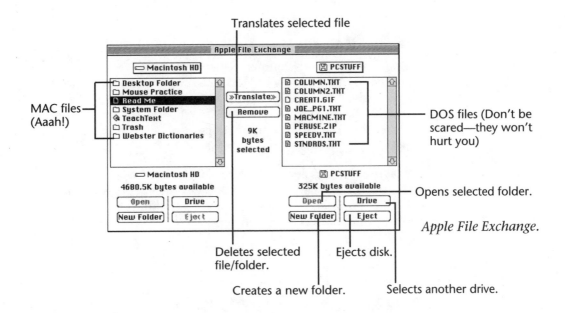

Translates selected file

MAC files (Aaah!)

DOS files (Don't be scared—they won't hurt you)

Opens selected folder.

Apple File Exchange.

Deletes selected file/folder.

Ejects disk.

Creates a new folder.

Selects another drive.

The other window shows the contents of your Mac's hard drive. Each scroll box has a set of navigating buttons beneath, to **Open** selected folders, create a **New Folder**, change **Drives**, or **Eject** the displayed disk.

Navigate to the file you want to translate and click on its name to select it. The Translate button becomes active. Click on the **Translate** button, and AFE translates the file from its original format to the format appropriate to its destination disk.

For a listing of the translations AFE will do, select **About AFE** from the **Apple** menu. Just so you know, AFE doesn't just do DOS. It also translates ProDOS (the Apple //e operating system) files and can do Mac-to-Mac translations.

AFE is pretty good about selecting the appropriate translation routine, but you can give it more specific information by selecting one of the translation protocols in the menu bar. The heading changes depending on what you're trying to do: Mac to Mac, Mac to MS-DOS, Mac to ProDOS, or MS-DOS to Mac, and so on.

By the Way . . .

If you work in an environment where you have to exchange files on a regular basis with DOS-based computers, you may want to check out one of the many translator packages that are available. Apple's Macintosh PC Exchange lets you mount PC disks on your desktop, open documents from them, and save to them, just like they were Mac disks.

DataViz has a package called MacLinkPlus/PC that comes with a cable you can use to physically connect your Mac to a DOS PC. You translate files back-and-forth through the cable, rather than on disks. Very convenient.

The Least You Need to Know

It's tough to cull everything you absolutely-positively need to know out of a chapter like this, but I'll give it a shot.

- ☞ Your use of the DAs and applications that came with your System software will vary depending on how you work and grow as a Mac user.

- ☞ DAs all have really obvious names, so reminding you of what each does would insult your intelligence. Just remember you can use them from within any application.

- ☞ *HyperCard* is like a digital and dynamic index card file. Way cool and fun.

- ☞ *Apple File Exchange* translates files between computer platforms (such as Mac, ProDOS, and even MS-DOS).

Chapter 13
Stuff You Need to Buy

In This Chapter

- ☞ Freeware, shareware, and commercial software
- ☞ Ways to seize freeware and shareware
- ☞ Major software categories, and what each can do for you
- ☞ Completely biased reviews of some of the big name applications

As you learned in the last chapter, your Mac came loaded with enough stuff to get you working and playing. As good as the DAs, TeachText, and utilities are, they aren't really suitable for major projects. They're the supporting cast, rather than the leading players. You'll need to get other software that's suitable to the task at hand. To that end, this chapter is a roundup of the major software types and categories.

After you rip through this chapter, you might want to run to Chapter 19 for some shopping advice.

Freeware, Shareware, and Commercial— or—No Money, Money, and Mo' Money

Freeware, shareware, and commercial are three software groups that have less to do with quality than they do price. You can find all kinds of software in all three groups.

Freeware is software written by programmers and distributed free of charge. There are literally thousands of freeware extensions, control panels, and DAs that do practical, useful, and even foolish things.

You'll never see a freeware store; mainly you'll find this software on *electronic bulletin boards* and other *on-line services*. You can also buy freeware disks from user groups in book-disk sets and from some mail-order companies. Generally, you'll find the most recent copies of freeware programs with on-line services and user groups.

On-line service or electronic bulletin boards are companies and just plain folks who (when you have a **modem**) let you access a wide variety of files and information on their computer(s).

On-line service generally refers to corporate entities, and everything you do with the service costs you some money. CompuServe, America Online, and Prodigy are on-line services. Electronic bulletin boards are usually smaller, home-grown service, and charge little or nothing for you to join them. We'll talk more about the services and communications in Chapter 17. Modems are also mentioned in Chapter 18.

Shareware is software that is distributed in the same open manner as freeware, but if you like and use the software regularly, you're supposed to send the author a *fee*. The money requested is generally much less (from $5 to $50) than what you'd pay for commercial packages , and it goes *right to the programmer*. It doesn't get filtered through some huge corporation.

By the Way . . .

One of the tackiest, *tackiest* things you can do is use shareware and *not* pay the fee. Don't be tacky.

Commercial software is what you see every time you walk into a computer store or open a Mac mail-order catalog. When you buy commercial products, you're not only paying for the software, but also the glossy manual, the research and development department's next five projects, all those ads you see everywhere, and extraneous, but pretty, packaging. Plus, you're throwing a nice chunk of change at the company's CEO.

By the Way . . .

In terms of finding freeware and shareware, one of the best things you can do for yourself is join a *Macintosh User Group*, or *MUG*. A MUG (pronounced like a coffee mug) is a collection of people of all levels of Macintosh skills. The idea of a MUG is best expressed by the mission statement of the BMUG (pronounced "BEE-mug"), the largest (and bestest, if you ask me) Mac User Group on the planet: We're in the business of giving away information.

You can find the name of a local MUG by calling Apple at 1-800-538-9696. You can get more information about BMUG by calling 510-549-2684, or writing to: BMUG, 1442A Walnut St., #62, Berkeley, CA 94709-1496.

Integrated Packages

Integrated packages are the Swiss Army knives of software. They're all called SomethingWorks, because you "get the works" with them. Each package includes an array of software you would normally have to buy separately: word processor, database, spreadsheet, painting, drawing, and communications. Some even have outlining and charting capabilities.

What makes them integrated is that the features of each module are available in most of the other modules. If you need a drawing while writing a memo, you can draw one. If you need a spreadsheet in a report, you can add one.

Different packages are integrated differently. Some use the idea of *frames*, where you draw a box in a document and specify that it is for the word processor, a picture, or a graph, and then the appropriate tools become available whenever you are working in that frame.

Publish and Subscribe is part of the new Mac technology introduced with System 7. It allows one application to share information and functions with another application. System 7 makes interapplication communication possible, but the software you use must be able to make use of it.

Others make use of System 7's *publish and subscribe* function. It allows you to create an item (say, a spreadsheet) in one module and *publish* it so it is available for use in any document that *subscribes* to it (such as a magazine). If you change the published spreadsheet in the spreadsheet program, all the documents that subscribe to it will get an updated copy.

What You Can Do with Them

You can do almost anything with an integrated package that you can do with its stand-alone counterparts. The difference is that since integrated programs have to fit all those applications into one tidy package, numerous high-powered features get dropped.

Almost none of the individual modules are as powerful as their stand-alone siblings. But, that isn't necessarily a bad thing, depending on what you do. For example, you may not need all of the features of Microsoft Word or Excel. The limited range of integrated functions may be enough for you.

If money is tight and you can't afford to buy all the stand-alones you need, a less expensive integrated package will let you work while you save to buy the higher-priced packages.

The Popular Packages

Microsoft Works was the first integrated package for the Mac. All the other integrated packages tried (and many succeeded) in knocking it off of its throne. I own it, and don't use it much. It lists for about $260, but you can find it by mail order for about $160.

By the Way . . .

Never buy version 1.0 of anything. Wait until there's a number after the period.

Version number—the (re)incarnation of the software. Version 1.0 is its debut. Version 1.2 fixes everything that should have been fixed before 1.0 was released. Version 2.0 is the next incarnation. Version 2.1 fixes the new incarnation, and so on. When the first number changes (1.0 to 2.0), it's called a **version upgrade**, a major overhaul. 2.0 to 2.1 means it's still essentially the same program, but now it works. Versions, such as 2.1, are sometimes called **bug fixes**. One more reason for sending in your software registration cards: when the company releases an upgrade to software you own, they'll let you know.

GreatWorks, from Symantec, is another one I own. GreatWorks makes the best use of Publish and Subscribe I've ever seen, and it's color-paint module does some pretty high-powered stuff. The last pricing I saw put it's list price at about $299, with a mail-order price of about $199.

ClarisWorks, from Claris, has the best overall integration of its modules. You can work with any module in any document, and the combination makes it a pretty fair replacement for a low-end page layout program. The integration makes it a good choice for people who don't want to go through the rigmarole involved with using Publish and Subscribe. I don't think the individual modules are as strong as GreatWorks' modules—but I might be prejudiced. ClarisWorks lists for $299, and you can get it mail order for about $199.

WordPerfectWorks, from WordPerfect, is a late entry into the integrated program wars. It has the full assortment of modules: word processing, database, spreadsheet, painting, drawing, communications, plus charting capabilities. WordPerfectWorks lists for $249, and you can get it mail order for about $149.

Word Processing and Page Layout

There was a time when these would have been two different categories, however, recent releases of both kinds of software have brought them closer together. Where once word processors were purely the domain of letters, reports, memos, and manuscripts, they've added enough graphic and layout features that you can actually use a powerful word processor like a page layout program.

The capability of an application to take a document created with another application and use it is called *importing*.

When an application has the capability to save (usually with the **Save As** command) a file in a format easily imported by another application, it's called *exporting*. Many applications come with a set of *translators* that allow them to import and export files easily in other application formats.

Meanwhile, page layout programs have improved in the text entering department. Once upon a time, it was usually faster to write your text with a word processor and *import* it into your page layout program. Now they handle text entering and editing much better.

What You Can Do with Them

Word processors and page layout programs are all about words, words, words. Their sole duty in life is to get your thoughts down on paper in as attractive a manner possible. In general terms, word processors are better for documents where the words are the main focus, however many word processors let you add pictures and graphic elements (such as lines and boxes).

Generally, word processors come with some sort of *spelling checker* and *thesaurus* built-in so you don't have to use a separate application to check yourself. They also allow you to set margins (the space around the words on all four sides of the page), tabs, line spacing—all the things you used to have to fiddle with knobs on a typewriter to adjust.

Also in general, *page layout* programs deal with words, but their strength lies in arranging the words on the page with style; using columns, boxes, headlines, graphic elements, and pictures. Newsletters, newspapers, brochures, and flyers are the kinds of things you'd create with a page layout program.

Page Layout programs give you some of the same features as a word processor, but their focus is on presentation: how those words look on the page. They give you complete control over columns, graphics (pictures, as well as lines and embellishments). They make it easier to create documents, such as booklets and brochures, where you aren't dealing with a standard 8 1/2 x 11-inch page, or you're folding it into new configurations.

The Popular Packages

Microsoft Word is the industry standard for word processing. Word boasts an impressive array of features: graphics capability, QuickTime compatibility (you can include a movie in your disk-based documents), voice annotation (you can actually attach spoken comments to your document, on disk only), an equation editor (for you scientific types), graphing, tables, and automatic indexing. It's very powerful stuff.

If you have the space to store it, and the memory to run it, and you can only afford one program, Word might be it. (They say a minimum of 2 megabytes of RAM with System 7, but that's wishful thinking. Four is more like it.) Microsoft Word lists for about $500. You can get it by mail order for about $300.

MacWrite Pro, from Claris, is another full-featured word processor that almost crosses the line into the realm of page layout. Feature for feature, MacWrite Pro compares favorably to Word: it does a lot of that good stuff that Word does and is also a big, fat program that can hog up disk space and RAM. MacWrite Pro lists for about $250, and you can get it mail order for about $170.

WordPerfect for the Macintosh, from WordPerfect Corporation, comes with a similar array of features and functions as Word and MacWrite Pro. Its features compare well and lists for about $500, with a mail order price of $290. Ask your local dealer to let you test drive it on one of their computers (you should always try before you buy, if you can).

WriteNow, from WordStar, is an excellent contender for word processing for two reasons: it boasts a full complement of features (though not as many as the higher-priced packages), and it's cheap. The advantages of

WriteNow are that it takes up less disk space than the other full-featured word processors, and it runs with less RAM. That makes it ideal for PowerBook users. The price doesn't hurt either. WriteNow lists for $70, and you can pick it up mail order for about $40.

Desktop Publishing is literally "publishing from the top of your desk," as opposed to having to pack up all your text and woes to send them to a typesetter and printer.

PageMaker, from Aldus, is the page layout program all others are trying to beat. PageMaker was introduced about the same time Apple introduced the first LaserWriter printer. The combination of the two resulted in the birth of *desktop publishing*.

PageMaker is exhaustive in its thoroughness. You can create a simple one-page flyer or an entire book-length manuscript. Its features include: powerful editing tools (including spell checking), professional color handling, and total control of almost every aspect of typesetting. PageMaker lists for a daunting $900, but you can buy it by mail order for less than $600.

Quark XPress, from Quark (the company, not the barkeep on "Deep Space Nine") is PageMaker's biggest rival. For a while, they were neck and neck. Then Quark kind of squeezed ahead with a few more features and more flexibility. Now they're pretty much neck and neck again. On average, Quark XPress and PageMaker are pretty evenly matched. Quark also lists for about $900, with a mail-order price of about $600.

Personal Press, also from Aldus, is a low-end version of PageMaker. Everything is predefined, so it's difficult to experiment. It comes with an assortment of *templates* (predesigned pages), so all you have to worry about is selecting the graphics and writing the text. It isn't anywhere near as powerful as PageMaker, but it's okay for folks who want to dabble in page layout without investing half a grand to do it. Personal Press lists for $200, and you can get it mail order for about $100.

Publish-It! Easy, from TimeWorks, is supposed to be a low-end page layout program, but its fleet of features (including a built-in database for creating form letters and mailings) put it way ahead of the pack of low-end products. I've used it and liked it. Publish-It! Easy lists for about $260, with a mail-order price of about $110.

Spreadsheets and Databases

Spreadsheets and databases are about manipulating information. Like word processors and page layout programs, these two do similar things with different kinds of data. Spreadsheets deal with numerical data (adding, subtracting, multiplying, and dividing columns of numbers). Databases deal with more word-based information (names, addresses, favorite colors, you name it).

Spreadsheets and databases are essentially information managers. They let you group bits of related information together, so you can look at various aspects without having to re-enter or reorganize the existing information.

What You Can Do with Them

How much you expect the spreadsheet to do for you will determine how much work you have to put in the spreadsheet (likewise for a database). If you expect a database of all the members of your family to keep track of important events, you'd need to enter individual categories for birthdays, anniversaries, and so on, rather than a big, mixed bag of important dates.

Creating elaborate, yet elegant, spreadsheets and databases is an art form, one that I haven't mastered well. I always want mine to do something I didn't anticipate when I designed them. For folks like me (with simple needs and little patience), the spreadsheet and database modules of an integrated package are probably enough. Others need the power of dedicated packages.

The Popular Packages

Excel, from Microsoft is the Word of spreadsheets. Part full-featured spreadsheet, it's also part page layout program, allowing you not only to do complicated and involved spreadsheets, but also to make them pretty as all get-out. Excel lists for $495, with a street price of around $295.

Lotus 1-2-3 for Macintosh, from Lotus, has all the high-powered features of its DOS cousin, which has been a business standard for over a decade. Lotus 1-2-3 lists for about $495, with a mail-order price of about $295. (Isn't it funny how competitive packages maintain competitive pricing?)

FileMaker Pro, a popular database from Claris, is aimed at business users because it allows information sharing across a network. FileMaker Pro also has extensive report-generating capabilities, allowing you to print out exactly the information you need. FileMaker Pro lists for about $400, and you can get it mail order for about $270.

Graphics Programs

Painting and drawing programs have been around as long as the Mac itself. They're graphic programs that let you draw and paint on your Mac's screen and save the graphics for use in your other documents. The pictures you produce (depending on the program) can be as simple as the stick-figures you drew in third grade, or as complex as a recreation of Edward Hopper's painting, "Nighthawks." There is an array of graphics programs to appeal to all levels of artistic skill.

Graphics programs tend to fall naturally into several general categories:

- **Drawing programs:** Create objects (a box, a circle, a line) that you can select and move around to create a picture, or in the case of computer-aided design (CAD) programs, a blueprint.

- **Painting programs:** Let you create bit-mapped images. Bit-mapped images (such as bit-mapped fonts) are collections of dots. They allow finer detailing than drawing programs. Programs for editing and enhancing photographic images fall (loosely) into the paint category.

- **PostScript-based programs:** Are generally referred to as illustration programs. PostScript illustrations, such as PostScript fonts, can be scaled to any size and still look good.

- **3-D Rendering programs:** Let you take basic two-dimensional images (showing height and width) and add simulated depth. (That's the third dimension—not to be confused with that dimension of sight and sound and mind, known as "The Twilight Zone.")

Naturally, the more a program tries to do, the more complicated it can be to use, and may require a more high-powered Mac to be effective. I wouldn't run a 3-D rendering program on anything less than a Quadra.

What You Can Do with Them

With the right application, and the right equipment, you can really do anything you like. You can create your own assortment of clip art for your reports and newsletters. You can create a logo for your business. You can do magazine-quality illustrations with a PostScript illustration program or draft the plans for a house or a machine with a CAD (computer-aided design) program.

Many graphics programs benefit from adding a *drawing tablet* to your Mac. A drawing tablet is like a cross between your mouse and a piece of paper. Instead of rolling a mouse around, you draw on the tablet with a stylus (a pen without ink), and your pen-strokes appear on your Mac's screen. I'll talk more about adding hardware, such as a drawing tablet, in Chapter 14.

Clip Art is a collection of graphic images meant to be copied and pasted into other documents. The term comes from the days when you could buy a book of illustrations, clip them out with scissors, and literally glue them on your pages. Now clip art collections come on disks, but you still copy and paste them into your pages.

The Popular Packages

This particular software category is already huge, and new programs are being introduced all the time. Any kind of exhaustive list of what's available, and what it does, could fill a volume on its own (and would go rapidly out of date). Since there are so many products, this is a listing of a few names from each category. Use the list (plus the comparison shopping advice from Chapter 19) to select the program that meets your needs and artistic skills.

MacDraw II, from Claris. Basic drawing, color. List: $199, street: $140.

MacDraw Pro, from Claris. Souped up MacDraw. List: $399, street: $280.

IntelliDraw, from Aldus. Intermediate/Advanced drawing. Funky tools. Color. List: $299, street: $200.

SuperPaint, from Aldus. Does paint and draw functions. Color. List: $150, street: $100.

BrushStrokes, from Claris. Huge selection of tools, ability to use add-ins from other major applications. List: $139, street: $100.

Painter, from Fractal Design. Advanced paint tools. Comes in a cool paint can. Recreates actual oil paints and pastel textures on-screen. List: $399, street: $280.

PhotoShop, from Adobe. Editing/enhancement software for scanned photographic images. High-powered, professional tool. List: $895, street: $550.

Freehand, from Aldus. Professional-quality PostScript image creation, full-featured and flexible. List: $775, street: $390.

Illustrator, from Adobe. A professional-quality flexible package from the people who created PostScript. List: $595, street: $370.

addDepth, from Ray Dream. Converts 2-D PostScript fonts and illustrations into simulated 3-D. List: $179, street: $125.

Ray Dream Designer, from Ray Dream. Similar to addDepth, but lets you create images from scratch as well. List: $299, street: $210.

Three-D, from Macromedia. Let's you create and render 3-D images and add *animation* for video production. Amazing. List: $1,495, street: $1,000.

Utilities

Utility is a catch-all phrase that covers a lot of territory. Generally, it means an application that does something useful but not necessarily productive (meaning that you won't hold a finished product in your hand when you're done). Utilities come in all shapes and sizes. The kind(s) you need really depend on what type of things you do with your Mac.

Disk Utilities

I've already mentioned some disk utilities that you'd probably find handy: Central Point Software's MacTools and Symantec's Norton Utilities for Macintosh. Both provide tools for painlessly backing up the valuable data on your hard drive. Both also try to repair damaged disks (including hard drives), and try to retrieve deleted files.

Most disk utilities also have applications devoted to *optimizing* or *defragmenting* your hard drive. A disk optimizer reorganizes all that data so that files and applications are stored together, so it takes less time for your Mac to find the information. You should make a *complete backup* of your hard drive before you use an optimizer on it, because if the optimizer goofs rewriting an important bit of System information, your hard drive is toast.

Fragmenting occurs when you save data to your hard drive, and your Mac has to stash it as quickly as possible. It writes it in whatever space it can find, which is not necessarily all together. You can wind up with files being **fragmented**: a bit-bit here, a bit-bit there. That's okay in terms of **writing** the file, but when you want to use that file later, you Mac has to search all over your disk to find all those bits, and it can slow your Mac down.

Finder Enhancements

As much as I love the Finder, there are always things I wish it would do better: format disks faster, find files faster, have more flexible menus, and even better desktop patterns. Never ones to slouch, the software companies leap into the breach trying to add more features to the Finder. There are dozens of commercial and shareware solutions to some of the Finder's quirks.

Virus Protection

A computer *virus* is a small bit of programming that (when you use the file it's hidden in) does something funny (such as put a silly message up on your screen) or something dangerous (such as overwrite all of your data files with gibberish). Either way, they're bad news. Since you don't see viruses before they strike, there's no way to tell if one will be benign or not. The better course is to avoid them, or destroy them before they can attack your system.

Central Point's MacTools package includes *virus detection* software. You can also get stand-alone virus protection with packages like SAM (Symantec AntiVirus for Macintosh).

However, the best virus detection program is absolutely free. Disinfectant, by John Norstad of Northwestern University (and hundreds of close personal friends), is an Extension/application combination that can detect and eliminate any digital cooties that may already exist on any of your drives (disk or hard), and prevent any from insinuating themselves into your system later.

The chances of a virus penetrating your Mac increase every time you use software or data from other sources. The more outside data and applications you load on your hard drive, the better your chances of catching a virus. If you do any of the following, you should have some form of virus protection:

☞ Trade disks with friends, colleagues, or strangers.

☞ Access a network's file library, or download files from an on-line service.

☞ Let someone else use your Mac with his or her own disks (you don't know where they've been).

The virus scares of the last couple of years have been big news. Hype and paranoia have turned virus protection into big business. That's not to say that viruses aren't a threat. You should have *some* form of virus protection if your Mac is vulnerable.

Compression Utilities

Another hotbed of growth in the utilities market has been *compression utilities*. Before compression utilities, when you started running out of space on your hard drive, you only had two options: deleting old stuff to make room for new, or buying a bigger hard drive.

Compression utilities free up space by removing repetitive data and replacing it with smaller place-holders so the files take up less space. When you decompress (expand) the file, the application replaces the place-holders with the original information, and you have your file back. The cool thing about compression utilities is that they do it invisibly so you hardly notice (hardly because it does slow things down a little). Instead of spending a couple of hundred dollars on a bigger hard drive, you can compress your old one for under a hundred.

Screen Savers

A *screen saver* is a utility that blanks your Mac's monitor after a set period of inactivity. Why? Because, if you leave your monitor displaying the same screen for an extended period of time, it can get burned into the chemical coating on the inside of your monitor. You will forever see a ghost image of that particular screen.

By far, the most popular screen saver is After Dark, from Berkeley Systems. It has a line of four versions (and counting): After Dark, More After Dark (MAD), Star Trek The Screen Saver, and The Disney Collection. I'm ashamed to admit I have them all.

Utility Popular Packages

Central Point MacTools, from Central Point Software. List: $149, street: $80.

Norton Utilities for Macintosh, Symantec. List: $149, street: $90.

Public Utilities, Fifth Generation Systems. List: $149, street: $100.

Now Utilities, Now Software: hierarchical Finder menus, better file and folder access during saves, and so on. List: $129, street: $85.

Connectix Desktop Utilities, Connectix. 16 utilities including security, power conservation, customizing windows and the Desktop. List: $99, street: $55.

Kaboom!, Nova Development Corporation. A replacement for your Mac's Sound Control Panel that lets you assign sounds to dozens of Finder functions, instead of just an alert sound. List: $50, street: $30.

Central Point Anti-Virus, Central Point Software. List: $70, street: $50.

Symantec AntiVirus for Macintosh (SAM), Symantec. List: $100, street: $65.

Disinfectant, John Norstad, Northwestern University. *Free!* You can get Disinfectant from most on-line services and MUGs, or send a self-addressed stamped envelope and an 800K floppy disk to: John Norstad, Academic Computing and Network Services, Northwestern University, 2129 Campus Drive North, Evanston, Illinois, 60208.

Stuffit Deluxe, from Aladdin Systems, is a manual compression utility for files or folders (as opposed to your whole hard drive). List: $120, street: $70.

Disk Doubler, from Fifth Generation Systems. Stuffit Deluxe's chief competition, with a similar range of functions. List: $80, street: $50.

Stuffit SpaceSaver, from Aladdin Systems, is a transparent hard drive compression routine. List: $60, street: $35.

AutoDoubler, from Fifth Generation Systems. Another transparent hard drive compression routine. List: $90, street: $60.

After Dark, from Berkeley Systems. The coolest. The basic module (*After Dark*) lists for $60, but you can get it for about $30 by mail order. *More After Dark,* gives you updated and totally new modules, but requires *After Dark*. List: $40, mail order: $26.

Start Trek: The Screen Saver, from Berkeley Systems, is a stand-alone spin-off of After Dark. Features funky characters, scenes, and sounds from the original "Star Trek." List: $60, street: $35.

Giggles & Yucks: Games and Stuff

Macs used to be pathetic machines if you wanted to play games. There wasn't much around except for some pretty bad freeware and shareware games. The computer that was thought of as a "toy" when it was first released, suddenly became too serious to play games. Thankfully, that situation has changed. The introduction of the Mac LC, with the optional Apple IIe emulator card installed (allowing the LC to behave like a IIe), brought a huge increase in sales of Macs to schools. Now there's an enormous assortment of educational titles available, too.

The Popular Packages

There's way, way too many to pick a few measly samples. Games aren't one-size-fits-all. They need to suit your personality. I like logic puzzles. You may like shoot-em-up war games. Do yourself a favor and browse the game and education aisles in your local software store. Buy yourself a treat, you earned it.

The Least You Need to Know

There are more kinds of software available for the Mac than you can, well, shake a Mac at. Here are the important things you need to come away with from this particular chapter:

- ☛ Freeware and shareware are great, cheap alternatives to the pricier commercial packages.

- ☛ Macintosh User Groups (MUGs) are an excellent source of freeware and shareware (as well as other information and help for you and your Mac). You should join one.

- ☛ If there's something you want to do with your Mac, there's probably a software package around to help you accomplish it.

- ☛ Learn how to shop for the software that meets your needs. Chapter 19 will help.

This page unintentionally left blank

Chapter 14

Hardware in a Nutshell

In This Chapter

If you thought the small sampling of software was a smorgasbord for your Mac, just wait 'til you get a peek at all the hardware goodies you can add on.

- ☞ Macintosh brain surgery: CPU upgrades
- ☞ What was that? Oh, yeah: adding memory
- ☞ Pedal to the metal: accelerators and math chips
- ☞ Scuzzy peripherals
- ☞ I hate meeces to pieces

Hiking the Upgrade Path

For starters, if you've had your Mac for a while (and the way Apple keeps cranking 'em out, anything over three- or four-months old is suspect), there might be a newer version of your Mac on the market. For example, the current version of my LC (only two-years old) is the LC III, or the educational model LC 520. I'm at least two upgrades behind.

Usually, when Apple releases a new model of an existing CPU (like the LC II to the LC III), they offer an *upgrade.* That is, you bring your Mac into an authorized Apple dealer, and they'll rip the guts out of your old Mac and install the guts of the new one. The price is usually a lot less than the price of a completely new machine—it still isn't cheap, but it's less.

Sometimes, when Apple releases a completely new Mac model meant to replace an older model in the Macintosh line (the way the Powerbook series replaced the Mac portable), they also offer an upgrade. But that's only if the innards of the new machine fit in the box of the old. Sometimes, the architecture is too different, won't fit, and your only option is to buy the new CPU, or remain satisfied with your current model.

By the Way . . .

Just because Apple replaces your current model with a newer, spiffier one doesn't mean you need or have to upgrade. The only compelling reasons to upgrade your Mac are:

- ☛ If keeping current in Mac technology is your bread-and-butter (like you're a consultant, a Mac-writer, or something).

- ☛ If your old model can't keep up with new software and peripherals, you should probably upgrade to a newer model.

- ☛ If you succumb to upgrade fever. That's when no matter what it is, if it's the latest and greatest, you have to have it.

"Because I can" or "because it's there" are not really good enough reasons to upgrade. If you keep upgrading simply because Apple and software companies keep releasing upgrades, you'll wind up in the poorhouse, babbling and drooling while you wait for your afternoon dose of Thorazine.

SIMMply the Best: Adding RAM

Short of upgrading your Mac to a newer, zippier model, the kindest thing you can do for your tired, overworked Mac is to increase its supply of random-access memory (RAM). You add RAM by means of SIMMS (single in-line memory modules). SIMMS are tiny cards (about four inches long) with eight or nine memory chips on them. Most Macs have a couple of slots built-in to accept SIMMS (some Macs have more than others).

Adding RAM is like sending your Mac to college: it will be able to work with larger applications, do more stuff with those applications, and create bigger and better documents—all without the hazards of Friday night fraternity parties and high tuition bills.

SIMMS are simple to install in all but the compact Macs (the Classics) and PowerBooks, so you can do it yourself. Most mail-order companies are kind enough to send you an easy-to-follow installation guide, sometimes even a video tape, to make the process even easier. But technically, installing RAM yourself voids your Mac's warranty. If you're at all squeamish about that, have the RAM installed by your Local Authorized Apple Dealer.

Each Mac's memory capacity is different. Different models of Mac also take different kinds of SIMMS (most use specifically Mac SIMMS, others use the same kind as DOS computers). SIMMS come in different memory sizes: 1, 2, and 4 megabytes (higher capacity chips are available, but hard to find). They also come in different speeds: 150 ns (for nanoseconds or millionths of a second; it's for how long it takes your Mac to access the memory), also 120, 100, 80, 70, and 60 ns. The lower the number, the faster the SIMM (and more expensive). The easiest way to find out which SIMMS your Mac needs is to ask.

If you're a do-it-yourself kind of person, mail-order companies are very good about specifying packages of SIMMS by Mac model and memory size. They'll also let you know if you need any special tools to install (like the special wrench you need to crack open a PowerBook or Classic). Best of all, their advice is free, and their prices are usually better than your Local Authorized Apple Dealer. Of course, you have to do the work yourself.

If you'd rather have root canal than poke around inside your Mac, call your Local Authorized Apple Dealer and let them do the work—if they don't know what kind and how many SIMMS your Mac can handle, well, we're all in big trouble.

Ahead Warp-Factor Seven: Accelerators and Such

Does your Mac seem poky and slow compared to some other Macs you've seen? Can you type faster than your word processor can process? Do you have to take a coffee break while your spreadsheets recalculate? Your Mac doesn't need vitamins or iron supplements: it needs a silicon supplement.

Math Coprocessors

If you do a lot of math-intensive work with your Mac (not only spreadsheets, but 3-D rendering, PostScript illustrations, and so on), your Mac may benefit from the addition of a *math coprocessor,* or *FPU* (for Floating Point Unit) *chip.* A math coprocessor takes away the burden of math (and it is a burden) from your Mac's central processor. With the central processor freed up to do other things, your Mac can zip along, but only with math-related applications.

Some Macs come with math coprocessors as a standard feature. Others come with an empty socket where you can plug one in. Still others won't accept a coprocessor at all. If your Mac won't accept a coprocessor, don't despair: you have other options.

Accelerator Cards

If your Mac is generally sluggish, you can add an *accelerator card* to give it a boost. An accelerator supplements your Mac's central processor by giving it another processor, or even bypassing your Mac's processor with a bigger, faster one.

The accelerator card goes into one of your Mac's expansion slots, which are empty sockets that accept cards that add speed or functions (such as an internal modem for communications) to your Mac. If your Mac doesn't have a socket for one, some accelerator cards come with a math coprocessor on the card, so the socket isn't an issue.

Here's the trouble with accelerators: they're expensive. In some cases, almost as much as a whole new Mac CPU. It's a case of think before your buy. If your Mac is so poky and slow that you think you want to accelerate, shop for the accelerator, but before you buy it, compare its price with the price of a more powerful Macintosh CPU. It may be less expensive (and more reliable) to cough up the bucks for a faster Mac.

Accelerators come made for specific Mac models, because some Macs have *NuBus* slots, others *PDS*, and still others have both. NuBus and PDS cards are not interchangeable.

There are different kinds of accelerators for different kinds of work: general accelerators speed up your Mac overall; video accelerators speed up the time it takes for your Mac to put information (especially QuickTime or photo-realistic still images) up on your screen. There are still others that speed up other processes.

SPEAK LIKE A GEEK

NuBus is a high-speed slot that accepts cards that work along with your Mac's central processor to supplement its functions. The information is fed along a data path called a *bus*, like your Mac's ADB (Apple Desktop *Bus*) that feeds your Mac information from your mouse and keyboard.

PDS (Processor Direct Slot) is a slot that feeds information directly into the central processor of your Mac, rather than through a bus.

Again, because of the variety of Macs, slots, and cards, your path of least resistance is to figure out what you want your Mac to do faster. Then call your Local Authorized Apple Dealer, Macintosh Users Group, or favorite mail-order company, and pick their brains for suggestions. Shopping well is half the battle (see Chapter 19 for shopping tips).

Talk Scuzzy to Me

If you aren't considering buying any peripherals right away, but want to know what your options are, skip this section and read about the hardware. SCSI is often confusing and troublesome to the biggest propellerhead. Don't hurt yourself unnecessarily. Wait until you have to read it, okay?

SCSI stands for Small Computer Systems Interface. It's another way of connecting peripherals to computers.

Many of the peripherals you'll be reading about are SCSI (pronounced "scuzzy"—what did you think I meant?) devices that require some special handling. Hard drives are SCSI devices, as are scanners. No matter what a SCSI device does, they all get connected the same way (that's what makes them SCSI), so here's a little SCSI primer.

You can hook up a total of six more SCSI devices to your Mac. (You can really install eight, but your Mac and its internal hard drive already count as two SCSI devices, leaving you only six available for add-ons).

Since your Mac only has one SCSI port, you connect SCSI devices to each other (they come with two SCSI ports), and only connect one of them to your Mac. That's called a *SCSI chain*, or sometimes, *daisy-chaining*.

Having all those devices connected can confuse the heck out of your Mac (and you), that's why each device needs to be assigned a *SCSI ID Number*. The SCSI ID Numbers are 0 through 7. Typically, your Mac's ID Number is 7, and its internal hard drive is 0. That leaves you with the numbers 1 through 6 to assign other SCSI devices.

The ID Number tells your Mac what order to check-in the devices at startup. Usually your Mac looks for ID number 0 first, then backtracks through numbers 6 to 1. The ID Number has nothing to do with the physical order that the drives are hooked together—put that thought right out of your mind. That would be too easy.

You set the external hard drive's ID number with some sort of button, wheel, or set of *dip switches*. Check your hard drive's manual for it's particular method of setting ID numbers.

Dip Switches are little teeny-tiny switches (such as microscopic light switches) that you have to use a pencil-point or other teeny-tiny thing to flip, because most fingers are too big to do it. They must have been invented by a dip.

Dip switches are a pain in the butt. Do yourself a favor: buy a hard drive that has an external *wheel-* or *dial-set SCSI number,* or a *push-button*. It'll say so in the ad, or if you're shopping in person, you can look for it. (Did I say this was easy? I don't think so.)

When you're connecting a chain of SCSI devices, the first and last devices have to be terminated. A terminator stops the signal that runs through your SCSI cables from bouncing back and forth eternally through the chain, giving your Mac a nervous breakdown. When the signal hits the terminator, it stops, and your Mac can get on with its life.

The first item in the chain is your Mac's internal drive. It's termination is built-in, and you never ever have to worry about it. The last item in the chain, the one that's physically farthest away from your Mac, should also be terminated. Nothing in between should be terminated.

Termination of a SCSI device is either *internal* (inside the device, and a pain in the butt—so avoid it), or *external* (on the outside of the case, usually a cap plugged into one of the device's two SCSI ports and very easy to change).

To remove internal termination, you have to open the device, and pull a little plug-kind-of-thing, or cut off a resistor-kind-of-thing. Don't try it yourself. Take it into your Local Authorized Apple Dealer. Better still, don't buy anything with internal termination, if you can avoid it.

The easiest termination to deal with is an on/off switch. Flip, it's on. Flip, it's off, just like the Clapper. I wish more manufacturers would use it.

One last thing: the total length of the SCSI cables in any chain shouldn't be any longer than about 20 to 24 feet. (That's why most SCSI devices only come with two- or three-foot long cables). Otherwise, the signal gets too weak before it reaches the end of the chain. You can add a *signal amplifier* somewhere in the middle of a longer chain. It boosts the signal so it can travel farther, but they, naturally, cost money. If you can avoid that, you can save some shekels.

By the Way . . .

Okay, one more one last thing: SCSI devices can be cranky. You can follow the rules to the letter, and it still won't work. If that happens, chuck the rules and try anything. (If you're adding one SCSI device, it's pretty painless. Even two isn't too bad. It's only when you get up to three or more that things get kind of wonky.)

Storage Space

After you've added RAM and given your Mac a dose of speed, you'll be working like a devil, right? You may run out of places to store all those wickedly brilliant documents you've been creating. Not a problem. You can add additional *storage space* any number of ways.

If your Mac's hard drive gets choked with data, despite your best efforts to keep up with housekeeping (see Chapter 10 for more on that), or the best efforts of your compression software (Chapter 13) to give you some elbow room, it may be time buy a new hard drive, or other mass storage devices.

Fixed Drives

The easiest way to add a new hard drive to your Mac is to plug in an *external* hard drive. An external hard drive is one that sits near your Mac. It's connected to your Mac through your Mac's SCSI port.

Installing an *internal* drive is a little more difficult because you have to open your Mac to do it. There's screws to screw, cables to cable, but, if you have the nerve, I say go for it. The biggest benefit of replacing your Mac's internal drive with a new, larger one (in addition to the extra space) is that you can still add six more SCSI devices. (Do I need to remind you again about how installing things inside your Mac can void Apple's warranty? I didn't think so.)

A hard drive is also called a **fixed drive**. Not fixed as in neutered, but fixed as in not removable. It means the magnetic media is fixed in place. It doesn't come out.

Hard drive capacity (internal or external) is measured in megabytes. By today's standards, 40 or even 80MB is pretty small, especially when you consider that a full installation of Microsoft Word takes up to 8 megabytes of space! That's 20% of a 40MB hard drive.

When shopping for hard drives, buy as large a drive as you can afford. I wouldn't get anything smaller than 40MB, and you can find hard drives that hold as much as a gigabyte (1,000 megabytes), and more. Trust me, sooner or later, you'll fill it.

Removable Media Drives

Removable media drives work like a hard drive, but with one difference: you can pop out the magnetic media when it gets full and pop in a new blank one—like a regular floppy disk. Imagine that infinite storage potential!

Removable media drives are a good idea for people who work on huge files that have to travel to another location. You pop out the media from your drive and toss it in your briefcase or backpack. No more lugging 30 or 40 floppy disks around.

Removable media drives come in several varieties and capacities, but they're all SCSI devices:

The *cost per megabyte ratio (or $/MB ratio)* is a good rule of thumb for deciding if a hard (or other mass storage) drive is really a bargain. All the other options have to be equal (warranty, ease of use, and so on). Sorry, but it involves math.

An 85MB hard drive, at $249 (249/85= $2.93 per megabyte) is not as good a bargain as a 170MB hard drive (with otherwise identical features) at $450 (450/170= $2.65 per megabyte). Of course, it's all meaningless if you only have about $249 to spend.

☞ **Bernoulli drives**, from Iomega Corporation, work with what looks like a big ol' floppy disk. They come in capacities of about 45, 90, and 150MB disks. The drives themselves cost (mail-order pricing) between $500 and $900. The Bernoulli disks cost about $160 each. The *cost per megabyte ratio* (the price divided by the number of MB of storage) only gets competitive with fixed hard drives if you know you'll use more than one or two Bernoulli disks.

☞ **SyQuest** drives work with cartridges as well, but come in capacities of 44 and 88MB. The drives themselves cost (mail order) between $400 and $550 (depending on capacity). The cartridges cost between $75 and $110. The cost per megabyte ratio is a little easier on the wallet, but you still need to use a few disks regularly to make it cost-effective.

☞ **DAT Drives** or **Digital Audio Tape** drives can hold enormous amounts of data (up to 2 gigabytes per tape). They're good for voluminous backup copies of large or networked hard drives. They're a little pricey for personal use, since they run between $1,000 to $2,000. There are other, less expensive tape drives that use standard data cassettes. (They can hold about 160MB of data and cost about $700.)

☞ **Optical Drives** work something like standard 3.5-inch disks with a big difference: they use *VHD* (*very high density*) disks that, when combined with the precision of an optically driven write-head, can store up to *21MB* per disk. Optical disk drives can also read and write to regular 1.4 MB disks, so in addition to the extra storage space, you also get a second high-density disk drive. Optical drives cost between $500–600. The optical mechanisms have special cleaning requirements, and I hate to clean.

If your circumstances make an ejectable media drive both necessary and cost-effective, go for it. Otherwise, a regular run-of-the-mill hard drive should be more than sufficient.

CD-ROM

CD-ROM drives (compact disc read-only memory) are SCSI devices that hold huge amounts (over 700MB) of read-only data. You can hold the entire contents of a multimedia (pictures, sounds, movies, as well as words) encyclopedia on one CD.

The advantages of CD-ROM drives are these:

☞ Huge libraries of reference and educational materials (excellent for children and students) are available.

☞ Lots of interactive games (if you're into gaming).

☞ The ability to play music CDs and Kodak Photo CDs (where you get your pictures back on disc, instead of on paper).

There are also disadvantages of CD-ROM. There are suddenly hundreds of drives to choose from, all with different speeds (an important factor) and capabilities:

☞ CD-ROM drives access data at between 180 ms (milliseconds, or thousandths of a second) and 400 ms. 180 ms. is fast, 400 is slow. Compare that to most hard drives that access data at an average of about 20 ms. CD-ROMs are slloooowww.

☞ Some drives also only come with one SCSI port (most SCSI devices have two for easy daisy-chaining) which is a pain.

☞ Some drives you buy are just the drives: you have to buy cables, connector kits, driver software, speakers, headphones, and anything else you might want separately. I hate that. When you're pricing them, make sure the price includes everything you need, or else the drive you think is a bargain could start running you big bucks.

☞ Most computer peripherals go in boom-or-bust cycles. Right now, CD-ROM drives are a boom item: everyone is making them, trying to cash in. That's good because prices are competitive, but that's bad because you have to do your homework so you can buy the drive that's best for your needs. Flip to Chapter 19 for shopping tips.

Input Devils—er, Devices

Anything that gets information into your Mac is an *input device*: a mouse, a keyboard, a microphone, a scanner . . . you get the idea. Some come already packaged with your Mac, but you may want to replace them. Others make nice additions because of the benefits they give you.

Mice and Trackballs

Mice are nice, but you can do so much more with them if they get a little more complicated: one button (for some) just isn't enough. Two- or three-button mice let you program specific commands to each button: say the first button is your basic click; the second button is a double-click (but you only have to click once); and the third button is something you use frequently. You can program it to send a command like ⌘-W to close a window, or a click-lock (like holding down the button) for dragging stuff around without wearing your button-finger down to a nub.

Trackballs, on the other hand, work like mice turned over on their backs. Instead of sliding the mouse around, you roll the ball of the trackball to move the cursor. Your hand remains pretty much stationary.

Buying a replacement mouse or trackball can give you (usually) a new control panel that can replace your original Mouse Control Panel. What they do varies from manufacturer to manufacturer, but generally they let you assign a *tracking speed* (how far the cursor moves in relation to how far you move the mouse or trackball), a click speed (how quickly you click), and (for a multibutton device) what number of clicks or other commands the additional buttons send when pressed.

By the Way . . .

There's a lot of confusion about which is better for your health: a mouse or a trackball. Does heavy mouse-use cause Carpal Tunnel Syndrome (a very painful condition that affects the tendons of your wrist and forearm)? Does a trackball alleviate the problem? Or is the whole thing one of those high-fiber-like hypes only to sell peripherals?

I don't know. I do know that a multiple-button mouse or trackball can make it easier for you to work. On the other hand, I'm not a doctor, and I've never played one on TV. In terms of how I work and whether or not it may cause Carpal Tunnel, I follow the medical advice of Groucho Marx's Dr. Hackenbush: "Does it hurt when you do that? Then don't do that."

If you have concerns about arm, wrist, or even neck or back pain when using your Mac, don't ask a computer geek, ask your doctor. That's what she's there for.

Drawing Tablets

If you've ever tried drawing a free-form shape with your mouse, you know that it's no substitute for a pen and paper. A drawing tablet gives you the same sort of control of your drawing as a pen and paper. (I talked about these briefly while talking about painting and drawing software in Chapter 13.)

A drawing tablet is an ADB device (like your mouse) that plugs into one of your Mac's ADB ports. It behaves like a pad of paper: you draw on it with a stylus, and the lines you draw show up on your Mac's screen in your painting/drawing program.

Drawing tablets come with many different functions and capabilities. The important thing to remember is that all the tablet capabilities in the world won't help you if the software you use can't make use of them. If you buy your software first, look for a drawing tablet that gives you all the functions it can handle. If you buy a super-duper full-featured tablet first, shop for software that can make use of the features, otherwise you've wasted money on the tablet.

Probably the easiest way to do it is to buy the painting/drawing program when you buy your tablet so you can be sure the two work together. Some mail-order places even offer you a deal on a set: the software with the best tablet for it. That can save you time shopping, and maybe even some money.

Keyboards

The best thing I ever did was add an *extended keyboard* to my Mac. An extended keyboard is longer than your normal keyboard. It has a number-pad for speedier entry of numerical data, arranged like the keys of a calculator. With practice, you can really speed up your numerical data entry.

They also come with Function Keys (you know, those F1 through F15 keys) across the top of the keyboard. With a utility, such as QuicKeys, you can assign all sorts of funky functions to the F-keys.

Apple makes several extended keyboards for the Mac, including that fabulous one that splits and bends (I think it even turns into a spy plane and an origami swan) so you can adjust it to your own typing comfort.

Apple's keyboards are expensive, though. Other manufacturers make keyboards for Macs too, and for less. Mine even came with a bundled copy of QuicKeys. Too cool.

Scanners

A computer scanner is a SCSI device that takes an image, either photo-graphic, graphic (like a line drawing), or type (text), and converts it to digital information you can display and play with on your Mac's screen.

Physically, there are two kinds of scanners: hand-held, or flatbed. A hand-held scanner is small enough to fit in your hand. You slowly, and carefully, drag it across the image you want to digitize. A SCSI cable links it to your Mac (or your SCSI chain). A flatbed scanner looks like a small photocopier: it sits on your desk and you lay whatever it is you're scanning on a glass plate. The scanner does its thing (also like a photocopier) and the image shows up on your Mac.

Hand-held scanners are less expensive than flatbed scanners. They're also more difficult to use—you need to have good eye-hand coordination, for one thing. Because they're small, you have to make several passes at whatever you're scanning, then stitch the pieces together with an editing utility (one usually comes with a scanner).

Flatbed scanners are easier to use, but expensive. You're also limited to stuff that fits on the glass plate: loose pages, photos, and so on. It's hard to scan things from thick books. For larger images, you can still scan parts and stitch them together. Flatbed scanners can usually be fitted with attachments that feed in multiple sheets, or even scan from slides or film negatives. They also cost extra.

Other considerations when selecting a scanner, include:

☞ Is it color (expensive), grayscale (less expensive), or black-and-white (practically cheap)?

☞ If its grayscale, is it real grayscale (256 shades of gray), or does it take a few shades of gray and *dither* them? If you want to work with photographs, avoid the ones that dither if you can. Look for ones that say "true 256 shades of gray" or "true grayscale."

If a person is in a dither, they're all confused. When a picture is **dithered**, the dots that make it up are all confused. The dots get jumbled and tinkered with so the eye is fooled into seeing many more shades of gray than are really there. Dithering reduces the quality of an image by making it look blurry.

☞ What's its resolution? *Resolution* is the number of dots per inch the scanner can create in an image. More dots improve the quality but are bad for the wallet.

☞ Does it come with OCR software? If you want to be able to scan stuff like quotations from books or magazines for use in reports and such, you need OCR software.

Monitors

Monitors come in many sizes, like their TV cousins. If you do extensive page layout work, you may want to get a two-page display. They're wider, so you can look at two full-sized pages at the same time.

If you're heavy into QuickTime, or do a lot of presentation work, a big ol' 21-inch color monitor can give you a better idea of what your presentations will look like on the big screen. If you're a Classic II or monochrome PowerBook user, you may have the option of adding a larger color monitor to supplement your small built-in screen. These are all options, and there are lots more.

You should know, before you shop, you may need to add a video card, to control the monitor, or beef up your Mac's built-in video by adding video RAM to get the most out of it. Some models of Mac may also need special adapters to add additional monitors at all. Check your manuals or ask at your local MUG, or Local Authorized Apple Dealer for advice.

Sound-in, Sound-Out

If you bought a new-ish Mac, you might not have gotten a microphone with it for recording your own sounds. That's too bad, but it can be fixed. For about $25, you can buy the microphone set that Apple used to include with their Macs. Of course, you can buy any old microphone with the small jack, and plug that into your audio-in port. Your Mac doesn't care.

The big advantage to buying Apple's microphone is that it comes with a *phono-plug adapter* that you can use to dub sounds from other sources (like the radio, audio, or video cassettes). If you have an older Mac that doesn't have an audio-in jack, you can still add your own sounds, but you need to buy a microphone package.

As long as we're on sound, you can also buy special computer speakers to give your Mac blazing sound. Or if you're the shy type, a pair of headphones (such as the kind you use with a WalkMan) will let you impress only yourself with sound. Either kind get plugged into the audio-out jack.

Video-In and -Out

With the advent of QuickTime, it's become very cool to use video clips on your Mac. For the practical-minded, they make for spiffy presentations. For toy-brains (like moi), they're just fun.

If you aren't satisfied with the selections of QuickTime clips you can buy, or if you need custom clips for a presentation, you can buy video boards that let you record your own clips from your VCR or camcorder. They're cards that you pop into one of your Mac's expansion slots. They give you both video-in and video-out ports. There are specific models for specific Mac slots (PDS or NuBus). Be sure you get the right one for your Mac.

When you're set up, you can also transfer your QuickTime creations to video tape (with the video-out port) to share your masterpieces with the Macintosh-impaired.

Baudy-Bits: About Modems

A *modem*, as I mentioned way, way the heck back in Chapter 2 (and will again in Chapter 18), is a device that allows two computers to talk and share files and information over common telephone lines. If you have access to two modem-equipped Macs (say one at work and one at home, or a desktop Mac and a PowerBook), you can stop schlepping disks back and forth between them.

With software (like *AppleTalk Remote Access*), you can dial up your home-based Mac from work (or vice versa) and access any file on the hard drive. On the road, you can hook into your job's network and check your e-mail (electronic mail), or just work like you were still in the office.

I didn't want to have to drag work and business into this. This is Macintosh. It's supposed to be the fun one. But, hey. You forced me into it.

Miscellaneous Hardware

There are many other goodies you can fling at your Mac. The above was just a sample. By the time you read this, there will have been whole new families of hardware introduced. You'll see CD drives that you can write to, instead of read-only. There will be fleets of add-ins for the new AV Macs to augment and accessorize the new voice and telephone technologies. Fleets of stuff. The only thing you can count on in the fast-paced world of technology is growth and change.

There are also tons of goofy stuff you can add: mouse-pockets that stick on the side of your monitor to hold your mouse when you aren't using it; dopey ears and stuff you can stick on your monitor to make it look like a monster or a dinosaur. It isn't really hardware, but it can be fun. And it's more fun to find them for yourself. My telling you everything would take all the mystery out of life.

The Least You Need to Know

- ☞ There are a lot of hardware upgrades available to rejuvenate a sluggish Mac.
- ☞ Many hardware peripherals (such as hard drives and CD-ROM readers) are SCSI devices.
- ☞ You can add up to six SCSI devices to your Mac.
- ☞ A big, fat, roomy hard drive would be a fabulous addition to any storage deprived Mac.

Part IV
The Macintosh Mystique

So far, we've seen how to set up a Mac and looked at the basic operations of the desktop and Finder; we've even tinkered with some of the basic applications and looked at the software and hardware you can add to your Mac to meet your specific needs. None of this is so terrribly dreadful. Like any new skill, it just takes a little practice before you get the hang of it. It's like learning to play the guitar: it hurts until you build up those callouses; then it suddenly becomes magic.

In this part, you will get a refresher on some of the things you can do to stay up-to-date with the Macintosh world and see what the future of your Mac looks like. You'll also get an entire chapter devoted to the special needs of PowerBook users.

Stop watching the clock. Pay attention until the recess bell rings. And spit out that gum, young man.

Chapter 15
Printer Prattle

In This Chapter

- ☛ Buffet o' printers
- ☛ Chauffeur-driven printers
- ☛ Cheap ($) printer tricks
- ☛ Choosing the Chooser
- ☛ Setting up pages
- ☛ Actually printing!

The only way to get that Great American Novel (or great American memo) you've been writing from your Mac's screen and into your hand is by printing it out. Printing can be, at once, the most rewarding and the most frustrating operation you perform. The two emotions are related: if it weren't so very satisfying to hold a crisp, clean printout (the result of your labors) in your hot, little hand, it wouldn't be so very frustrating when things go wrong.

Let's try and head some of that frustration off at the pass by arming you with a six-shooting squirt gun (no real guns for me, thanks) full of printer preparedness.

Printer Types

The simplest path to pain-free printing is with an Apple printer. Because Apple designed the computer as well as the printer, you get everything you need to hook that bad-boy up and just print away. Other manufacturers' printers will work with your Mac. However, unless it's a model specifically designed to work with a Mac (such as Hewlett-Packard's LaserJet 4M for Mac), you have to go through some Byzantine maneuvers to get a *third-party* printer to work with your Mac. We'll talk a little bit more about hooking up a non-Apple printer in a minute. First let's do a basic overview of your printer choices—in case you haven't bought one yet.

Over the years, five different types of printer have evolved. Of these, only three have really survived: *dot-matrix*, *inkjet*, and *laser* printers.

SPEAK LIKE A GEEK

The third party is not the party you go to after the first two. Third party refers to a company that isn't you and isn't Apple. Most often, they're referred to as *third-party developers.*

By the Way . . .

The two that went the way of the Dodo bird are the daisy-wheel and thermal printers. Daisywheel printers worked like typewriters, with a full character set (letters and numbers) on a wheel that looked like a mutant daisy. They were great for text, but couldn't really print pictures, so they died out.

Thermal printers used special paper that changed color when the hot print-head touched them. The words looked *burned* rather than printed. The combination of special paper and ugly results killed them.

Dot-Matrix Printers

Dot-matrix printers are old and venerable machines. They've been around about as long as computers themselves. They work by means of an arrangement of 9 or 24 pins in a *print head* (the moving portion that holds the ribbon and the pin assembly). The print head moves along the paper. The pins poke out and strike the ribbon. The ribbon strikes the paper, and dots are left behind.

Usually when you look at an ad for a printer, you'll see *printer resolution* described as *300 dpi* or *360 X 360*. Clear as mud, eh? What that means is the first printer prints 300 *dots per inch*, which is a fairly standard print resolution; though you will see some laser printers that can print from 600 to even thousands of dots per inch. The second printer is a dot-matrix printer that is capable of printing a matrix 360 dots high by 360 dots wide. That's lots o' dots, and a fairly standard resolution for 24-pin dot-matrix printers. The higher a printer's resolution, the better the printed page will look—and the higher the printer's price tag.

The print head leaves an arrangement of dots in a small, defined area that form the letters, numbers, and lines of your document. That's the dot *matrix*, and the source of the name.

The more pins you have in the print head, the denser packed the dots in the matrix, and the better the print quality. Therefore a 24-pin printer can give you better printout than a 9-pin. The number of dots that fit in the matrix is called the printer's *resolution*, and it's one of the few times that being dense is actually a good thing.

Apple's ImageWriter line of printers are dot-matrix printers, but there are hundreds of other brands. Most of the other brands, however, are geared toward the DOS side of computing and require those Byzantine maneuvers I mentioned earlier. The attraction of dot-matrix printers, overall, is that they're cheaper (but not much cheaper) than inkjet printers, and loads cheaper than laser printers. But they're also noisy buggers.

Inkjet Printers

In theory, inkjet printers work much the same as dot-matrix printers: there's a print head that moves back and forth across your paper leaving a matrix of dots to form lines and letters. In practice, however, there's one big exception.

Instead of pins striking a ribbon, the print head of an inkjet printer spits (eeeewww) those ink dots directly onto the paper to form your letters and lines. Because the spray of ink delivered by the print head is finer than the dots made by a dot-matrix printer, the resolution of an inkjet printer may sound the same (300 or 360 dpi) as a dot-matrix printer, but the quality looks better.

The attraction to inkjet printers is that they're quiet, the output is good, and they're a reasonable substitute if you need, but can't afford, a laser printer. However, there are a few drawbacks. They tend to be slow, and if you use the optional coated inkjet paper, the ink can smear if you handle the page too soon after printing. Plus, the coated paper (which keeps the ink from being absorbed into the paper, which in turn distorts the shape of letters), is expensive.

Apple's StyleWriter and StyleWriter II are both inkjet printers. Hewlett-Packard, among others, makes a line of inkjets especially for the Mac (the DeskWriter line), some of which print in glorious *color*.

Laser Printers

I know it's showing my age, but I remember when lasers were purely the stuff of science fiction. Now they're all over the place, thankfully without the destructive capability of their science fiction cousins.

Laser printers are the best, yet the most overrated, printers available today. They use laser beams to affix a black powder (*toner*) to the page in the shape of your letters and lines. Because the laser beam can be controlled so accurately, and the toner can be so finely ground, even laser printers with a 300 dpi resolution produce a page that looks better than one printed on an inkjet or dot-matrix printer with a higher resolution.

Since laser printers can fool the eye into seeing more detail than other, higher resolution printer-types, the laser printer is the best output device available for personal and business use. The print just looks better, crisper, and more professional.

If you haven't taken the plunge and purchased a printer yet, I'll talk about what kinds of printers are good for what kinds of jobs in a few pages. In the meantime, there are a few more things to consider about printers and printing before we get there.

Let Me Drive

Every bit as important as how (and how well) the printer gets your masterpiece on the page, is how (and how well) your Mac gets your page to the printer. The job of getting your Great American Novel (or memo) from your Mac to your printer is the job of the printer *driver*. The printer driver, like the driver of a car, issues instructions for the machine to follow. These drivers, also known as *Chooser extensions*, live in the Extensions folder inside your System Folder.

There are two kinds of printer drivers: those that rely on QuickDraw (built into your Mac's System software); and those that rely on Adobe PostScript. QuickDraw and PostScript are known as *page description languages*, a hoity-toity way of saying they get your printer to print what you've created on the screen (sometimes called *WYSIWYG* (pronounced "WIZZY-wig") for *What You See Is What You Get*).

QuickDraw is built into your Mac's System software. It's the same thing that draws and redraws everything you see on your screen. If your printer driver relies on QuickDraw (and most of them do), then your Mac does most of the heavy math that figures out which dot goes where on the page.

PostScript, on the other hand, is used mainly in laser printers, you'll see and hear them referred to as PostScript printers. PostScript isn't part of

Don't get confused. In addition to the PostScript page description language, we'll also be talking about PostScript *fonts* and *Adobe Type Manager (ATM)* that let you use PostScript fonts on a non-PostScript printer. These are three different but interrelated things.

your Mac, rather it lives inside the printer on a chip. When you print, the page is sent to the printer, and PostScript figures out where the dots go.

Every printer made specifically for Macintosh comes with an appropriate driver. Apple even goes so far as to provide you with all the drivers for all of their printers along with their System software. As I said earlier, you can use a non-Apple, non-Macintosh printer with your Mac, but it takes some work.

Non-Apple, Non-Macintosh Printers

There are three problems that stand in your way of hooking up a printer aimed at IBM-compatible machines. First, they don't come with printer drivers for Macs. Second, they don't come with the round-ended serial cables to plug into the printer port on the back of your Mac. Third, many of these printers are *parallel* printers (as opposed to the *serial* printers Macs require).

Parallel and *serial* are distinctions based on how the printers receive information from the computer. Parallel printers receive bits of information in sets of 8 bits. Most IBM-compatible computers come with *two* parallel ports, so parallel printers are popular for them. Serial printers receive bits of information one at a time. The Mac's built-in printer port is a serial port, and the source of this particular problem.

Two terribly clever companies have side-stepped these problems for you. The first one, GDT Softworks, in the lovely state of Washington, puts out what they call Power-Print. It's a collection of drivers that print on over a thousand non-Mac printers. It also comes with a converter cable that converts your Mac's serial output into parallel output. The second one, Orange Micro, has taken a different tack entirely. Rather than provide another driver, OrangeMicro will sell you a converter cable and software that fakes your Mac into thinking it's printing to an Apple ImageWriter printer.

The biggest advantage to buying a non-Mac printer is that they tend to be less expensive up front. However, they may not be less expensive once you add the converter gew-gaws and consider the dollar value of your pain and suffering. If you already have an IBM-compatible printer, or someone wants to give you their old one, then it can be a great savings to you. Whether the extra effort and any savings you might gain are actually worth it for you, only you can decide.

Choosy Users Choose the Chooser

Regardless of what printer you end up with, you need to tell the Mac what and where it is. To do that, you use the Chooser. It's one of the handy-dandy little items in the menu. When you select **Chooser** from the menu, you'll be presented with a window similar to the one shown here. (You may have different printer drivers.)

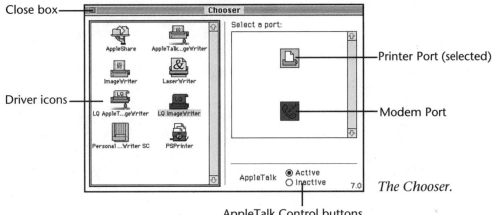

Close box

Driver icons

Printer Port (selected)

Modem Port

AppleTalk Control buttons

The Chooser.

Looking at the Chooser (clockwise, from the top left), you'll see a window that displays the icons for all of the printers and other Chooser selectable devices, like modems. If you have more drivers than fit in the scroll window, you can scroll through the list to find the one you'd like to select. When you select a printer icon, the right half of the display changes to accommodate the needs of that particular printer.

To select a printer's icon, simply click on it.

Click on the icon for the port you want to connect your printer to. Depending on the type of printer you've selected, the bottom third of the right side of the window will be different.

Background printing is accomplished by means of another little program called PrintMonitor, which is launched automatically when you have the Background Printing option turned on. We'll talk more about PrintMonitor in a bit.

In its simplest terms, a *network* can be as small as one Mac hooked up with one laser printer via AppleTalk. At its most extreme, a network can be dozens of Macs hooked up to each other, as well as to several printers. If your network consists of one Mac and one printer linked by AppleTalk, the instructions here are enough to get you printing. If you're on a more complicated network, check with the network administrator (whoever manages the beast) to verify what you need to do to print.

If you have a **Setup** button, clicking on it brings up a window or dialog box where you can tell your Mac necessary information about the chosen printer. If a **Background Printing** option is available to you (and it's turned on), control of your Macintosh is returned to you before the print job is completed. You don't have to wait for the entire thing to print before moving on to other work.

Finally, the *AppleTalk* control buttons are at the bottom right of the window. AppleTalk is Apple's built-in network communications feature. Many of Apple's laser printers rely on AppleTalk to pass information from your Mac to the laser printer.

If your printer is connected via AppleTalk (check your printer manual to be certain), be sure that AppleTalk is *active* before you try and print. If it isn't, click on the radio button in front of the word **Active**. You'll get a message warning that you must restart your Mac before AppleTalk can be activated.

Once you have the Chooser set up to accommodate your printer, you may close it by clicking on the **Close box** in the upper left corner. If you've changed anything, you'll get a warning that you've changed printers with the Chooser, and you should adjust your Page Setup settings. The next section explains how to do that.

Page Setup

The **Page Setup** command tells your Mac what kind of paper you'll be printing on. To use it, select the **Page Setup** option from the **File** menu. You'll see the dialog box similar to the one shown in the following figure. (The options available to you will vary slightly from printer to printer or from program to program.) You'll notice that the dialog box is specific to the printer selected in the Chooser.

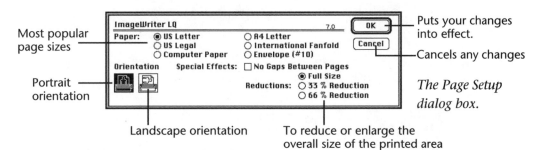

Most popular page sizes

Portrait orientation

Landscape orientation

To reduce or enlarge the overall size of the printed area

Puts your changes into effect.

Cancels any changes

The Page Setup dialog box.

The top third of the dialog box is dominated by the paper options. These are standard no matter what printer you use.

Another dialog box option is the *Reduce or Enlarge* text box. You can type in the percentage you would like each page of your current document reduced or enlarged to.

The most commonly used paper sizes are in the body of the dialog: *US Letter* (8 1/2 x 11-inches), *US Legal* (8 1/2 x 14-inches), *A4 Letter* (8 1/2 x 11 2/3-inches, a size more common in Europe), and *B5 Letter* (another standard size in Europe, 7 x 10-inches).

To select one of these sizes, simply click on the radio button in front of the paper size of your choice.

By the Way . . .

"Reduce or Enlarge" is badly phrased. It seems to say you should enter the amount you want the page reduced or enlarged. This is wrong! If you want each page *reduced* 25%, you don't enter 25%. Instead, you enter 75%, because 100% minus 25% is 75% (100-25=75). (Who said this math crap wouldn't be useful after you left school?) If you want to *enlarge* each page by 25%, you'd enter 125%.

Below the Reduce or Enlarge option are the *Orientation* icons. The icon on the left, where the person is standing full length on the page, is called *portrait orientation*. A page in portrait orientation looks the way you normally think of an 8 1/2 x 11-inch piece of paper (taller than it is wide). The icon on the right, where the outline of a person is cut off at the waist (ouch) is *Landscape orientation*. Landscape turns the page so that it is wider than it is tall: 11 x 8 1/2-inch.

Portrait is the *default* (or preset) orientation, so only change it if you want to print in landscape. If you change the orientation of a document, it stays that way until you change it again, but only for that specific document. If you want to print several documents in landscape orientation, you must change the Page Setup for each one.

Next come the Printer Effects options. These vary from printer to printer, so check your printer's manual if you're not sure what your options do.

Finally, the dialog box has buttons. You'll click on the **OK** button when you're through making changes to the page setup. **Cancel** abandons any changes you may have just made and closes the dialog box. **Options** brings up an additional dialog box that lets you add some special effects to your printed page. You can select any combination of these options that you care to, or none at all. The options vary depending on your printer's capabilities. Check your documentation if you can't figure out what one of your options is.

When you've chosen the special effects (if any) you want to inflict on your document, click on the **OK** button, or press the **Enter** key, and you'll be returned to the Page Setup dialog box. If you're done with that one, too, click on the **OK** button, or press **Enter**, and you'll be back at your document and ready to print.

Printing (Finally!)

Now that your Mac has been informed of all your printing choices, you can finally print out a document. If you don't often change printers, paper size, or add special printing effects, you may not have to tinker with the Chooser or Page Setup settings again for a long time. So let's print while the printing is good.

Printing a Document Within an Application

When your application is running and your document is open, click on the **File** menu. If everything is set to your liking and your printer is turned on, select the **Print** command. You'll get a dialog box like the one shown here.

ImageWriter LQ			7.0	Print
Quality:	⦿ Best	○ Faster	○ Draft	Cancel
Head Scan:	○ Bidirectional	⦿ Unidirectional		Options
Page Range:	⦿ All	○ From: ☐ To: ☐		
Copies:	1			
Section Range: From: 1	To: 1		☐ Print Selection Only	
☐ Print Hidden Text	☐ Print Next File			

The Print dialog box.

As before, some of the features and functions of the dialog box will vary. Some programs, like Microsoft Word, add their own special functions to the Print dialog box. Check with your application's documentation if you want to know the particulars.

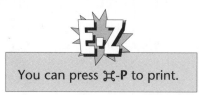

You can press ⌘-P to print.

When your dialog box options are set to your liking, click on **Print**, and in a few minutes or so (depending on your printer and the length of your document), you'll have a nice, crisp printout to ooh and ahh over.

Printing a Document from the Desktop

Yes, Virginia, there is a way to print a file you've already saved without having to open the application that created it. First, you click on the document's icon to select it. Then, you select **Print** from the **File** menu (or press ⌘-**P**). Your Mac automatically fires up the application that created the document, opens the document, and presents you with the Print dialog box.

You can mess around with the settings, and then click on the **Print** button (or press **Enter**) when you're finished. Your file prints, and your Mac automatically shuts down the application, neat as can be.

From the desktop, you can print the contents of the currently active window. This is way helpful for keeping track of what you have. I try to keep a current printout of all the junk I have cluttering up my System Folder, particularly the Extensions and Control Panels folders.

To print the contents of the active window, do one of these two things:

☞ If the window's in *Icon* or *Small Icon* view, select **Print Window** from the **File** menu. Repeat the process for each folder in the original window (so you get a full printout of contents).

☞ If the window's in *View by Name*, click on the arrow in front of each folder icon to expand the view to include all items in nested folders. Select **Print Window** from the **File** menu.

Monitoring PrintMonitor

If you have the option of *background printing*, you'll need to deal with *PrintMonitor*. It's a wee bit of a program that lives in the Extensions folder that's inside your System Folder. PrintMonitor accepts the printing chores you send it and handles them while you move on to bigger and better things.

When you print a file, all of the printing data is printed to disk in a folder called *PrintMonitor Documents* located in your System Folder. As soon as it's done printing to disk, control of your Mac is returned to you. This is called *spooling* a file (don't ask me why). Then, working quietly in the background, PrintMonitor then picks up the spooled file and *downloads* it to your printer.

You don't need to be printing something to access PrintMonitor. You can open it like any other application. Locate the PrintMonitor icon inside the Extensions folder in your System Folder, and double-click on it. You'll see the PrintMonitor dialog box shown here.

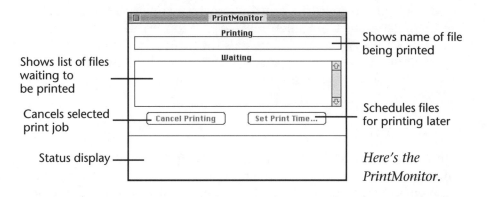

Shows list of files waiting to be printed

Cancels selected print job

Status display

Shows name of file being printed

Schedules files for printing later

Here's the PrintMonitor.

When you're actually printing something, all those blank spaces you see in the figure get filled in, as follows:

The first box, labeled *Printing*, shows you the name of the file currently being printed, as well as the name of the printer it is printing on. Below it, the *Waiting* box shows you what files are queued up to print after the current file.

The **Cancel Printing** button stops the current file from printing or removes a selected file from the *Waiting* queue. To cancel a file, simply click on its name to select it, and then click on the **Cancel Printing** button.

It may take a second or two for PrintMonitor to register the **Cancel Printing** command. Don't panic.

> ## By the Way . . .
>
> When you cancel the printing of a file with the **Cancel Printing** button, the spooled file is deleted from the PrintMonitor Documents folder. If you change your mind and want to print it again, you have to go back to the original application and reissue the print command.

If you want to *pause* the printing process (while you run to the bathroom or get a snack or something), select **Stop Printing** from PrintMonitor's **File** menu. That stops the print job without deleting the spooled file. When you get back, select **Resume Printing** from the **File** menu (it's where *Stop Printing* was before), and the print job continues.

How's It Going?

Underneath the buttons in the PrintMonitor dialog box is the **Printing Status** box (it's empty in the figure) that gives you some helpful information when you're printing. The first thing it tells you is the name of the file being printed (it really wants you to know this—that's why it tells you three times). Next, it tells you the number of pages left to print in that document. Finally, it once again tells you the name of the document you are printing, and its status. The status information is usually delivered in short little phrases: **looking for printer**, **initializing printer**, **preparing data**, and finally **printing**.

When the current file finishes printing, it's like the Mad Hatter's tea party: Everything in the queue moves up one space, and the process starts all over again. If there's nothing else waiting to be printed, the display goes blank. If PrintMonitor is working in the background (it's not the active application), it shuts itself down automatically and goes away. If it is the active application, it sits there until you click on something else (the desktop or another application), and then it scurries away, back into its hole until you call it up again.

The Least You Need to Know

Here's a quick recap of what you need to remember about printing:

- ☛ You need a printer to print. Duh. The kind of printer you use is completely up to you.

- ☛ You have to have a driver (appropriate for your printer) installed in the Extensions folder inside your System Folder, in order to print.

- ☛ The Chooser (on the menu) tells your Mac what printer (and printer driver) you are using, and where it is connected to your Mac.

- ☛ Use the **Page Setup** command (on the **File** menu) to tell your Mac what size paper you'll be printing on, and what orientation it will be in.

- ☛ You can print an open document from within an application with the **Print** command on the **File** menu, or by pressing ⌘-**P**.

- ☛ You can print a document from the desktop by selecting its icon and issuing either of the print commands.

- ☛ PrintMonitor handles your background printing tasks (with an appropriate laser printer) so you can print on demand, set a specific later time, or postpone the printing indefinitely.

This page unintentionally left blank

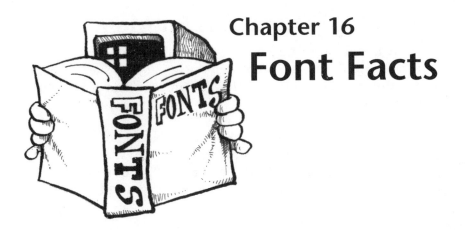

Chapter 16
Font Facts

In This Chapter

- ☞ The two basic font technologies: bit-mapped and outline fonts
- ☞ How to install fonts on your Mac
- ☞ How to manage your fonts so you can save space and memory
- ☞ Font do's and don'ts and an invitation to break the rules

Before you read any further, you should know that I am a serious font-freak. I love 'em. The more the merrier; the weirder the better. Fonts are slightly schizophrenic. On one hand, they're mundane, every day things: the alphabet, numbers, symbols, and punctuation. On the other hand, each font has its own personality, style (or lack thereof), and color.

A single chapter isn't going to give you the skills you need to raise font use to an art form—it would take a big, fat, hairy book the size of the *Oxford English Dictionary*, and even then, there's no guarantee you'll become a font artiste. However, I will introduce you to the basics of fonts. It may not be enough to make you an artiste, but it will certainly have you using fonts more effectively, and maybe put you in touch with the artiste within.

In The Beginning, There Was Bit Map

When Macs were first released, the concept of a graphical, icon-based interface was radical and new. In order to get the desktop on the desktop, menus fonts in the menu, et cetera, all the different fonts had to be built into the System software.

SPEAK LIKE A GEEK

There are many words used in computing to distinguish one kind of dot from another. In a printout, dots are simply called *dots* (as in *dots per inch*) when they make up letters and lines. On your monitor, each dot is called a *pixel*, borrowed from the terminology of television design. It's a contracted form of *picture element*. In drawing, and in fonts, a dot that is part of a letter or line is called a *bit* because it takes one bit (the smallest unit of memory) to create and place that dot somewhere.

At the time, the simplest way of doing that was to create each letter, number, and symbol of each font in a way that would be easy for your Mac to draw on the screen or print on a printer. The easiest way of doing that was to draw the letters the same way your Mac would: one dot at a time.

Since each dot in a letter is called a bit, and each letter is formed by drawing a map to tell your Mac where to place the dots, the earliest fonts were called bit maps. Because these bit-mapped fonts were first designed for use on your Mac's screen, they're also referred to as *screen fonts*. The terms are used interchangeably.

The trouble with bit-mapped fonts is that, since they're a collection a square-ish dots trying to form round-ish letters and numbers, the letter shapes would often look kind of lumpy and jagged. Lumpy letters are hard to read, especially at smaller sizes (for fonts, that's *point size*). At larger point sizes, the lumps get even more pronounced. You can see what I mean in this figure.

Lumpy Bit-Mapped Letters.

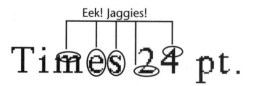

Eek! Jaggies!

Times 24 pt.

The words in the figure were done with 24-point Times (a standard Mac font), and then enlarged to show the detail. The lumpiness (often called *jaggies*) is most noticeable in the curved portions of the S, the 2, and even the diagonal part of the 4, which looks like a staircase instead of a straight line.

The most you need to remember about point size (unless you get hot and heavy into fonts) is that a *12-pt.* font is about equal to the size of type you'd get from a typewriter, and the size you'll probably use most often. Anything much larger, or much smaller, would be reserved for special uses, like big headlines or tiny captions (like the chapter names throughout this book).

SPEAK LIKE A GEEK

Point Size is a term borrowed from typesetters. One *point* is approximately 1/72 of an inch. Point is abbreviated *pt.* (as in 12-pt.).

For each common point size (like 9-, 10-, 12-, and 14-points), there was a plain bit-mapped font file, one per size. If you needed special styles (like **bold**, *italic*, and ***bold italic***), your Mac manufactured them by thickening or slanting the plain bit maps. That added another level of lumpiness to the fonts, making them even harder to read.

Generally, though, the jaggies were bearable if you had all the sizes you needed to do your work. Because bit-mapped fonts only came in fixed point sizes, if you needed to use, say, *12-point Venice,* but only had the *14-point* version installed, the jaggies would get completely out of hand.

Nice ——

Nasty ——

Venice Font Sample
Venice ▼ 12 ▼ **B** *I* U ▲▼ ▦▥◪ ◁ ☰ ☷☲
This is what Venice looks like with the proper sized bitmap installed (14 points).
This is what Venice looks like without the proper sized bitmap installed (12 points). Notice the unevenness of some of the line thicknesses here compared to those in the 14 point sample.
271 Chars	Normal	◀ ▨ ▶

Venice font sample.

Since the Venice bit map is only available in 14-points, when you specify it in 12-points, your Mac gets creative and tries to squeeze and compress the bit map it has to imitate the bit map you need. As you can see from the sample, the Mac isn't very good at imitations. The lovely calligraphic lines and flourishes of Venice at 14-points get pretty well trashed at 12-points. The invention of *outline* fonts changed all that.

You tell what sizes of a font you have installed very simply. When you pull down the **Font** menu in any application, you'll usually see the sizes you can choose from (although some applications put them in a separate menu). The font sizes that appear in *outline* characters (like 12-point) are installed and look beautiful.

The font sizes that appear in *solid* characters (like **12-point**) are not installed, and your Mac creates the size from the closest-size bit map, or uses an outline font if available.

Shapely Fonts

Instead of telling your Mac where each dot goes to shape a letter, an outline font gives a mathematical description of the letter's shape (an outline) that your Mac can then fill in. Outline fonts are like digital coloring books; all your Mac has to do is stay within the lines. The following figure shows the kind of outline that outline-style fonts provide, then how they get filled in.

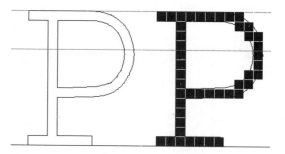

Font outlines.

The **P** on the right of the figure isn't really an accurate representation of how the outline gets filled in. You can see how some of the dots fall outside the outline (in the curve), and parts of the outline aren't filled-in. Outline fonts do a little more fiddling to fill the outline a little better. That's the blessing and curse of outline fonts.

Since the font outlines are purely mathematical, it's very easy for your Mac to fudge a number here and there to come up with the point size you need. Outline fonts are sometimes called *scalable fonts* because their size can be scaled up or down to meet your needs.

The math required to scale a font takes time, even for a computer. So, to keep your Mac from spending all of its time calculating the curves of S's, outline fonts work in tandem with their bit-mapped brothers and sisters. In fact, each outline font you have comes with a series of bit-mapped fonts at specific sizes. They also come with specific outlines for **bold**, *italic*, extended, and compressed formats. It improves the look of the type on the page, but all the additional font outlines can start to clutter up your Font folder (more about that in a little while).

If you select a font at a size available in bit-mapped format, your Mac uses that one first. If you goose the size up (or down) to one that isn't installed, then your Mac resorts to the outline font. There are two competing outline formats. One is *TrueType*, from Apple. The other is *PostScript*, from Adobe Systems. Each has specific benefits and drawbacks in terms of their use.

PS: It's PostScript

PostScript fonts, from Adobe, have been around about as long as there have been laser printers. They were originally made to live inside your printer's ROM (read-only memory) or be downloaded to its RAM (random-access memory) to make your laser printed output as crisp and clear as the technology allows.

As I mentioned before, PostScript fonts have two parts: the bit-mapped font that turns up on your screen (so you'll know what your printout will look like), and the part that lives in your printer, or in your Mac waiting to be downloaded.

The part that goes to the printer (called a *printer font*) is the actual *font outline* and had no effect on what you saw on your screen. You still had the jaggies imposed by the limits of bit-mapped screen fonts.

Then Adobe introduced *Adobe Type Manager* (*ATM*) that does two great things for Mac users. First, it lets your Mac use the *printer* fonts to calculate *screen* fonts in sizes you don't have a bit map for. The immediate benefit is a less lumpy type on your screen.

Additionally, ATM lets you use PostScript fonts on non-PostScript printers (like dot-matrix, inkjet, and some lasers) so you'd get some of the clarity and crispness of PostScript without having to shell out big bucks for a PostScript laser. They are two big benefits. The only drawback to using ATM is that it can slow your Mac down noticeably, and it can hog up your memory (RAM).

By the Way . . .

You can get Adobe Type Manager direct from Adobe for $7.50 by calling Adobe Systems at 1-800-521-1976. You get ATM, a couple of nice fonts, and pile of offers to buy other fonts at reduced pricing. What a bargain!

The dirt is that Apple used their TrueType fonts to put the fear of competition into Adobe. This $7.50 deal is a make-nice, kiss-kiss gesture on Adobe's part. Who really cares about the infighting behind it, if it saves you some bucks?

True(Blue)Type

TrueType, from Apple, is the new kid on the block. TrueType fonts were introduced with System 7.0. If you're running System 7.0 or later, you have TrueType and don't need anything extra. (System 6 users need to get the *TrueType INIT* from their local authorized Apple Dealer).

TrueType looks good, both on the page and on your screen, but there weren't many TrueType fonts around. It was a good idea, but without practical use. Now, suddenly, there are hundreds of TrueType fonts around, with more being released all the time.

The big advantage to TrueType is that you don't need anything extra to use them, just fonts. The drawbacks are that there still aren't as many TrueType fonts as there are PostScript, and if you buy a PostScript printer, you'll need to deal with PostScript fonts—at least if you plan on using the fonts built into your new printer.

> ### By the Way . . .
> TrueType and PostScript fonts get along fine on your Mac. You can use both if you want.

A Field Guide to Font Icons

Once you go poking around in your Font folder (System 7.1) or System file (System 7.0 and earlier), you'll probably want to know which type of font is which. It's easy to tell them apart, simply by looking. Let the next figure be your guide.

TECHNO NERD TEACHES

Adobe's fonts currently come in three variations: *Type 1*, *Type 3*, and *Multiple Masters*. Type 1 fonts are probably the ones you should stick with, unless you get heavily into fonts. Type 3 fonts are more for design professionals who use them in graphics, rather than text. Multiple Master fonts are for design pros: they're fonts that you can tinker with to create hundreds, even thousands of variations (in the boldness of bold, for example). Only real font freaks need apply.

There are also two versions of ATM flying around: *ATM* and *Super ATM*. Super ATM has more functions (and therefore costs more). The biggest thing about Super ATM is that it uses Multiple Master fonts to create substitute fonts if you try to open a document that uses fonts you don't own.

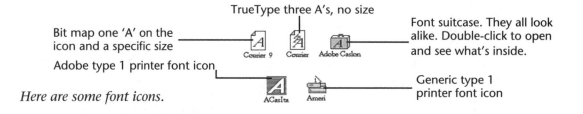

TrueType three A's, no size

Font suitcase. They all look alike. Double-click to open and see what's inside.

Bit map one 'A' on the icon and a specific size

Adobe type 1 printer font icon

Here are some font icons.

Generic type 1 printer font icon

Bit-mapped fonts only have one **A** on their icons and a point size after their names (such as *Courier 9* in the figure). All bit-mapped font icons look pretty much the same, whether from Adobe, Apple, or somebody else. TrueType fonts have three A's on the icon and no point size in the name (such as *Courier* in the figure). However, they specify **Bold**, *Italic*, or ***Bold Italic*** in the name.

Adobe PostScript printer fonts have a stylized **A** (for Adobe) as their icons, and many have seriously abridged names (such as *ACasIta* in the figure, which translates to *Adobe Caslon Italic*). PostScript printer fonts from other sources may have specialized icons. Many come with a generic icon, a LaserWriter with a **1** (like *Ameri* (for *American*) in the figure).

Ins and Outs of Fonts

Since the history of fonts is speckled with innovation and change, there are different ways to install and remove fonts in different versions of the Mac's System software. System 7.1 is the latest and greatest, so let's start there and backtrack.

System 7.1

What a piece of cake: drag the font icons you want installed from their disks into your Font folder. When you're done, restart your Mac. To remove fonts, reverse the process: drag the font icons out of your Font folder and onto a disk, holding folder, or into the Trash. Restart your Mac. You won't even break a sweat.

System 7.0

Installing fonts in 7.0 is still pretty easy, just not as easy as in 7.1.

1. After making sure that you're only running the Finder (quit any open applications), find your System Folder.

2. Drag the font icon(s) you want to install, and drop them on the System Folder.

3. You'll get a message saying something to the effect **Fonts should be stored in the System file, so I'm gonna put them there, Okay?** (The message varies according to the kind of font you're installing. Bit-mapped and TrueType fonts go in the System file, the PostScript *outline* (or printer) fonts go in the Extensions folder—don't worry, your Mac knows where they all go.)

4. Click on the **OK** button, and your Mac takes care of the rest. When it's done copying the fonts into your System, simply restart your Mac.

To remove fonts:

1. Open your System file, and drag the fonts you want to remove out of it. They can go onto a disk, into another folder, or into the Trash.

2. If you're removing PostScript fonts, drag the matching outline/printer fonts out of your Extensions folder, too.

3. Restart your Mac.

Pre-System 7

For System versions before System 7.0, things are a little more complicated. You need to use an application called *The Font/DA Mover* that came on your original System disks. As you may have guessed, you also use it to install *Desk Accessories* in your System. Its icon is a little moving truck (isn't that cute).

You launch the Font/DA Mover like any application. When the application opens, you'll see a screen like the one shown here.

The Font/DA Mover.

The scroll box on the left displays the fonts already installed in your System file. Click on the **Open** button under the right scroll box. You'll get a standard Open dialog box. Use it to navigate to the fonts you want to install in your System file. Click, or Shift-click, on the font name(s) in the right scroll box that you want to install. When you select a name, the **Copy** button goes from gray to black.

When you have the names of all the fonts you want to install selected, click on the **Copy** button. Font/DA mover installs them for you. When it's done, **Quit** the Font/DA Mover, and restart your Mac.

To remove fonts, click, or Shift-click, on the font name(s) in the left scroll box (the ones already in your System). Click on the **Remove** button. When you've removed all the fonts you want out of there, **Quit** the Font/DA Mover, and restart your Mac.

By the Way . . .

In my (not so) humble opinion, the ease of installing fonts and DAs into your System with System 7 more than makes up for the annoyance of upgrading and learning the new System version. If your Mac can handle it (that is, if it has 4 megabytes of RAM, a hard drive, and a SuperDrive floppy drive), it's easier to mess around with System 7 than previous versions. You might want to think about it.

Font Management

Here's the trouble with fonts: the more you load into your System, the more memory (both RAM and storage memory) they take up. If you turn into a font freak (like me), that can spell trouble unless you have a huge hard drive and mountains of RAM. Here are a couple of ways you can manage your fonts to keep them under control.

Keep Track of What You Have

The first step to managing your fonts is keeping track of the ones you own—especially if you don't keep them all installed all of the time. One way to see what a mystery font looks like (with System 7) is to double-click on its icon. System 7 opens a window displaying a sample of the type.

TrueType fonts shows you a variety of sizes. Bit-mapped fonts only show you the size of the font you clicked on.

This works well enough, but it isn't always convenient to go digging around double-clicking on fonts to see what they look like. I've found it easier to keep a binder full of printed pages of samples of all the fonts I own. They specify the font name, the point size of the sample, and run through the alphabet (upper- and lowercase) as well as all the numbers and symbols.

There are two ways to do this. One is to use a word processor to create and save a document of all the characters. When I install a new font, I open the sample document, select all of the text (⌘ A), and change the old font to the new one. Then I print it out, and slap it into my binder. The other way is with a font utility. You can find *freeware* utilities that give you more information about a font than you'll ever need.

Whether you do it yourself, manually, or use one of the many utilities for printing out font samples, a binder of samples is a great way to remember what you have, and what they look like. Especially once you break the 20 or 30 font level.

Saving Memory

I have mentioned it before, but it bears repeating: fonts take up memory. You might not see it directly, but you may notice that your System

Software RAM usage (when you check it with **About This Macintosh** in the menu) is getting kind of piggy.

One way to trim it back is to remove fonts you only use once in a blue moon from your System, then reinstall them when you need them. Sure it's work, but it's pretty easy if you're using System 7.0, and even easier with 7.1. Another way is to buy and install Suitcase, from Fifth Generation Systems.

Suitcase invented the Font folder before Apple ever thought of it. Suitcase is an application that manages your fonts, sounds, and Desk Accessories (three of my favorite things—right up there with raindrops on roses and whiskers on kittens). You can store them anywhere on your hard drive that you like, outside the System Folder.

The great thing about Suitcase is that it lets you specify a set of fonts, sounds, and DAs to open every time you start your Mac. Then, once you're up and running, Suitcase lets you open temporary sets for a special project, for a particular application, or just on a whim. You can see the Suitcase dialog box and some of the set of fonts and stuff I have set up in the next figure.

The Suitcase dialog.

The great benefit is that the size of your System Software's RAM usage only increases when you add stuff, and can actually shrink (gasp!) when you knock stuff out. Suitcase does take some setting up, but it isn't difficult, and boy, does it cut down on font, sound, and DA craziness. I think my Mac would explode without it.

Adobe Type Reunion

Another way to squeeze some extra space out of your Mac when you have piles of PostScript fonts installed is by using Adobe Type Reunion. The problem with PostScript fonts, as I mentioned before, is that not only does each font have at least two pieces (the screen and printer fonts), there are also separate fonts for bold, italic, and bold italic. All these different styles make up a font *family*, and can include such esoteric variations as: *semibold* (lightly bold), *heavy* (extra bold), *light* (thinner than the regular), *oblique* (mildly italic), and then combinations, such as *light oblique semibold*. Yikes! Each of these font variations takes up space in your font menu. To make matters worse, some of the names don't hang together alphabetically.

That's a problem. It's awkward to have to go sifting through a jam-packed font menu trying to find all of the variations on a PostScript font. It also wastes time. Adobe Type Reunion changes that.

Type Reunion reorganizes your font menu (in most applications) so that font families are represented by only one entry in the main menu, with a submenu to display all of the variations. Oh, it makes the heart sing!

By the Way . . .

As long as we're on the subject, you should be aware that some companies, when advertising fonts or laser printers that come with fonts, put in letters six-feet high that the package includes OVER 100 POSTSCRIPT FONTS!

It isn't necessarily a lie, so much as bending the truth a little. What they're doing is counting individual fonts, rather than font families. So, in truth, you are getting 100 fonts, but six or ten of them are, say, Helvetica variations. Saying OVER 100 POSTSCRIPT FONTS! sounds better than saying OVER 15 FONT FAMILIES!

Speed Up Your Laser Printer's Print Time

Now that your Mac is filled up to its blow-hole with fonts, you're going to be tempted to use them, right? Well, you should know that using many fonts in a document can slow down your printing time unbearably, or stop it entirely. Here's why: Most laser printers come with an assortment of fonts built into their read-only memory (ROM). Having the font already in the printer makes it print faster. If you use a font that isn't in your printer, your laser and your Mac enter some heavy negotiating:

Laser: Hey! This says use Bodoni. I ain't got Bodoni. You got it?
Mac: Wait a minute, let me look.
Laser: Okay, but hurry it up.
Mac: Got it! You want it?
Laser: Yeah, send it down.
Mac: Sending it.
Laser: Getting it.
Mac: Got it?
Laser: Yeah, got it.
Mac: Good.
Laser: Hey! This says use Bodoni Bold. I ain't got Bodoni Bold. . . .

It happens faster than that, but still, you may be old and gray before they're done schmoozing about fonts (thank goodness they don't gossip,too).

If you load a document with too many fonts (and don't ask me how many too many is; it depends on your printer's memory), the printer's memory can get so full of font outlines that it doesn't have any room to process the actual document. It sits there chattering back and forth with your Mac about how cool all those fonts look.

There are two ways to avoid this back-and-forth chattering. The first way (for maniacal font freaks only) is to attach a hard drive to your printer (if it has a SCSI port, like the one on the back of your Mac). You can then *download* all of your fonts that fit on the drive, and your printer never has to ask for them again.

Most of us, however, aren't so heavily into fonts (or rich enough) to just throw another hard drive at our printers. A cheaper way to do it is to download the fonts you regularly use (or ones you know you'll use today) to your laser printer's RAM. This isn't a permanent fix. It'll have to be redone every time you turn your printer on, because things in RAM go away when you turn off the power.

You download fonts to your printer with one of two utilities: either the Apple Font Utility (on the Tidbits disk from your set of original System disks), or Adobe's Font Downloader, which comes with any Adobe font you buy.

In general, both do similar things: download fonts and PostScript files (documents you've *printed to disk*, you'll recall from last chapter) to your printer. Both give you a catalog/directory of the fonts already in your printer's memory and allow you to restart your printer without having to turn the power off and back on.

Apple's Font Utility lets you print font samples, add and remove TrueType, and gives you several options if you have a hard disk attached to your printer. Most importantly, it let's you stop your LaserWriter from printing out that wasteful startup page every time you turn the power on. Simply select **Start Page Options**, and tell it to stop that right now.

Adobe's Font Downloader lets you assign a *password* to your printer (so no one else can change the fonts), clear the cache of fonts you've previously downloaded so you can download some more, and shows you the status of your printer (whether its idle, preparing data, printing, and so on). Personally, I wouldn't mess with the password unless you're in a crowded work space and paranoid, or have kids using your Mac (in which case you should be paranoid). Seldom-used passwords are too easy to forget.

Some Fonting Tips

When selecting fonts for various projects, I like to hold the KISS rule in mind at all times: Keep It Simple, Stupid. I like to keep the number of fonts in any document to a manageable number, like two, maybe three. I figure, if I can't get enough variety out of different point sizes and combinations of bold and italic, well, I'm not going to win any design prizes anyhow.

If I go for two fonts, say one for text and another for headings and subheadings, then I try to contrast them as much as possible while keeping them harmonious. I am prone to novelty fonts for headings, so I like to keep my text font tasteful, like Palatino.

I like to use large words set in an interesting typeface, rather than using a picture. I think it attracts more attention than a picture, anyhow. If I do go for some sort of graphic, I still keep it simple: never underestimate the power of a well-placed line.

That's what I like to do. Other people like to do different things. You can go to your library or bookstore and find some books on design to learn all of the finer points (I've been tempted to write one of my own), but your own taste is the final deciding factor. It's like what that jazz great, Les Paul, used to say (and I'm paraphrasing here): If you make a mistake, but it works, then it's not a mistake—it's jazz.

The Least You Need to Know

Fonts are tough. They're deceptive. They only take a couple of minutes to master in terms of the technoid stuff: where they go and how to tame them. But you can spend a lifetime combining them, arranging them, making them pretty, and still not learn everything there is to know about them. They're an adventure.

Here's the least you need to know to get you started on your adventure:

- ☞ Bit-mapped fonts come in specific sizes and are sometimes called screen fonts.

- ☞ Outline fonts (like TrueType and PostScript) can be used at any size, but still use bit-mapped fonts for basic sizes.

- ☞ Fonts go in your Font folder in System 7.1. For System 7.0, they go in your System File (and PostScript printer fonts go in the Extension folder). For any earlier System version, they go in the same places, but you need to use the Font/DA Mover to install them in your System file.

- ☞ Managing your fonts can spare you hassles and time.

- ☞ When using fonts in your documents, work with the KISS rule, but live for jazz.

Chapter 17

Ac-cen-tu-ate the Positive . . . An-tic-i-pate the Negative

In This Chapter

- ☞ The Mac-Scout's motto: always be prepared
- ☞ Building a people network
- ☞ Working your people network
- ☞ The shape of Macs to come

Right now, I'd be comfortable with you closing this book and getting on with the business of using your Macintosh. Not happy, mind you, just comfortable. I think you've absorbed enough information that you can go on your merry Macintosh way. Nothing bad will ever happen. Your Mac will startup first time, every time. You will never hit a snag in an application. Files will never get damaged. System software upgrades will be compatible with every piece of software you own.

However, cynic that I am (and I seem to get more cynical every day), I know that this is not the best of all possible worlds. Poop happens. This chapter is about dealing with it.

Since no book can anticipate every single thing that could go wrong with your Mac, in this chapter, you'll discover some resources to help you out when poop happens. You'll also get a peek at the future of Macintosh, because whatever Apple does in the near future will certainly have an impact on the kinds of problems you'll have to deal with.

X Marks the Spot

Everyone knows how to deal with a crisis reactively: the poop hits the fan, and you freak out. You just react to the crisis.

Right now, you may be primed for a major freak-out. You go chugging along, using your newly acquired Mac knowledge happy as a clam, and blam. Your Mac goes berserk, and you freak. I don't want you to freak. I want you to be *proactive*. That means that you try to anticipate the crises before they happen, either to avoid them, or to be prepared when problems eventually happen.

Keeping a fire extinguisher in your kitchen is proactive. Marshalling your personal resources in the event of a crisis is also proactive. In fact, you may have already done a few proactive things without even knowing it. If you sent in the registration card on your Mac and any software you bought, that's proactive. You've let the companies know that you bought their product and you may come looking for help if something goes wrong.

If you bought an AppleCare service contract to keep your Mac's warranty up and running for an extra couple of years, that's very proactive. But there's more you can do.

Join the Mac Community

One thing's for sure: computer geeks love to talk shop. Most of us do, anyway. It makes us feel smart. When you're in your local computer store (buying disks, or just cruising the new software titles), talk to folks. Ask their opinion on stuff.

Befriend a salesclerk, preferably one who knows his stuff about Macintosh. Introduce yourself. Learn his name and say hello when you walk in. Always ask for his help when you're ready to buy something; he'll really appreciate that if his paycheck's based on a percentage of the sales. If he knows you, he'll be more likely to help you in the future.

By the Way . . .

Salesclerks often get advance information about new software and hardware and demonstration copies of applications. They may let you play undisturbed on their Mac so you can try stuff out before you buy it.

MUGs-head Revisited

In Chapter 13, I briefly talked about the benefits of joining a Mac Users Group (or MUG): getting access to libraries of freeware and shareware, but there's more. Joining a MUG puts you in touch with many people who are in touch with many people who are in touch—ad infinitum—with many Mac users.

There probably isn't anything that can happen to your Mac that hasn't happened to at least a couple of other people in your MUG. Even if, by some outrageous twist of fate, something new and completely bizarre happens with your Mac, it will be reassuring to pick up the phone and hear a calm, rational voice say, "Hmm. That's bizarre, but don't panic. Let me see what I can find out." And you sigh with relief knowing that you're not alone with a problem.

MUGs also publish newsletters with news that's important to Macintosh users. Sometimes the big, glossy magazines can be a little out-of-touch with the needs of us every day computer users.

Magazines

Another way to anticipate difficulties is by subscribing to a Mac magazine. There are three, right now, you can pick up at your local newsstand: *Macworld*, *MacUser*, and *Mac Home Journal*.

By the Way . . .

There are other Mac magazines, but you won't find them at your newsstand, such as *MacWeek*; they're geared toward Mac professionals, programmers, and the like. Since each of them appeals to different types of Mac users, I'd pick up one of each and read them, then subscribe to the one (or two) you like.

Getting a magazine (and reading it) can keep you abreast of the latest developments in the Mac community. You'll also get reviews of software and hardware, upgrade announcements, and columns devoted to various tips and tricks that could help you out of a jam.

The Life On-Line

If you have a modem, you can also make all kinds of contacts through electronic services and bulletin boards. I know I've talked about them before, but they're just so useful.

I've often solved big, big problems with the help of people I've never met, just by posting a note in an appropriate area of America Online (such as the Hardware and Mac Operating System Forums), and other services. Mostly, it's been application, or peripheral specific, but that's because when your Mac itself takes a nose-dive, it's hard to connect to a computer service.

On-line services and bulletin boards are an excellent resource for help and moral support. I won't beat it into the ground, though. Well, maybe just a little.

Computer Shows

Computer shows are another great place to meet all kinds of computer users. They're the traveling sideshows of the 90's. If you live in, or near, a big metropolitan area, chances are one or two will pass your way each year. You'll see ads in your local paper or flyers in the computer store.

They aren't always the best for Mac users (since a lot of them focus primarily on DOS machines), but there are some for us, such as the traveling MacShow. In addition to vendors getting you to buy junk, there are usually workshops and discussion groups about all kinds of uses for your Mac. At the good shows, some of the workshops are basic; some are advanced and specialized. There's always something for every level of Mac user.

If a traveling Mac show never hits your neck of the woods, and you can afford to travel, there's always Macworld. Macworld is a huge exposition that seems to be held almost daily somewhere in the world. There are also shows held in Canada, Japan, and other fun-filled locations around the world.

This exposition is put together by *Macworld* magazine, and it's the showplace where all the Macintosh-related companies try to unveil their new products. (I say *try* because often in the rush of getting things ready, they often leave out little details, such as getting their product to work— not that I'm bitter or anything.)

Working Your Network

Once you've surrounded yourself with as many Mac friends as you can muster, you're in a prime position to compare notes, receive advice and help, and grow into a Macintosh guru in your own right. It won't take long.

> ### By the Way . . .
> Your best troubleshooting tool when you hit a snag is your telephone. Call you Mac friends. Call the clerk you be-friended at the store where you bought the troublesome product. Call technical support at the company that makes that pesky product. (For more on getting good technical support, see the appendix.)

The nature of Macintosh is such that once you master a concept, you can usually apply it across the range of Macintosh applications and hardware. Then, one day soon, you'll be expected to return the favor and help another Mac novice go along and get along. Won't that be nice.

The Shape of Macs to Come

There's an old Chinese curse that goes: "May you live in interesting times." In terms of Macintosh, the times are interesting, indeed. There are some big, big changes lurking on just the other side of the horizon. Some of the changes have already started, in small ways, that might pose some sticky puzzles for old-school Mac users.

In August '93, Apple introduced the first AV Macs: the Centris 660AV (now called a Quadra) and the Quadra 840AV. The AV stands for audio-visual. Macs have long been a playground for sound, and lately a playground for movies. The AV Macs feature an even better aptitude for sound and motion. AV Macs come with built-in video-in and -out jacks, eliminating the need for a separate expansion card. They can also dial and answer your phone, and take a message.

They also make use of Apple's new PlainTalk voice recognition and generation system. With PlainTalk, you can tell your computer to do something, and it will. Very Hal 9000. Very *Star Trek*.

While the AV Macs are still Macs, they're a small first step in the process of change. Apple says that most of the new Macs introduced will have these AV capabilities. The technology is staggering to someone who remembers a time when there was no such thing as a personal computer, much less one that talks (and you don't have to be that old to remember, either).

Couple the AV Macs (with their emphasis on telephony, sound, and video) with the new Newton MessagePad, "the first in a family of *communications assistants*" according to the Apple press kit, and Apple's plan to introduce its own on-line information service, and you can see where Apple thinks its future is. It's like that scene in *The Graduate*, only instead of whispering the word "plastics," the old guy says "digital information."

Apple is spinning a web of communications, an information and communication network that (of course) will be easiest to access with—you guessed it—Apple consumer electronics. As their plans take shape, you can probably (and this is just guesswork on my part) expect to see new, generic Mac and Newton products introduced and then quickly upgraded to spiffier, more focused machines. They'll have to sell them fast, and sell a lot, if only to recoup their research and development costs.

Throw in the long promised PowerPC, the Mac that's supposed to break the price and application-sharing barrier between Macs and DOS machines, and you can see that Apple's plan is to carpe diem: seize the day. PowerPCs are supposed to start turning up in mid-1994.

Start saving your pennies, though. Even if the PowerPC does lower the price of a Mac to that of an IBM knockoff, the only Macs with an upgrade path to the new technology will be the ones that run on a 68040 central processor. Right now, that's the pricier Quadra line.

Apple says that the new Macs, even the PowerPCs, will be running with a variation of System 7.1, probably with new extensions (System *enablers*) thrown in to help bridge the technology gap, but that's sure to change as the PowerPCs squeeze out the older Mac line. Eventually, as the old Macs fade away, Apple will introduce an operating system that takes full advantage of the PowerPC's new and more powerful architecture.

So What?

What does that mean to you, now? Maybe nothing. Maybe everything. Apple is preparing some major changes in the way Macs work. Along with change, there's always a period of awkward adjustment: New things that don't quite work right; old things that used to work on older machines, but don't on the new; and things that sounded good in theory, but are kind of wonky in practice. Change can be traumatic and problematic.

The point is, in order for you to decide if you want to play along, you'll have to know what's up Apple's sleeve. Staying tied into the Mac community is one way to do that.

If you decide to play their Power(PC) game, then you'll need the help and support of others who might have a better handle on the rules of the game. If you decide not to play, you'll definitely need the support of your peers as applications and hardware stop being backward-compatible with older Macintosh systems.

Besides, once you're hooked-in to the Mac community's grapevine, you can just sit back and watch the poop fly, all smug and self-satisfied because you saw what was coming and purchased a plastic slicker and a big umbrella.

The Least You Need to Know

☞ Every Mac user you meet is a potential resource for you. Learn how to win friends and influence people.

☞ I can't say this often enough: Join a Macintosh users group.

☞ When you run into a problem you can't handle, pick up the phone.

☞ The computer times, they are a-changing. You have to stay connected to the Mac community if you want to keep up.

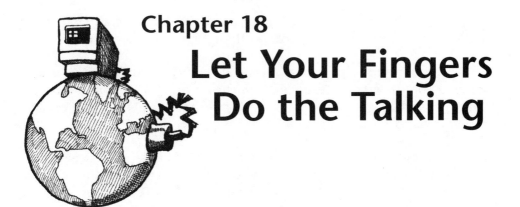

Chapter 18
Let Your Fingers Do the Talking

In This Chapter

- What modems are and how they work
- What communications software can do for you
- What electronic services are out there, and how to access them
- Some on-line communications and etiquette tips

In telecommunications, the two components, hardware and software, are so perfectly entwined that you can't talk about one without the other. So, you'll hear about both. In this chapter, you'll learn about getting your Mac in touch with the whole, big, wide, wonderful world of digital communications.

Let's begin, shall we?

You Gotta Getta Modem

Modems are almost mystical. One little piece of hardware, one little piece of software, and suddenly you have the ability to be in two places at the same time. You can be all cozy and warm in your own little corner of your own little room, and at the same time, you can be inside a computer at a remote location chatting with folks, or doing a pile of other cool stuff.

Simply by making a phone call, you and your Mac can be hooked into a computer on the other side of your hometown, or even into an international network of computers. How is this possible? It's the mystical combination of hardware and software.

The communications software takes and interprets the things you type (commands, text, even mouse clicks) and converts that digital information into discreet, little packages of data. The little packages of data get sent to the modem that converts the data to sound pulses. The modem may compress them, then shoot them out through your phone lines to the computer at the receiving end.

The receiving modem reverses the process: unpacks the little packages of data, expands them if necessary, and then hands the information off to the software at that end. The receiving computer then deals with the information you sent—executes that command or click, or shares what you typed with whomever might be waiting for it.

With a modem and the appropriate software (there are different kinds, which I'll spell out in a minute) you can:

- ☞ Access a local bulletin board to get (and share) information, as well as freeware and shareware files.

- ☞ Access a national (or international) on-line service.

- ☞ Access another modem-equipped computer at work, at school, or even at a friend's house.

Modem Varieties

Modem technology has blossomed in the last couple of years. Where once you could only choose from slow, pokey, or super-pokey-slow modems, now there's a huge range of speeds—and some spiffy extra functions you can get, too. Modems are classified two ways: first, how fast they transmit data; second, by where they get installed.

Modem speed is measured in *bits per second* (*BPS*), or *baud rate*. Most commonly, you'll see modems advertised as being 1200, 2400, 9600, or 14,400 BPS or baud.

1200 BPS is considered snail-slow these days. 2400 BPS modems are considered the low-end. 9600 and 14,400 BPS modems have become fairly standard in the last year, because with error correction and data compression features, you can transmit data wicked-fast.

The differences in where the modem gets installed are pretty obvious:

Internal modems go right *inside* your Mac. They have no outer cases, no frills, only a bunch of circuits and chips on what looks like a plastic card.

External modems sit on your desk, *outside* your Mac. The only physical attachment is with a cable that plugs into your modem or printer port (you can skip back to Chapter 2 if you need a refresher on your Mac's ports and what they're for).

Modems can also be further distinguished by any additional features they have: what else they do besides communicate with other computers. The added functions, naturally, are also phone-related.

You can get a modem that doubles as a *fax machine* allowing you to send files to another fax machine right from your Mac's screen. They're called (*duh*) *fax modems*. You can choose a fax modem that only sends faxes to a fax machine (a *send-fax modem*); or one that receives faxes as well (*send and receive fax modem*, or simply a *fax modem*.)

Technically speaking, a modem's baud rate isn't exactly the same as the number of bits per second it transmits. However, the distinction is fine, and only applies in certain circumstances. You don't need to worry about it. You can use the two terms pretty much interchangeably. Some snooty propeller-head may correct you, but just slap him.

Not all BBSs and on-line services can deal with the high speed (9600 BPS and faster) modems. If you can, check it out before you log on for the first time. If you can't check it out, don't panic. Most modems will automatically step down to the appropriate speed before they connect to another computer.

There are three drawbacks of fax modems. They're great for sending a memo or letter you've written on your Mac, but there's no way to send a fax from a piece of paper—they only deal with digital information. If you need to fax a paper document, you need a regular fax machine.

The second drawback is that when you receive a fax, you receive it as a *picture* of the document, not a text file that you can work with. Some fax modems, (such as the Global Village PowerPort line) come with *OCR* (optical character recognition) software that translates the picture of text into actual, editable text.

The third drawback is that with a fax-modem you either have to leave your Mac and modem turned on most of the time, or you have to baby-sit the machine whenever you think you're going to get a fax.

Some modems also give you a digital answering machine with *voice mail* capabilities. You've dealt with voice mail, I'm sure: "Press 1 for customer service. Press 2 for a company directory. Press 3 to leave a message." Pretty annoying to talk to, but I guess it's convenient for the user (and cheaper than hiring a receptionist). I can't imagine many home-users needing voice mail, unless you run a home-business, or have teenagers in the house who refuse to miss a single message.

SPEAK LIKE A GEEK

Proprietary is the property of, or specific to a particular computer or service. America Online and Prodigy are also called proprietary because you need their software to access their services and because the software won't work for any other service.

Enter and Sign-on Please . . .

When you buy yourself a modem, the manufacturers know you want instant gratification. They always include a generic telecommunications program, and often software or coupons for free trial time on a major service, such as America Online or CompuServe. You may get two kinds of telecommunications software because some on-line services (such as America Online and Prodigy) require their members to use special *proprietary* software to access their service.

Some services, such as CompuServe, can be accessed two ways, either with generic communications software or with their proprietary software (for CompuServe, that would be CompuServe Navigator, or CompuServe Information Manager).

By the Way . . .

The generic communications software that comes with your modem may be a freeware or sharware package, or it may be a scaled-down version of a commercial package with an offer to upgrade to a full-featured version at a special price. You don't have to buy one right away. Wait.

Because you do want instant gratification when you unpack a modem, you're also very vulnerable to anything that sounds like a good deal. Wait. The coupons may be a good deal, but the product might be something you don't need. Once you get some experience on-line, you'll know what kind of features you need. You may not need anything more than that generic package. If you get into telecommunications, you may need something more high-powered. Don't buy one until you know.

Once you have the modem and software installed, and a phone line hooked up to the modem (installation varies, so be sure to read the manual that came with it), you're ready to roll.

Whether you're using generic software to access a local bulletin board, or proprietary software for a big service, you have to do a couple of things before you can dial into a board.

Setting Up

For generic communications software, "setting up" might mean telling it where the modem is installed, what baud rate you want to use, and what phone number(s) to dial for what service. The setup procedure varies somewhat from modem to modem, software to software. Check the software, or modem manual for details on how to configure your particular brand.

Proprietary software also requires some initial setup. In addition to the same kinds of information a generic telecommunications program would need, you'll also have to let the service know how you're going to pay for it: that means credit card information, too.

While I can't give you setup and configuration specifications for every kind of telecommunications software out there, I can certainly show you the kinds of information you'll need to supply to most applications. The next figure shows the set-up dialog box for America Online's software.

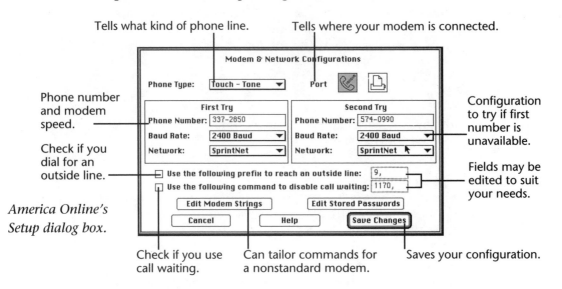

Tells what kind of phone line.

Tells where your modem is connected.

Phone number and modem speed.

Check if you dial for an outside line.

America Online's Setup dialog box.

Configuration to try if first number is unavailable.

Fields may be edited to suit your needs.

Check if you use call waiting.

Can tailor commands for a nonstandard modem.

Saves your configuration.

As you can see from the figure, your software needs some basic information to function:

- ☞ The kind of telephone line you'll be using (Touch-Tone or rotary dial), so it knows how to dial out.

- ☞ What port your modem is plugged into, so it can send the information to the right place.

- ☞ What phone number you want it to dial to reach the other computer, or on-line service.

- ☞ What speed you want your modem to operate at (most are switchable from its highest speed down to about 300 baud).

The Network entry is only applicable to big services that let you call a local phone number for access. Even though America Online's computer is in Virginia, you'll dial a local number to reach it. My local number gives me access to SprintNet (a national phone network for computer users), which patches me in to Virginia, while only making a local phone call—much less expensive than calling long distance.

The check boxes are for specifying particular dialing prefixes if you need to dial a special number to get an outside line (like from work), or if you have call waiting and want to disable it while you're on-line.

TECHNO NERD TEACHES

You should *always* disable call waiting (if you have it) before using your modem. The clicking sound an incoming call makes can disrupt the flow of information to or from your computer and knock you off-line. You'll have to start over with whatever you were doing. Very annoying.

You can add **1170,** to the beginning of any phone number your Mac is dialing (like: 1170,555-1212) to disable it. In some areas you may have to use ***70,** to disable. The comma (,) makes your computer pause before dialing the rest of the number. The pause gives your phone a chance to accept the command before dialing the rest of the number. You can manually disable call waiting on a regular telephone by dialing either 1170 or *70 before you dial a number to talk to someone, too.

Hayes Compatible is a term that identifies a modem that conforms to the standard set of modem commands developed by the Hayes Corporation. Hayes compatibility is fairly standard among modems. I wouldn't mess with one that isn't—it can complicate your life unnecessarily.

The Edit Modem Strings button lets you change the commands (like dial, hang up, and so on) your software issues to the modem. For most modems (if they're Hayes compatible) you won't have to change anything.

The Edit Stored Passwords button lets you automate your logon sequence. It can save you a few seconds here and there, but it also removes all the protection a password affords you: any geek with access to your computer can log on to your account, run up your phone bill and service charges. In short: *Unless you're the only one with access to your computer, don't store your password.* Any time you save will be offset by the money you'll lose if some doofus decides to use your account.

A *screen name*, literally, is the name that appears on the screen whenever you "speak" to someone else on a service. Try to pick one that suits your personality. My screen name on America Online is Piv—say "hello," if you see me.

Signing On

Once your stuff is set up, you're ready to dial out and *sign on* (also known as *logging on*) to a bulletin board. What happens then varies from service to service, but generally a few standard things happen:

- ☞ When you connect to the service, you'll be asked to identify yourself.

- ☞ Sometimes, you'll be asked to choose a *screen name*.

- ☞ If it's a pay service (such as America Online or CompuServe), you'll have to register and set up a method of payment (usually a *credit card* number that will be billed monthly).

- ☞ When you register with a new service, you will also be asked to provide your real name (not your screen name), address, and telephone number for verification. Some local bulletin boards may get confirmation of the information by phone before you can use the service. It's a security precaution on their part.

☞ After you provide your name, you'll be asked to enter a *password*, that's your "open sesame" to the service. No one will be able to log on to your account (including you) without that password. Make sure it's one you can remember without writing it down somewhere.

☞ If you don't have to be verified (with a phone call from your local bulletin board's SysOp), you should be done—go on and explore. Learn. Have fun.

Around the World in 80 Ways

There are thousands upon thousands of bulletin boards in the world. Some are easier to find than others. You'll get information on the big commercial services when you unpack your modem. The little one's are harder to find.

Local Boards

Local boards come in all shapes and sizes. Some can only take one user at a time, others can take dozens. Many of them are geared to special-interests of their users: specific brands of computers, operating systems (like MS-DOS and System 7), computer games, sports, hobbies, sexuality, you name it.

There are three easy ways to find out if there's a bulletin board in your area:

OOPS!

America Online, Compu-Serve, and Prodigy are commercial companies that rely on credit cards to handle the high volume of payments they receive. Registering yourself with them is pretty much the same as using a credit card in a department store. You can be pretty sure all they're interested in is getting paid for what you're buying from them.

Local bulletin boards usually don't accept credit cards. If someone on-line asks for your credit card number (like in the course of normal conversation, or trying to sell you something) DON'T GIVE IT OUT. Credit card numbers are just as valuable as cash money—more so, in some cases. You wouldn't hand over your wallet to anyone who asked for it, would you?

SysOp is short for System Operator. That's the propel-ler-head in charge of the bulletin board. It's pronounced "SIS-op."

☞ **Ask.** Ask members of your local MUG. Ask at your local computer store. Ask at your local college computer club. Just ask.

☞ **Read.** If you have a local computer newspaper, or if your MUG publishes a newsletter, some local bulletin boards may advertise (though the ones that advertise probably want you to pay to join) or get mentioned in an article about modems or telecommunications.

☞ **Look.** If you join one of the major services, such as America Online, look in the area devoted to telecommunications, or other special interest area. There's usually lots of listing for lots of bulletin boards across the country.

When you find one local bulletin board, log on to it. There's usually a listing of other local bulletin boards.

America Online

If you haven't noticed, America Online (*AOL* for short) is my favorite service. I use it a lot. (If you decide to sign up, drop me a note there, my screen name is Piv.) AOL is ideal for beginners: it has an excellent Mac interface, it's easy to find your way around, there's live help available most of the time, and the staff of Guides (those who do the helping) are well-trained, very helpful, and loads of fun.

The monthly membership fee of $9.95 includes five hours of use each month, and additional time is $3.50 per hour. The rates are effective 24-hours a day, seven days a week. Special holidays (like Christmas and the Fourth of July) are free whether you've used your five hours or not.

You can pick up an access kit for free by calling 1-800-227-6364 (tell them I sent you). Or you can buy a kit in book and software stores, which comes with a complete manual (very helpful) for $19.95, and includes 10 hours of free usage.

CompuServe

CompuServe is the oldest and largest of the on-line services. It has millions of members world-wide. It is an excellent service, but it isn't as easy to navigate as America Online, nor are there as many opportunities for getting assistance if you run into trouble.

You can sign on to CompuServe without special software (the information probably came with your modem), but I wouldn't recommend it for a beginner: there are no menus, everything is done with typed commands. Ack.

You can pick up a proprietary software package for CompuServe in most book and computer stores. The CompuServe Information Manager lists for about $50, but you can pick it up mail order for $25. The CompuServe Navigator lists for about $100, but you can buy it mail order for about $50. After the initial software investment, CompuServe charges a flat rate of $8.95 per month for basic services, with additional charges for extended packages. They always warn you before you try to enter a service that costs extra.

(You can drop me a note here, too. My CompuServe address is 70713,3554—think you can remember it?)

Prodigy

Don't like it.

I know there are die-hard Prodigy fans out there who take umbrage at that, but that's how I feel. I tried it a couple of times on a friend's computer. Too many ads crammed in your face (you could watch television and see fewer commercials), too many time-wasting levels to go through to find stuff, no files to download, too much censorship, too expensive . . . you get the idea.

People have been abandoning Prodigy in droves, especially since service hasn't improved and prices have gone up. It's gotten so bad that America Online has recently had to put in a special area exclusively for Prodigy refugees.

You can find Prodigy startup kits in computer and book stores, if you're curious, but really, the other services are so much better. I can't (in good conscience) even waffle and say, "it's good except. . . . " I just don't like it.

Miscellaneous Others

The "Big Three" are not the be-all and end-all of information services. A peek inside the coupon envelope that came packed with your modem tells you that much. There's lots more out there.

Don't think that because it wasn't mentioned here that a service isn't worth investigating. These three, plus any local boards you find, are a great place to start. Since this book works under the assumption that you're an absolute beginner, I don't want to overwhelm you with choices. Once you get comfortable with the on-line world, you might be interested in exploring AppleLink (Apple's own service), InterNet (the international scientific and educational network), or one of hundreds of others.

The Least You Need to Know

It would take a whole book to clue you in to the wonders that await you on-line. This was merely a taste. The least you should remember from this section:

- ☞ Modems connect you to a vast electronic world.
- ☞ Modems can be internal or external; if you're buying an internal one, ask to be sure it's appropriate for your Mac model.
- ☞ With a modem, you need some kind of communications software, either a generic one for general telecommuting, or a proprietary package to access an on-line service, such as America Online.
- ☞ Your software needs to be configured for your modem, type of phone line, and the service you are using. Check your manual.
- ☞ You can find the phone numbers for local bulletin boards by asking at your local MUG, computer store, or in computer publications.
- ☞ Have fun!

Chapter 19

When the Going Gets Tough, the Tough Go Shopping

In This Chapter

- ☞ Lots o' lists of things to do (fair warning)
- ☞ Before you think about shopping
- ☞ Preparing to shop
- ☞ Shop 'til you drop
- ☞ What I've got
- ☞ What I'd get (if someone else was footing the bill)

Okay, so I've really tantalized you with all this blather about junk you can add-on to your Mac. Computer users are easily tantalized: all you have to do is promise to eliminate some annoying problem, or add a nifto-swifto capability that wasn't there before. Like the old saying goes: *Build a better Mac mouse, and the world will beat a path to your door.*

Unfortunately, there are a lot of add-ons and applications that promise Mac users the world, but only deliver the marshy parts of New Jersey. That's because manufacturers and sales people want you to buy what they have to sell. If they have to exaggerate the positives a little, and overlook the negatives a lot, well, that's Marketing (with a capital M).

This chapter is devoted to making you a little cynical when it comes to shopping. I hope to poke a hole in the lovely gauze of hype and advertising that surrounds most products (not just computer accessories). I'll talk about what you should do before you buy, what to do when you're ready to buy, and I'll even engage in a little healthy fantasy by telling what equipment I have now, and what I'd buy if someone else was paying for it.

Before You Buy

Because somehow, someone found out you own a Mac, you've wound up on a billion mailing lists. Today, you received a catalog the size of the Manhattan Yellow Pages from company Mega MacMonger (just call 1-800-PAY-MEEE), and already the pages are dotted with drool. You're lusting after a million dollars worth of stuff. What do you do?

PUT THE CATALOG AWAY.

Catalogs are designed to make you want stuff. Never mind what you want, you know you want everything. Shush that inner child who's stamping his feet and screaming "Gimmee gimmee." Now is the time to think about what you need.

I make a little list which I keep near my Mac. When, in the course of human events, it becomes apparent that I need something (that will make my life easier, or make my Mac work better), I add it to the list. When there are a couple of things on my list, I'll look them over to see if they are things that I really need. If not, I cross them off the list. (I've crossed a CD-ROM drive off my list every month for the past year. I really want one, but I don't need it yet.) If, after I eliminate wants that are masquerading as needs, there's anything left on the list, I prepare to shop.

First, I'll take a quick check of my finances to see how much I can afford to spend, then whether or not I have the cash, or the space left on a credit card.

I set my price limit first. Only then will I pull out the Mega MacMonger catalog and see how much what I need costs. If I can't afford it, I put the list and catalog aside and start saving up for it, either by setting aside the cash, or paying down a credit card. There's nothing more frustrating than obsessing over a new computer gadget that I can't afford.

On the rare occasions that I can afford it (or must, sometimes you just have no choice), I start my pre-shopping drill. It's a couple of simple steps that make me an informed shopper. Mostly, I do it to save time and money, but it also ticks-off sales clerks, and that's a good thing, too.

I go through this process with everything I buy, from software to complete computers. The more expensive the purchase, the more thoroughly I do my homework. I'm cheap that way.

Ask the Man Who Owns One

I know a few Mac users: my brother for one, people I've worked with, and electronic friends on America Online and CompuServe. When I start lusting after a product, such as a hard drive or other big-ticket item, I'll call them or drop them a note on-line.

Here's what I ask them:

- ☞ What's the make and model of yours?
- ☞ Where did you get it?
- ☞ What did you pay for it?
- ☞ Were you happy with the product, and if not, why not?
- ☞ Were you happy with the company you bought it from, and if not, why not?
- ☞ If you had it to do all over again, would you buy the same thing? If not, why not?

I always go to the people I know (whose opinions I respect) first. That gives me a place to start, either with products and companies to look at, or products and companies to avoid like the plague.

The Reviews Are In

Whether or not I've wrestled an opinion out of people I know, my next step is to go to the magazines: *MacUser*, *Macworld*, and *Mac Home Journal*. I'll pull out back issues and see if they've reviewed the particular product I'm interested in, or if they've done a round-up review (such as "10 PostScript Laser Printers Compared").

I'll read everything on the product, or class of product, I can find.

> ## By the Way . . .
> I don't read the magazines to buy the products they recommend. I find that most magazines have way different priorities from mine. I've found myself buying stuff that reviewers hated, because what seemed a horrible problem to the reviewer didn't bother me at all.
>
> I read reviews and roundups for the factual information: components, speed, price, problems. The opinion stuff is just opinion after all, and totally subjective. I give the reviewer's opinion a fairly low weight in my buying decision.

After I weigh all the reviews, from my friends and magazines, then I sit down and decide what I'm going to get.

Settling for the Best

Sometimes, circumstances dictate that you settle for a product that meets fewer of your needs than some other. Price is usually the deciding factor.

In general, I try to get the most from my money that I can. I'd rather spend a little more money for something that will grow with me and meet my future needs (either real or imagined), than spend less money on something I'm going to have to replace in six months. I'd rather just wait out the six months and get exactly what I need, rather than throw good money after bad in an effort to make-do.

This is especially true of hardware: why buy a hard drive with only enough storage space to hold you for the next six months? As soon as you add new software and store some data files, you'll run out of space again. I waited until I could afford to buy a bigger hard drive, one that would hold me for a year or two.

So, the advice here is: "Get as much as you can while staying close to your budget." If you can't afford to buy something you can grow with, it might be better to wait until you can.

When You're Ready to Buy

So you've weighed your options (and your wallet or purse), listened to your friends, and read the reviews. You're ready to put your money where your Mac is. Where do you go?

With Apple trying to penetrate the so-called "Consumer Market" by putting the Performa line and Newton's into more traditional stores (as opposed to "Computer Stores"), your shopping opportunities have increased dramatically.

Each kind of store has its own advantages and disadvantages. Let's look at each kind, talk about the differences, and then you can choose the shopping experience that best suits your needs.

The Educational Market

Apple pretty much pioneered the educational market with the Apple and the first Macs. To this day, Apple still has a very strong educational distribution channel, and it discounts heavily.

If you work in education, or your child goes to a Macintosh college (that is, a school where they require all students to have a Macintosh), then you might just be eligible for special educational pricing on Macs, software, and peripherals. Good for you!

Before you do anything else, find out what kind of deals are available for faculty, staff, or students (depending on which one you are) for hardware and accessories. Sometimes, all you have to do is flash your student or staff I.D. in the college store, and you get deep discounts on everything Macintosh. On other campuses, you may have to contact an Apple representative directly, or place orders through a specific staff member. Check with your school for details, but check there first. You have nothing to save but money.

Malls, Stores, Superstores

The way shopping has evolved in this country, you're most likely to find a store that sells Macintosh computers, accessories, and software in or near a mall. You can find Performas and all the to-go-withs (software and accessories) in Sears, office supply chains (such as Staples, OfficeMax, and so on), and in shopping "clubs" (such as Sam's Club). You can find the rest of the Macintosh line, plus Mac stuff from other companies, in local computer stores, and in national chain "super stores," such as Micro Center and Computer Warehouse.

The main advantage of shopping locally is that the store is nearby. If you're lucky to be in an area with many stores, you can comparison shop and even buy pieces at different stores based on price. If your local store claims "We'll beat any advertised price," you should definitely take advantage of the offer.

When shopping locally, you have the advantage of being able to test drive software and hardware, question a salesperson, and—should something go wrong—make a return without having to ship the defective merchandise across the country for repair or replacement.

The disadvantage of local stores is simple: overhead. Part of every dollar you spend in a retail store goes to pay the rent, the utilities, the sales staff, mall security . . . you get the idea. Prices may be appreciably higher. Super stores try to offset the cost of overhead by going for volume; they sell more stuff at lower prices and hope that quantity makes up the difference.

You may also (in noncomputer stores, like Sears) not have access to a knowledgeable salesperson. That can definitely cause trouble. If the clerk doesn't know what you're talking about, how can he offer you merchandise that meets your needs? Or that even works with your computer? Of course, the closeness of the store to your home makes it easier to return or exchange things, but how much running back and forth are you prepared to do?

There are ways to protect yourself:

☞ Select a reputable store: one that's been around a while and is likely to still be around a while. A great returns policy is meaningless if the store has gone out of business.

☞ Before you buy anything, check the store's returns policy. Get it in writing, if you can.

☞ If a clerk says he'll make an exception to the returns policy for you (because you're so nice), definitely get it in writing, and be sure to get the clerk's name.

☞ If you can, pay with a credit card. You can always try to get the card company to withhold payment if a dispute develops.

☞ Try to make your purchase on a weekday, or when the store will be open for the next two or three days. There's nothing more frustrating than discovering a problem when the store is closed. (It's happened to me—over a three-day weekend, no less.) You'll have to sit and grind your teeth until the store is open again.

☞ Save all of your receipts, and don't fill out warranty/registration cards until everything is working satisfactorily. Some stores won't accept returns unless everything (even little slips of paper) is in the original condition.

Mail Order: An Overnight Affair

You've seen them (or you soon will) scattered throughout the Macintosh magazines: mail-order companies that sell everything you can possibly want for your Mac, including complete new Macs. Their prices are good, and many offer overnight delivery for almost immediate gratification.

The advantages of going the mail/phone-order route are numerous. You'll generally find lower prices, because they aren't maintaining glitzy stores. You can also save money on sales tax, if you're ordering across state lines (at least until the Feds or State governments figure out a way to plug the loop hole). Philadelphia has a 7% sales tax. On a $200 hard drive, I'd pay an extra $14 if I bought it in town.

A lot of mail-order places have a knowledgeable staff to take your order. They can help you make up your mind and answer any simple questions you might have. Additionally, many mail-order places have toll-free technical support lines you can call and ask heavy-duty questions before (and after) you buy. I like that.

The disadvantages, however, are just as numerous.

- ☛ You can't try things before you buy them. You pretty much have to know what you want before you pick up the phone.

- ☛ Returns policies are a little more strict. Many places charge a restocking fee (except on damaged or defective goods), and you must call for permission to return things.

- ☛ There's no way to judge a mail-order company's reliability from its ads. There just isn't. You can, however, get hints: read the policies closely. If it looks like it is nickel-and-diming you to death with service charges and restocking fees, run away. If it has a 900-number for ordering, run away. 900-numbers always seem vaguely slimy to me. I mean, really: making you pay $2 a minute for the privilege of spending your money—ack!

- ☛ There are no authorized Apple mail-order retailers. That means that the company hasn't been vetted and approved by Apple, and that means no training from Apple about products, service, or repairs. I don't say that's a good thing or a bad thing. It's just something you should know, and a risk you should be prepared to take.

I've been lucky. I've dealt with a few of the larger companies (MacConnection, Mac's Place, and MacWarehouse) and have had nothing but good experiences. MacConnection helped fixed a problem that was a result of my own stupidity (blush), with no hassle and no extra charges. Mac's Place replaced a defective hard drive overnight, painlessly. Needless to say, they've both gotten repeat business from me.

Mistakes happen. It's how mail-order companies correct these mistakes (yours or theirs) that is the measure of their greatness. I'm usually willing to pay a little more at a place (mail order or walk-in) where I get excellent service. A painful shopping experience is still painful, even if you save a buck.

I don't recommend that novices buy whole computer systems by mail order. There are too many switches and rip-offs that can happen, especially if you're not wise to them. They can happen in a local store, too, but locally you can wring someone's neck, scream, or cause a scene if you need to. That's hard to do effectively by letter or phone.

Sometimes, you don't have a choice. Again, there are ways to protect yourself:

- ☛ Ask your Mac-friends who they've dealt with and who they keep dealing with. Ask them why, too.

- ☛ Check the Macintosh magazines. Consumer columns and Letters to the Editor are often ways of hearing horror stories about shady companies.

- ☛ Consider what's normal. A mouse comes standard with every Mac. They're one of the things that makes a Mac a Mac. If a mail-order place tries to tell you that the mouse is optional, hang up the phone. They're ripping you off.

- ☛ Scour the fine print in ads. Don't pay extra for using a credit card, for overnight shipping, or for placing an order.

- ☛ Don't pay by check. Even reputable places hold your check until it clears the bank: that's only prudent. Once they have your money, however, you have no recourse. Use a credit card so you can at least try to withhold payment should a dispute arise.

- ☛ When you're placing an order, take names. Write them down. Have the salesperson confirm your order. Be clear and be sure you've understood (and been understood) to avoid any confusion over what you ordered.

- ☛ Take notes, too. Good notes help you sort out a problem with the company, or document a claim with your credit card company should you need to withhold payment.

- ☛ This is extreme, but if you're the cautious (read: paranoid) type: record your phone conversation when you place your order. You can get a microphone that sticks on the ear piece of your phone to record both halves of the ordering process.

If you do, tell whomever you talk to that you are recording while you are recording and *before* you get down to business! Otherwise, it's horribly, horribly illegal. I'd hate to have to visit you in the slammer.

Single Platinum Mac Seeks Same

If your budget won't allow you to buy new, don't despair. Bargains can be had in the used computer market. You can find ads for used equipment in the want ads of your local newspaper or local computer newspaper or newsletter, if you have one. In the Pennsylvania, Delaware, and New Jersey area, we have *The Delaware Valley Computer User.* It's good, and it's free!

Other good sources: bulletin boards at your local supermarket, high school, college, and, if you use a modem (see Chapter 18), a local electronic bulletin board. You can also turn up leads on used stuff if you belong to a Macintosh User's Group. The real propeller-heads in these groups are always upgrading their equipment and selling off the old stuff.

The advantage of buying used is price. You can get some real bargains. The disadvantages are the same as for buying a used car from a classified ad: you don't know the person you're dealing with, and (if you don't know a good bit about computers) you can pay way too much for a real lemon.

There isn't a lot you can do to protect yourself after the purchase, unless your local laws provide protection. Even so, resorting to the law is mighty tiresome. It's best to protect yourself before you hand over the cash.

- ☛ Try the machine or component out before you buy it, preferably at your home, and for a few hours if not for a day or two. Make sure the disk drive drives, the monitor monitors, the mouse mouses: check the obvious.

- ☛ Check for signs of damage or abuse. Heck, check for dust: anyone who tries to sell you something without cleaning it first has no idea of how to take care of things.

- ☛ If you can, look under the hood. Lots of dust, dirt, and other riffraff inside a computer (while not necessarily evil) is another sign of poor maintenance.

☞ If you don't know what to look for, bring someone along who does. Buy him or her a nice lunch as a bribe.

☞ Ask if you can have a 30-day warranty (in writing) in case the dingus blows up when you get it home. If not 30, try for 15, 10, or 7 days—even 48–72 hours. Anything to give you a little extra leeway.

☞ Make sure you get a transfer of ownership (just a signed note saying what you bought) if hardware is still under a manufacturer's warranty, or if you want to re-register the software in your name.

☞ If you're buying used software, make sure you get the original manuals and disks. If you get photocopies of the manual and duplicate disks, you have a software pirate (arrgh, maties) on your hands. That's horribly illegal, unethical, and just not nice. Don't encourage it.

Computer Brokers

No, these aren't people who break computers for a living. These are companies that buy up other companies' (and individuals') computers, refurbish them, and resell them. Or they're companies that lease computers, then sell old models when they upgrade their line of machines. They're like used car lots for computers.

The advantage of going through a broker to buy used equipment is that (since they refurbish the machines) they usually offer limited warranties. You can find them advertised in large metropolitan newspapers (you can pick up the *New York Times* just about anywhere these days), or in *USA Today*.

Computer resellers are cropping up everywhere there are businesses that rent computers, so you may even be able to find them listed in your local *Yellow Pages*. Treat them like you would any mail-order company, taking the same precautions listed above.

What I've Got Now

Okay, I know you're just breathless with anticipation. This is a listing of the hardware and major software I have, followed by a listing of the stuff I'd get if I had a sugar-daddy to bank roll my digital fantasies.

I'm including it for two reasons: first, to debunk the idea that you have to have some kind of super-powered system to know a lot about Macintosh. You don't, thank you very much. Second, because I think it helps you see what kind of possibilities exist for mid- and low-end Mac models.

Hardware

- Macintosh LC with 10 megs of RAM and a 40 meg internal hard drive.

- 13-inch Apple color monitor.

- Datadesk 101e extended keyboard.

- Kensington TurboMouse trackball.

- DataPlace 120 meg external hard drive partitioned into three drives: One for Applications, one for Graphics, and one (tiny) partition for System 6.0.7 in case I ever have to write about it again.

- Apple's microphone.

- Labtec external speakers (because there's nothing like a Mac going "Boing" in faux stereo).

- NEC P2200XE 24-pin dot-matrix printer.

- Apple LaserWriter Select 310 PostScript laser printer with 5.5 megs of printer RAM. This is one I bought against the advice of reviewers, and I'm perfectly happy with it. It's slow, but it gives me an excuse to run out for coffee.

- Global Village Communications TelePort Gold high-speed fax/modem. I adore Global Village's line of modems. I wish I owned stock in the company.

Principle Software

My hard drives are choked with software. Some of it I only use once in a while. I won't bore you with that. This is stuff I use every day:

- ☛ System 7.1 (I held out until after I started writing this book before I upgraded from 7.0.1.)

- ☛ Apple's Macintosh PC Exchange, for dealing with DOS disks. (It isn't the best, but it met my minimal needs for the least money.)

- ☛ Baseline Publishing's INIT Manager, because I'd crash constantly without it.

- ☛ Adobe Type Manager, because no Mac should be without it (not when you can get it for just $7.50 to cover shipping and handling).

- ☛ Fifth Generation Systems' Suitcase 2.1.3, because I am a font and sound freak. I have entirely too many fonts and sounds installed for my own good, and Suitcase lets me easily rotate sets of each in and out of use as I need or want them.

- ☛ MicroFrontier/Timework's Color It! 2.0 for tinkering with graphic images.

- ☛ Kevin Mitchell's excellent shareware program GIFConverter 2.3.2, for other graphic-image tinkering.

- ☛ Microsoft Word 5.1a, for big writing projects.

- ☛ Symantec's GreatWorks 2.0 integrated package, for less complicated things.

- ☛ America Online 2.0. I go into withdrawal if I don't check my mail at least twice a week.

- ☛ CompuServe Information Manager 2.2. (but I understand there's a brand new version just released). I use CompuServe because the rest of the world hasn't wised up to how cool America Online is.

- ☛ Timeworks' Publish It! Easy 3.0. I don't particularly like it, but I don't need all the bells and whistles of Aldus PageMaker and don't feel like paying $600 for that one.

☛ Berkeley Systems After Dark screen savers—all of them. Yes, I am a toy-brain.

☛ The usual assortment of games: Lemmings, 3 in Three, Solitaire.

What I'd Buy with Someone Else's Money

This is my wish list right now, but I'm fickle. It's subject to change at any moment. If someone wants to try and bribe me with some of this, well, you're welcome to try, but don't get your hopes up.

First, I'd like a new Mac: either a Performa 600CD, or one of the new Quadras, like the 660AV with all the audio (there's that CD again) and video gewgaws. They're more powerful than my spunky LC, but more importantly, they have more growth potential. The LC has been a discontinued model for more than a year now, and there's an LC III and an education-only LC 520.

Then I'd like another Mac: a PowerBook 180, fully loaded. I'd settle for a used PowerBook 100, kind of loaded, but this isn't my money I'm spending.

I'd immediately upgrade both Macs' memory to their full capacity: The Quadra 660AV can take up to 68 megabytes of RAM. I don't think I could ever use all that memory, but I'd sure give it a try.

I'd go for a larger monitor, too, 16-inch or 21-inch. I get tired of paging through long manuscripts. Since I'm spending someone else's money, maybe I'll get two: a 16-inch color monitor, and then a monochrome full- or two-page display. Or how about a one monitor that does both; something funky like the Radius Pivot: the monitor swivels so it can be either long or wide.

Then I'd add one of the Apple's new ergonomically designed keyboards and a mouse—not because of the ergonomics, just because they look cool.

I'd want to add another external hard drive: either a big, fat one with over a gigabyte of storage; or one with ejectable media, such as a SyQuest or Bernoulli. That way, when I fill up one cartridge, I could just pop in another.

With all that storage memory, I'd have to get into Kodak's PhotoCD (you know, where you drop off a roll of film and get back a CD-ROM disk of pictures). Picture files are real memory hogs, both in storage memory and RAM.

I'd also need a color scanner, preferably full page, with Ofoto, OCR software, and Adobe PhotoShop for some serious photo tinkering. I'd create my own *National Inquirer Of The Weekly World/Not Necessarily The News*-type photos of Satan's face in a storm cloud and space aliens with senators, without the inconvenience having to leave my home.

Because I'm such a toy-brain, I'd have to buy a camcorder to create my own QuickTime video clips and presentations. I can't think of why I'd need them, but they look like fun.

I'd also load up on CDs, both music and ROM, just because I could use them with my built in CD-ROM drive. I think it would be great to have the 1812 Overture blasting out of my Mac. Since I'm such a font freak, I'd include the Adobe Type On Call CD, and any other complete font libraries I could get my hands on. While I'm at it, I'd lay in a supply of educational and entertaining CDs in case my godsons stopped by and wanted to play.

There isn't much other software I'd add right away. I'd definitely add AppleTalk Remote Access (ARA) so I could control my desktop Mac from the road with my PowerBook. I might also pop for PageMaker 5.0 (just to have something else to use all those fonts with) and maybe one of the 3-D font effects generators.

As for anything else, well, I don't wish more than a few months in advance. Like Dorothy said when she landed in Oz, "My, things come and go so quickly here." (Or something.) The technology changes so rapidly, it doesn't pay to plan too far ahead.

That's my wish list. What's yours?

The Least You Need to Know

Remember these little tidbits whilst doing your shopping:

- ☞ Don't buy on impulse: do your homework.

- ☞ Protect yourself however you can when you make a purchase.

- ☞ Don't forget the potential savings if you qualify for educational-market purchases at your school.

- ☞ Buy to anticipate your future needs, as well as your present ones.

Chapter 20

On the Road (With Charles Kurault Nowhere in Sight)

In This Chapter

- ☞ Dealing with airports and airplanes
- ☞ Checking out hotels and motels
- ☞ File synchronization tips
- ☞ More shopping and dropping
- ☞ PB & J (PowerBooks and Junk)

PowerBook users have special concerns, the biggest being ways of keeping their PowerBooks up and running as long as possible before their batteries croak. To make y'all happy, here's a special little chapter all your own, with tips and tricks for making your computing on the road just a little less harrowing.

In this chapter, you'll get tips for dealing with airport security, airlines, hotels, and motels. You'll also get some tips on keeping the files on your PowerBook and desktop Mac synchronized, so you always have the most recent version of a file handy.

Airport Security

The biggest pain in the butt, when traveling with a PowerBook, is getting through the bloody airport metal detector and X-ray security check. (I always forget and wear a metal belt-buckle, so security has to poke me with a hand-held metal detector in embarrassing places. Not that I enjoy it, or anything.)

If you're a savvy business traveler, you're carrying everything you're bringing with you: a garment bag, or overnight case, plus the obligatory briefcase, and perhaps a whole separate bag for your PowerBook and accessories. (How many arms do you have, anyhow?)

Your plan is probably to pass off the garment bag to a flight attendant, jam the overnight bag in the overhead compartment, and keep your precious briefcase and PowerBook stowed under the seat until you can take them out and work—if you can convince airport security that none of your work tools is a bomb in disguise.

The easiest way to muscle your way through security is to drop everything but your PowerBook case on the X-ray belt. Hand your PowerBook and accessories (disks, and so on) over to the security person and say you want it hand-searched. That will spare your disks (including your PB's hard drive) and accessories from an X-ray bombardment. You will be asked to power up your PowerBook so security can see that it actually works and isn't a device of terrorism masquerading as a Mac.

You can turn it on and off for the guard; however, that's going to drain your battery needlessly (spinning up the hard drive, then powering it down). If you plan to work while waiting for your flight to be called, you can (before you hit the security desk) power up your PowerBook and then put it to sleep with the **Sleep** command under the **Special** menu.

When you get to security, then all you have to do is open the lid and touch a key: your PowerBook will snap to attention. When security is satisfied, use the **Sleep** command again to conserve your battery until you're ready to work.

Up in the Air

When you get onboard the plane, you can work until they tell you to prepare for takeoff. Then your PowerBook must be stowed (in the overhead compartment, or under the seat in front of you), at least until you're in the air. Put that bad-boy to sleep (I almost said "put that puppy to sleep," an unfortunate choice of words), or turn it off if you plan to snooze and not work.

By the Way . . .

Airlines, of late, have gotten all kinds of weird when it comes to using electronics in the air. Some ban the use of radios, even with headphones. Others don't want you to use a laptop computer. Unfortunately, none of the airlines seem to agree on what they don't want you to use. If you know you have to work in the air, check with the airline for their rules before you buy your ticket. Nothing's more frustrating than having to work, and then being told you can't. It will give you gray hair.

The Bates Motel

"Norman? Norman? You evil child, put that computer away and come help your mother. . . . "

Hotels and motels that cater to business travelers have been getting more and more understanding of folks who tote around laptop computers. If your PowerBook has a fax or modem, when you make reservations, be sure to ask for a room that has an accessible phone jack to plug into—not the typical hotel jack where you can't unplug the phone.

Before you leave on your trip, also be sure to get a couple of local access numbers for any on-line services you may use (such as America Online or CompuServe).

Get in Sync

One of the most trying things about computing on the road is remembering which files are the most recent versions of documents you use on both your PowerBook and desktop Mac. Short of using a synchronizing utility (more about them shortly), you can do a couple of things to make the chore less of a chore.

First, you can use the Views Control Panel's **List Views** options (shown in the figure), and set your options to show date and comment information.

List Views from the Views Control Panel.

Click these.

When you're ready to move the current version of file between your computers, select **View by Name**, and then **View by Date** with the **Views** menu in the Finder. Your files will sort themselves out by the date/time that's automatically stamped on every file when you save it. Your most recent files will float to the top of the list (as shown here).

```
┌──────────────────────────────┐
│ ▓▓ ▓▓▓▓ Manuscript ▓▓▓▓ ▓▓   │
│ 25 items    38.7 MB in disk    10.4 MB ava│
│ ──────────────────────────── │
│ Last Modified                 │
│ ──────────────────────────── │
│ Tue, Oct 5, 1993, 12:30 PM   ⬆│
│ Tue, Oct 5, 1993, 10:12 AM    │
│ Mon, Oct 4, 1993, 10:13 PM    │
│ Mon, Oct 4, 1993, 9:41 AM     │
│ Sun, Oct 3, 1993, 7:26 PM     │
│ Sat, Oct 2, 1993, 12:51 PM    │
│ Fri, Oct 1, 1993, 3:33 PM     │
│ Fri, Oct 1, 1993, 1:55 PM     │
│ Thu, Sep 30, 1993, 10:19 AM   │
│ Wed, Sep 29, 1993, 10:35 PM   │
│ Sat, Sep 25, 1993, 10:55 PM   │
│ Thu, Sep 23, 1993, 3:50 PM    │
│                              ⬇│
└──────────────────────────────┘
```

Files sorted by last modified date.

Second, you can attach comments to any file, which will also be displayed (if you select **Show Comments** in the Views Control Panel). To attach comments to a file:

1. Click on the file icon to select it.

2. Select **Get Info** from the **File** menu (⌘-**I**).

3. When the Info window appears (shown in the following figure), click in the Comments box to activate it, and type in a reminder.

4. Close the Info window. Your comments will be displayed whenever you change the view to **View by Name**.

Get Info window with comments.

You can also apply a set of naming strategies to help you recall which file is most recent. You can number your files like application versions: **Text 1.0** for a first version; **Text 1.2** for an intermediate phase; **Text 2.0** for a total revision. If that sounds too much like work, you can get applications that will synchronize your files for you automatically—it's still work, though.

If you ever rebuild your desktop, be aware that rebuilding erases all of the comments you have attached to files. (You can get a shareware utility called CommentKeeper, available on-line and from MUGs and shareware libraries, that will save your comments.)

PowerBook Utilities and Other Doodads

The instant success of the PowerBook line left it wide open for third-parties to try and fix the foibles of portable computing. There are scads of utilities, hardware add-ons, and effort-saving devices you can spring for.

In addition to getting yourself a comfortable carrying case (that's padded to protect your PowerBook) that will hold all this junk, there are some very handy items you can get.

PowerBook Utilities

Utilities aimed at PowerBook users are a burgeoning field. There are dozens of packages already. The current crop of utilities all seem to address the same half-dozen or so concerns of the common PowerBook user: making batteries last longer; keeping tabs on battery charge; security; cursor control; speedy access to information about your system; and file synchronization.

To make batteries last longer, the utilities give you faster and better control of your PowerBook's automatic sleep settings. Some will let you set different sets of conservation tools, (such as controlling your monitor's display,—a very power-hungry device) for different computing situations, even different applications. All of them provide an Instant Sleep command that bypasses the one in the Special menu, saving you time and battery power.

> ## By the Way . . .
> To keep track of how well your batteries are performing, there's usually some sort of monitor function built-in: either to keep track of your battery's usage (so you know when its time to buy a new one), its charge (so you know when to plug that puppy in again, its condition (totally draining the battery before recharge extends battery life), and to let you know that the battery isn't charging at all (very bad news).

Security functions generally provide password protection, either at startup, when you "wake" a sleeping PowerBook, or both. The goal is to keep casual observers from accessing your information when you aren't looking.

All the PowerBook utility packages give you help finding the PowerBook's cursor (which tends to vanish during periods of inactivity). Some let you set a larger cursor, so it's easier to find; others will find it for you whenever you touch the trackball.

They also all enhance the PowerBook's battery display—since the one that Apple provides isn't entirely honest (it will tell you you're out of juice when you could actually keep on working for a bit). Different packages add other displays: time and date clocks; computing time left to the battery; disk activity; and even whether AppleTalk is active.

Only a few of the current line of PB utilities give you minimal file-synchronization. Generally, that's better handled by a stand-alone synchronization utility.

Since the PowerBook utility packages vary greatly in their usefulness, it's silly for me to try and recommend one because I don't know how *you* use your PowerBook. Besides, by the time you read this, there will be a dozen new ones. As always, shop for the package that gives you the tools you need at a price you can afford. The current batch of utility sets list for $100–$130, and you can find them for about $50-$80, mail-order pricing.

Synchronization Utilities

Like the PowerBook utilities packages, file-synchronization has become big business. Software developers have realized that many people working on PowerBooks use the laptops as travel machines, and rely on desktop Macs and Duo-docking stations when at home or in the office. That presents the problem of knowing which hard drive has the latest-greatest version of any given file. Sometimes, you've even made intermediate changes to two versions of the same document.

All of the stand-alone file-synchronization utilities provide you the means of specifying which files and folders on which of the Macs you access are to be kept current with your PowerBook's files, and which are not. All of them are more-or-less comparable in terms of basic functions, while some have extra whiz-bang features, such as automatic virus checking (a nice touch) and the capability to synchronize two Macs via floppies, since not everyone has access to a network.

By the Way . . .

Since synchronicity is a newly created software category, as of this writing, all the sync utilities are in their first incarnations (version 1.0, or 1.something). None particularly distinguishes itself over the others.

If you need one, shop to meet your current needs. If you only think you might need one, keep your eyes on the reviews and advertisements. Now that there's some competition going, someone is bound to release a 2.0 knock-your-socks-off package that does everything but your dinner dishes. Applications advance in spurts like that, especially when the field is running neck and neck. Most of the synchronization utilities list in the $100–$130 range, with mail-order pricing around $70–$80.

PowerBook Hardware

The kindest hardware additions you can give your PowerBook are similar to those mentioned in Chapter 14: more RAM, a bigger internal hard drive, a modem, and an external monitor, keyboard, and mouse for those times when your PowerBook isn't on your knees.

Additionally, there's some PowerBook-specific junk that may make your life easy: an extra battery or two; a free-standing battery conditioner (one that drains the battery completely before recharging it, to extend the battery's life), and a security kit (such as a bicycle chain or lock) that will let you anchor your PowerBook to some immobile piece of furniture to keep it from traveling without you.

By the Way . . .

There are hardware enhancements that range from the sublime to the ridiculous. I hesitate to mention the car cigarette-lighter attachment that lets you recharge your batteries while you drive. In theory, it's a great idea. I know, however, that some smacked-fool will be sitting in traffic, talking on a cellular phone while keying appointments into his PowerBook, and doing everything but watching the road. With that cheery thought in mind, happy trails.

The Least You Need to Know

- ☞ Check with your airline (before you buy your ticket) to be sure you can use your PowerBook in flight.

- ☞ Make sure any hotel you make reservations with is computer friendly.

- ☞ PowerBook utilities and accessories can make your life on the road much easier.

**Special bonus: virtual text page.
(There's virtually no text on it.)**

Chapter 21
Installing System Software

In This Chapter

- ☛ How to install System software
- ☛ How to re-install System software
- ☛ Custom installations

Do you have your hands on a Mac without System software installed, or else something is all boogered up in the System already installed on your hard drive? I've said it before and I'll say it again: *don't panic*. There's no reason. You can fix it.

Extra Steps When Reinstalling

If you're reinstalling your System software to eliminate a suspected (or confirmed) corruption problem, there are some extra steps you have to take. Naturally, if you're installing from scratch, you may skip blithely ahead to the next section, "Installation Included."

If you're reinstalling, here's what you need to do first:

When you restart with the Install disk (or any bootable floppy, for that matter), you may get a message that says something like: **Your Macintosh is set to run with 32-bit Addressing turned on. This version of the System can't deal with it. If you want to proceed, click on Continue.** If you get this message, click on the **Continue** button. This will restart your Mac again, and disable 32-Bit Addressing in the Memory control panel. Your Mac will also spit out the Install disk in the process—just pop it right back in.

32-bit Addressing is the option available on most Macs that allows them to access and use more than 10 megabytes of RAM. You turn it on and off (if your Mac can handle it) through the Memory control panel.

1. Dig out the set of white System disks that came with your Mac (or if you were very good, the backup copies you made).

2. Start your Mac, if it's off, and disable whatever virus protection program(s) you may have installed. If it's a Control Panel (such as Central Point Software's CP Anti-virus), turn it off. If it's an Extension (such as Disinfectant), drag it out of the Extensions Folder and onto the desktop.

3. Restart your Mac (using the **Restart** command under the **Special** menu).

4. After the startup sound, insert the disk labeled **Install** from your set of System disks. It has a scaled-down version of the System software installed so you can run your Mac from it.

5. When your Mac has gone through its startup thing, and you find yourself once more at the desktop, double-click on your **Hard Drive** icon to open it (if it isn't already open).

6. Navigate to the **System Folder** and open that, too.

7. Since you're reinstalling because of a corruption problem, you want to throw away the alleged troublemakers to make sure the corruption is not passed along to your newly installed System. Click on the **System** suitcase icon, and drag it into the **Trash**.

8. Next, click on the **Finder** icon, and drag that into the **Trash**, too.

9. Now, empty the Trash by selecting **Empty Trash** from the **Special** menu.

With the most likely suspects removed from your System Folder, proceed with the rest of the installation instructions detailed below.

By the Way . . .

If you're upgrading your System software, you may see a message that says you already have a newer version of the file than the one you are about to install. Unless you're reinstalling to replace the file mentioned in the warning, it's generally better to leave the newer file installed. Click on the **Newer** button, and the file will remain unchanged. If you click on the **Older** button, the older version of the file will be installed.

The reason why you get the 32-bit Addressing message is simple: System 7.x doesn't fit or run very well on a floppy disk, even a high-density disk. Many bootable disks (that is, disks with System software on them) use System 6.0.7, because it takes up less space. 32-Bit addressing, however, was introduced with System 7, and older versions of the Mac's System don't know what it is, much less what to do with it. Hence the message.

Installation Included

If you haven't been following along, because you're installing from scratch, you need to start (or Restart) your Mac with the disk labeled **Install** in the disk drive.

When you reach the desktop, open the Install disk's window by double-clicking on its icon. Scroll around in the window until you spot the **Installer** icon shown on the following page. Double-click on it to fire up the Installer program.

The Installer icon.

When the Installer opens, you'll be presented with the Welcome screen. To proceed, click on the **OK** button. That puts you right into the Installer's **Easy Install** option. The Easy Install assumes you don't want to be bothered (or you're too intimidated to be bothered) to select the exact installation you want.

Easy Install dialog box.

If you are installing from scratch and have no idea what your custom options are, simply click on the **Install** button, and skip the section on custom installations. When you're done installing, turn to the "Junk You Can Throw Away" section in Chapter 11 and decide which junk can be thrown away.

The next time you need (or want) to reinstall your System software, you'll feel better about choosing a custom installation. If this is a reinstallation you're doing, and you want to customize the installation, click on the **Customize** button.

Custom Installations

Clicking on the **Customize** button changes the Easy Install dialog box to the one shown here. By scrolling through the list in the upper left corner, you can click on one basic installation, or you can Shift-click to select several installation options.

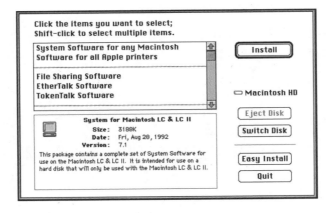

Click the items you want to select;
Shift-click to select multiple items.

System Software for any Macintosh
Software for all Apple printers

File Sharing Software
EtherTalk Software
TokenTalk Software

Install

⊷ Macintosh HD

Eject Disk

Switch Disk

Easy Install

Quit

System for Macintosh LC & LC II
Size: 3188K
Date: Fri, Aug 28, 1992
Version: 7.1

This package contains a complete set of System Software for use on the Macintosh LC & LC II. It is intended for use on a hard disk that will only be used with the Macintosh LC & LC II.

Custom Installation dialog box.

As you can see in the lower left corner of the figure, I chose the basic installation for a Macintosh LC or LC II. By scrolling through the list of options, you can choose an installation based on you model of Mac, or you can customize by selecting only the things you need.

If you find all these options confusing, you can (without regret or feelings of inferiority) click on the **Easy Install** button and go for the full installation without any thinking on your part. It's okay.

If you want to install System software on a disk or hard drive other than the one named beneath the **Install** button, click on the **Switch Disk** button, and navigate to the hard drive you want to install to, or insert the floppy disk you want to install on.

When you've selected the disk (or hard drive) to install on, and the options you want installed, simply click on the **Install** button, and a-waaaay we go.

Don't be afraid. You'll notice that almost every screen shown throughout this section gives you the opportunity to Quit the Installer, or Cancel the installation once it's begun. You aren't working without a net.

Doin' the Floppy Shuffle

When you click on the **Install** button, your Mac will think and churn, think and churn, deciding what all it needs to install to make your Mac happy.

By the Way . . .

To keep you informed of what it's doing, the Mac shows you a status screen.

System 7.1 comes on six high-density floppy disks (seven, if you count the **Before You Install** disk). It comes on eight or nine disks if you have QuickTime and AtEase, too. When you click on the **Install** button, the Installer decides what disks it will need, and lines them up in the status display. You're bound to have to shuffle floppies around, inserting and removing them from the disk drive.

To save yourself some time, stack the disks in the order they're shown in the status display; that way you won't have to go searching for a disk each time your Mac asks for one.

When your Mac needs the next disk in the series, it will spit out the current disk in the drive, and flash the message shown here (of course, the name of the disk will change). Simply remove the ejected disk, and pop in the one requested. The installation will proceed along its merry way.

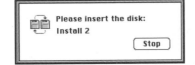

Installer disk request.

When the installation is nearly complete, your Mac will request that you insert the disk labeled **Install** again. It wraps up a few things, tidies up after itself, and you're done.

To celebrate, your Mac will throw the message shown in the figure up on your screen.

Remember to turn your virus protection back on (if you have it) after you Restart. Turn on the **Control Panel,** or drag the extension back into the **Extensions Folder** and **Restart** yet again.

Installation Successful!

Click on the **Restart** button, and you're good to go.

The Least You Need to Know

☛ Remember to turn off or disable any virus protection programs you may have running.

☛ Restart and immediately pop the Install disk into the drive.

☛ When in doubt, choose **Easy Install.**

☛ Remember to turn back on any virus protection programs you may have shut down to install.

Recycling tip: tear this page out and photocopy it.

Appendix

I Think We're All Bozos on This Bus

Proactive planning is fine for difficult situations beyond your experience, but hey, what about the run-of-the-mill things that go bump in your Mac? Many of them are easy to fix. Here comes a pile of them, along with some theory to let you figure out what's going on when the problem isn't specifically covered here.

In this appendix, you'll find solutions to most of the common Mac ailments that may afflict your Mac. You'll also get some specific tips on getting good customer service and technical support from the companies you buy from. I also hope you'll get a solid grounding in how Macs work, so you'll be able to search and destroy problems on your own.

Before You Panic

Macs are, in some respects, just like babies: sometimes they spit up for no good reason. It doesn't mean your Mac is sick if something weird happens, it could simply be an odd collision of circumstances that threw your Mac for a loop.

Before you go packing it up to drag into your nearest Authorized Apple Service Center, there are some things you can try before you panic.

Check the Obvious

Your Mac won't start. Your communications software can't connect to your favorite bulletin board. You can't get a certain file to print. Your external hard drive doesn't want to mount.

They all sound like serious problems. In some cases, they may be. In others, they aren't. Before you reach for the phone, check the obvious:

☞ Is everything plugged in and turned on?

☞ Are cables connected securely to your Mac and the peripheral?

☞ Are the correct cables plugged into the correct peripherals?

☞ If it's a monitor problem, (no picture, say) check the contrast and brightness controls, as well as the above.

By the Way . . .

I once had to make three trips to a computer store trying to get my brand new LaserWriter Select 310 to print. I tried everything you'll read here, plus more. (I also hurled some colorful language at it that you probably will never see in print.) Even the technician at the store was flummoxed because it always worked there. To make a long story short, it turned out to be the printer cable. I had the wrong kind, but no one noticed because Mac cables all look kind of alike. Trust me here, if professional tweaks can be faked out by a cable, so can you. *Check the obvious!*

☞ Are you using the right software for the hardware (the correct printer driver in the Chooser, the right telecommunications software for the service, and so on)?

☞ What's the dumbest thing you could have forgotten to do? Check that, too.

Start Again

If something strange happens while you're working on something, stop. If you can, save everything (⌘-**S**), quit (⌘-**Q**) any and all open applications, and **Restart** your Mac.

Sometimes, a heavy-duty work session, with a lot of opening and closing (and reopening) of applications and documents confuses your Mac. A restart is like a slap in the face to your Mac. It forces it to clear out its memory (which is why you save your work before restarting) and load your documents and applications again from scratch.

If the problem recurs, then you have to start sniffing around for another solution.

Rebuild Your Desktop

Your Mac keeps track of everything on every disk by building these big, fat, invisible files that are collectively called *The Desktop File*. Sometimes, the information in the Desktop File gets screwed up, mismatched, or disconnected. Your Mac might tell you it can't find an application that you know is right under its digital nose. Some of your file icons might become boring generic ones.

When your Desktop File gets screwy, it's like Wednesday on the "Mickey Mouse Club"—anything can happen. You have to tell your Mac to rebuild its Desktop File.

Restart your Mac while holding down the ⌘ and **Option** keys. When you reach the desktop, you'll get a notice saying **Are you sure you want to rebuild the Desktop**. Click on **OK**. The message repeats for every disk, hard drive, or hard drive partition on your Mac.

To rebuild the Desktop File on a floppy disk, hold down the ⌘ and **Option** keys while you insert the disk in your floppy drive.

OOPS!

If you use the **Get Info** command to attach comments to any of your files, rebuilding the desktop will delete those comments. You'll have to redo them.

Zap Your PRAM

That's pronounced "pea-RAM," not "pram" like a baby carriage. PRAM is where your Mac stores parameter information: how you like the time and date displayed and other custom settings you use Control Panels to set. If your PRAM goes wonky, you Mac doesn't know how to behave. So you have to administer another open-handed slap across your Mac's face.

This time, as you **Restart**, press **Control-Option-P-R** (you might have to get a friend to help), and hold them until your startup screen blinks. That clears the parameter setting and starts you with a clean slate: that means you need to open your control panels and reset them to your preferred settings.

I could never remember how to zap PRAM until I noticed the letters made a nice little mnemonic device. Simply remember COPpeR, (Control-Option-P-R) as in pennies, or "You'll never take me alive, COPpeR!"

Reinstall Suspicious Applications

If your problems persist, try reinstalling the suspect application. Delete all of the application files (they can be scattered all over your hard drive, and in your System Folder). Be sure to delete the application's preference file(s) in your Preferences folder. Reinstall the application, following the directions in your manual.

If you suspect your System software, you can reinstall that too. Check Chapter 21 for details.

When All Else Fails

(Re)read the manual. Who knows, there may be some useful information in it.

Okay, Now You Can Panic . . .

Just kidding. You really don't have to panic. If things still aren't working, pick up the phone and call technical support.

Technical support, typically, means the part of a software or hardware company devoted to answering technical questions about their product. I expand the definition to include anyone I can call in a pinch—user group members, Mac-friends, and so on—especially because many companies have added 900-numbers, pay-per-minute technical support lines.

Before you pick up the phone, there are a few things you should have handy:

☛ A list of any error messages you received.

☛ A list of everything you tried to fix the problem yourself.

☛ The make and model of the hardware in question, or the name and version number of the software.

☛ Your system configuration: Mac model, System software version, amount of RAM, any and all peripherals, and what port they are connected to.

- A list of the other software that was running all the time, including version numbers.

- A list of the contents of your System Folder: especially your Extensions and Control Panels.

- A pen and paper for taking notes.

If you have all that together, take three deep breaths, and calm down. You're ready to dial.

Making the Call

When you call technical support, the first thing you should write down is the name of the person helping you: if you have to call back about the same problem, ask for her by name so you won't have to explain everything all over again. The person you spoke to will probably remember you (with a little prompting—after all, they take many calls).

Remember: be nice. Those people are there to help you. They didn't write the software; they didn't build the hardware. Be fair and give them a chance.

Call from a phone that's close to your Mac so you can try suggestions right then and there, without having to run back and forth or play telephone tag.

Also, be clear and precise: "I'm having trouble with the Mac so-and-so hardware/software, model/version number. I'm using it on a Mac LC with 10 megs of RAM and a 40 meg hard drive running System 7.1. When I try to do this, this happens." He will ask questions, such as what applications were you running, what extensions. That's why you should put all that system information together before you call.

You should write down all suggestions and the results. If it works, you have it on paper for future reference. If it doesn't, you have it on paper so you know what you've tried. This is sleuthing, a process of elimination.

Nine times out of ten, you'll get a solution. Tech-support people answer many calls, see many of the same problems, and know what to do right away. Sometimes, it takes a while—he may even have to chase down another technical-type and call you back.

I Can't Get No Satisfaction

Technical support people are people. Some are good, some are bad, some are having a bad day. If you can't reach a satisfactory resolution with one, ask to speak to a supervisor. Keep taking names, keep on moving up the chain of command until you hit the CEO, if necessary (not that the CEO will know how to fix your problem—if he or she does, buy stock in the company). Chances are you'll never have to go that far, but . . . who knows?

You can always resort to letter-writing campaigns by the members of all the MUGs you've joined, and phone calls to the Better Business Bureau. Meanwhile, you should be working the network we talked about establishing in the last chapter, calling on your other resources.

In Specific

That's the course of action you should take when you run into unusual problems with specific hardware or applications. More often than not, though, you'll run into a problem that's purely a function of the peculiarities of your own Mac. Here are some specific problems with specific solutions.

Plenty of Nothin'

If you fire up your Mac, only to have it sit there and stare at you with its one big eye (no startup bell, no monitor, no nothing), it's time to check the obvious again: is it plugged in, turned on (don't forget to check the switch on your power strip)? If that's not it, check the cables: make sure everything is connected properly. If that doesn't get it, you have a serious dead-Mac situation on your hands. Call the para-Mac-ics.

Floppy Disk Icon with a Question Mark

An icon of a floppy with a question mark is your Mac's way of asking where the System Folder is. If you start up from an external hard drive, make sure its plugged in, turned on, and connected to your Mac's SCSI port.

If you start from an internal hard drive, try turning your Mac off for, oh, about fifteen or twenty seconds, and try it again. If that doesn't do it, try it again, but zap your PRAM (look earlier in this appendix for more information). If that doesn't get it, pop in your rescue disk, or the Disk Tools disk from your original set of System disks. Both should have startup information so your Mac will run.

When your Mac starts from the disk, one of two things will happen: either your internal hard drive will finally mount, or it won't. If it mounts (its icon shows up on your desktop below your rescue disk), you need to install (or reinstall) your System software. Something boogered it up so badly your Mac can't read it.

If it doesn't mount, your internal hard drive is boogered up in general. You can try taking a pass at it with Disk First Aid, but if a hard drive won't mount, most utilities can't touch it. Call for help.

Ballad of the Sad Mac Café

Usually, when you start up, the first thing you see is a little smiling Mac: that's good. If you should ever see a sad Mac, that's bad.

Your Mac puts itself through a series of self-tests at startup. It smiles when it passes, and frowns when it doesn't. It also throws an arcane and oblique error message up on your screen. Write it down, just in case.

Try restarting from a rescue disk: it may be a problem with your System software. If it starts up, and your hard drive icon mounts, it's your System software, and you need to reinstall it (see Chapter 21). If it starts, but your hard drive doesn't mount, there's something physically wrong with your hard drive. Call for help.

If it still gives you the sad Mac when you restart from the rescue disk, there's something wrong with your Mac itself. Call your Local Authorized Apple Dealer, and read off a copy of the error code; let them figure it out.

Not Your Usual Bong Sound

Every Mac makes some kind of **bong** sound when it starts up, even if you've turned down your Mac's volume with the Sound Control Panel (unless you have something plugged into the audio-out jack, such as speakers, that aren't turned on).

If you hear any other sound (such as four notes), there's something wrong. Usually you'll get this four-note samba when you've just installed something: new SIMMS, a new SCSI device, or an expansion card. The notes mean that whatever you just installed, is installed incorrectly—try again.

For SCSI problems, check the "General Scuzziness" section near the end of this appendix for more information. For any other kind of hardware, check your manual, and try reinstalling it.

Problems in the Finder

Sometimes, your Mac will start up fine, only to give you grief when you try to do something. Here are some of the more common problems.

Disappearing Files

Usually, if a file disappears abruptly (say, while you're copying it onto a floppy, or moving it into another folder), usually it's because your finger slipped off the mouse button while dragging it, and it landed in that same place all of your odd socks go from the dryer.

Luckily, your Mac has a **Find** command (⌘-**F**) in the **File** menu. Tell your Mac to look for that puppy by name, or by other criteria (such as part of the name, kind of file, and so on) when you click on the **More Options** button. If you can't remember anything about the file, you'll have to dig around in folders manually to find it. Sorry.

Can't Empty Trash

The Trash isn't smart: it lets you throw away almost anything. The only things it won't let you throw away include:

☛ **Locked files:** You have to unlock them first, in the file's **Get Info** window (⌘-I).

☛ **Files from locked disks:** You have to unlock the disk. Eject the disk (⌘-E), flip the disk's locking tab, and reinsert it in your disk drive.

☛ **Files that are in use:** For document files, use the appropriate application to close the documents. For extensions or control panels, simply drop them in the Trash, and leave them there until the next time you start your Mac; they won't load from in the Trash, and you can empty it then.

System Errors

System Errors are also known as *bombs* or *crashes*. Your Mac has a minor nervous breakdown and with its last breath before passing out, it throws a polite, but useless, **Sorry, a system error occurred** message on your screen. (Don't confuse system errors with a system *freeze*, where everything seizes up: you can't move the mouse, select a menu, nothing. I'll talk more about system freezes later.)

Throw your hands up in disgust, and restart your Mac. You can try to click on the **Restart** button in the message, but that almost never works. If you have one, use your Restart switch (on your keyboard), or reach behind your Mac and turn the power off for a few seconds. There isn't much else you can do when it happens. Everything you were working on is gone except for what you already saved to disk.

You can do some things to prevent bombs and crashes, though. They usually happen for one of three reasons:

☛ **Memory:** The application you were using ran out of memory (RAM); check out the "Digital Amnesia" section of this appendix for more help.

☛ **Software:** The application might be badly written, or might not be compatible with your version of the System software. (If this is the case, call the company. Follow the steps in the "Now You Can Panic" section). Or you may have an extension/INIT conflict (see the next section). Or something's screwy with your copy of the application or your System software (you may have to reinstall them).

☞ **Hardware:** If your Mac crashes when you tell it to do something with a piece of hardware (save to your hard drive, print, and so on), the hardware may be at fault. As always, check the obvious first. Try turning the peripheral off and then on again. If the problem involves your hard drive, it may need its driver repaired or to be reformatted.

Sibling Rivalry: Extension and Control Panel Conflicts

Extension and Control Panel conflicts cause most of the grief in the Macintosh universe—at least in my Macintosh universe. Actually, the main culprit is usually an extension (or as we fossils call them, INITs). Control panels only enter into it when they have an extension component (you might not actually see it).

For a variety of reasons, not all extensions and control panels get along. Sometimes, they fight over the same scrap of memory. Sometimes, they try to fiddle with the same bit of your system (such as the menu bar), and sometimes, they just crash.

When you have an extension conflict, you'll know it. Right after you load in a new extension, your system will start crashing on a regular basis. It will crash either right at startup when the two extensions collided, or as soon as they both try to fiddle with whatever they fiddle with.

To fix an extension conflict, first you have to isolate the two extensions that are causing the trouble. The first one is easy: it's the last one you installed. The other one is harder. (Don't flinch now.) Pull all of your extensions (except the new one) out of your Extensions folder, and out of your System Folder (leave them on the desktop, or drag them into an empty folder). Restart your Mac.

If your Mac starts up okay, add one extension, and restart again. (If your Mac crashes on startup, that new extension is bad, bad, bad. Trash it and get on with your life). Add an extension, and restart. Add an extension, and restart. Repeat the process until your Mac crashes. The last extension you added before the crash is the other troublemaker.

Now you can do one of two things. Either throw out one or the other of the troublesome extensions, or learn to juggle extensions. Sometimes, changing the order of the conflicting extension load can resolve the problem. Try getting one to load first, the other last. If that doesn't work, reverse the order.

You can change your extension loading order by adding letters to the beginning of their names (they load alphabetically). Add an A to the beginning of the extension you want to go first, a B to the second, and so on.

> **By the Way . . .**
>
> Special characters work, too. An exclamation point (!) loads before a file starting with an A. A bullet (•), made with the Option-8 key combination, will load dead last.

It's another case of trial and error. It's tedious and time consuming, but it is also effective. If all this sounds too involved, you can always try an INIT/Extension manager (such as the aptly named INIT Manager, from Baseline), which makes the whole process a lot simpler.

Problems Within Applications

Yes, believe it or not, sometimes weird things happen even in your favorite application. Even the most stubborn, un-Mac-like application will grace you with an occasional error message before it poops out. Here are a few of my favorites.

Application *X* Has Unexpectedly Quit

Well, that's bloody helpful. Unless you fell asleep at the keyboard, you probably saw your document zip into nothingness.

The likely suspects: the application ran out of memory (skip to the "Digital Amnesia" section); got into a fight with another open application (you might want to close that one, if practical); or the application isn't compatible with your version of the System software (you need to upgrade whichever one of them is older).

Microsoft Word Prefers 6 Gigabytes of Memory, Only 28K Available

More memory difficulties. In this particular instance, you have too many applications open at the same time. Close some, preferably in the reverse order you opened them (last to open, first to close). That frees up enough RAM for the greedy application to open. Skip ahead to the "Digital Amnesia" section of this chapter for other memory tips.

If you get that message with no other applications open, you need to buy yourself some RAM, or you're going to be one irritated little sucker. Check out Chapter 19 for details on buying RAM.

Absolute Zero: System Freezes

Absolute zero is the temperature at which matter comes unglued. A system freeze is what happens before you come unglued. Your screen locks up, and you can't do diddly. Kiss your unsaved work good-bye. Like a System Error (discussed earlier), it's hard to recover from a freeze, but you can do something.

Press the ⌘-**Alt-Esc** key combination. If it works (it doesn't always work), you'll get a warning saying **Do you want to force the application** *(Whatever it Is)* **to Quit? All unsaved changes will be lost.** Like you have a choice. Click on the **Quit** button. The cranky application will quit, but any other open applications and documents will be spared.

Do yourself a favor: save any other open documents, and quit all the applications that are still open. Then, restart your Mac.

By the Way . . .

Freezes usually happen with a build up of crud in your Mac's RAM. If it happened in one application, it may happen in others. Save yourself the heartache, and restart.

The Bomb Party

Applications crash for pretty much the same reasons you'll crash in the Finder. You might want to sneak back to the "Problems in The Finder" section and review. Before you do, let me say this: there are different error codes for application crashes vs. Finder crashes vs. any other Macintosh mishap. None of them make any sense to human beings.

You can, if you enjoy that sort of punishment, get tables of error codes and figure out what they all mean. They don't mean squat to the likes of you and me—well, at least not to me. I wouldn't know an "unimplemented trap" if I got my foot caught in it.

Do yourself a favor: write down the error code, and call the technical support line at the company that wrote the program. Let them figure it out.

Problems with Documents

Sometimes, your Mac can behave like a cranky three-year-old. It stamps its digital feet. It holds its digital breath. It whines: "I don't wanna, and you can't make me!"

Don't you believe it. In most circumstances, you *can* make it.

Application Missing and Other Snotty Remarks

Sometimes, when you double-click on a document's icon to launch the application that created it, you'll get some variation on the **Application Missing** message. Your Mac either offers to open the document into TeachText, or it sits there like a schlub.

If you know deep down in your heart that the application is hiding somewhere on your hard drive, *find* the application's name with the **Find** command on the **File** menu. When your Mac uncovers it, launch the application by double-clicking on its icon and trying to open the document with its **Open** command. If that doesn't open it (or even if it does), I'd rebuild my Desktop File (as explained in the beginning of this chapter).

If you know you don't have the application in question, you can always launch the closest application you have (a word processor for a text file, a painting program for a paint file, and so on), and try to open the document with that. If all else fails, there's always TeachText. It can open some truly ornery files (as long as they're small, under 38K).

Document Cannot Be Opened

Occasionally, even if you have the right application, a file can't be opened. They get damaged, somehow, and unreadable. This is when a set of disk utilities comes in handy. Many of the utilities packages come with a file repair utility that will try to fix a file with spit-and-bailing wire so you can open it one last time and save a new and improved copy.

If the file is total garbage (it happens sometimes), the utility can at least try to salvage some of the data from the file so you won't have to recreate all of it.

Not Enough Memory to Open Document

Either you've run out of RAM overall, or your application needs to have its memory allocation changed to deal with this document. Whichever, you'll need to take some of the steps outlined in the "Digital Amnesia" section of this chapter.

File Is Locked

You can't do much more than read a locked file. That's why you lock them, for protection. Sometimes, like hiding a valuable thingy in a very safe place, you forget that you did it. Don't be ashamed, it happens to all of us. Unlock the file with the **Get Info** command in the **File** menu in the Finder.

Problems with Floppies

So it doesn't catch you by surprise, the answer to most of these will involve one of the utilities on your Disk Tools disk, from your System software set, or a commercial disk utility.

Disk Unreadable . . . Initialize?

That could mean you grabbed an unformatted disk. If you're sure you did, simply initialize it.

If you inserted a disk that you know has data on it, and your Mac says it can't read it, **Eject** it. Your disk has been damaged and become unreadable. Take a whack at it with Disk First Aid, and see if it can be saved.

Please Insert Disk *X*

This was more of a problem with the earlier releases of System 7. I haven't run into it much with 7.1. If you build up a couple of disk icons on your desktop by ejecting disks (⌘-E) rather than putting them away (⌘-Y), when you finally try to put one away, your Mac will keep asking you to insert one or all of the other disks.

You can make it stop by pressing the universal Macintosh stop command: ⌘-. (period). Your Mac will probably get huffy and put the disk away anyhow.

By the Way . . .

Of course, you can avoid this problem by putting your disks away, rather than ejecting them, unless you're copying between two disks.

Operation Could Not Be Completed Because of a Write Error

Your disk drive burped while writing a file to disk. Try and save it again. If it doesn't work the second time, the disk may be bad. Save the file to a different disk. Take a pass at the bad one with Disk First Aid to see if it is bad, and if it can be saved. If it can't, see if you can salvage any data with a file recovery utility and throw that bad-boy away.

Disk Full

What time is it when an elephant sits on your fence? Time to get a new fence. What time is it when you can't fit any more on a floppy disk? Time for a new floppy.

If you get this message when saving to your hard drive, you might want to read the section on compression utilities in Chapter 13, the section of Chapter 11 on System junk you can throw away, or the section on shopping for a hard drive in Chapter 19.

Disk Won't Eject

You've tried to put a disk away, either with the **Put Away** command (⌘-**Y**) in the **Special** menu, or you dragged its icon into the Trash. The icon went away, but the disk didn't come out of the drive. Yikes!

Don't panic. If you don't need the disk (or the drive), leave it there until you shut off your Mac. The next time you restart, your Mac will eject it (unless it has a System file on it). This isn't especially good for the disk, or the drive, but it works.

If you do need the disk or drive right away here's what you do: straighten one end of a pretty sturdy paper clip, just to the first bend. Gently, but firmly, insert the straightened part in the little hole to the right of your disk drive, and push. It will spit out the disk.

Disk Is Locked

Like a locked file, you can't do much with a locked disk except read its contents. You can't save to it, and you can't delete anything from it. That's why you lock it.

If you do have to do anything other than read a file from the disk, eject it from the drive, push open the locking tab on the back, and reinsert it in the drive. Voilà. Remember to lock it again when you're done, because you probably locked it for a reason.

Problems with Hard Drives

Most of the problems that can happen to floppy disks, explained above, can also happen to your hard drive (after all, it's only a big floppy disk). Because of the complications added by the extra hardware and the nature of SCSI devices, some other problems may crop up.

Where's the Drive?

If an *external* hard drive's icon fails to appear on your desktop, there may be a couple of things wrong:

☛ Check the obvious: plugged in, turned on, cables connected (and to the right port).

☛ Check your SCSI savvy (for details flip back to "Talk Scuzzy to Me" in Chapter 14, or "General Scuzziness" in this appendix).

☛ Did you turn on your external hard drive before you turned on your Mac? If not, turn the drive on, leave it on, and restart your Mac. (Or if you have one, you can use a disk mounting utility to mount the drive.)

☛ If that doesn't do it, try testing the drive with Disk First Aid, or updating it's driver software with Apple's SC HD Setup utility.

☛ If that doesn't get it, you may have to reformat your drive (explained in Chapter 10—I hope you've been backing up your data regularly), or there may be a mechanical problem you'll need to get serviced.

Sloooowly, I Turned

Sometimes, the files on your hard drive seem to take forever to load. The problem may be caused by file fragmentation, where bits of your files are spit up all over your hard drive. To fix file fragmentation, you need a disk utility package that includes a *disk analyzer* (to see if your disk is fragmented) and an *optimizer/defragmenter* (to fix the problem). These utilities are discussed in Chapter 13.

Digital Amnesia: Memory Problems

Random-access memory (RAM), or the lack of it, can cause you all sorts of hassles, especially with memory-greedy System 7 (remember, we're talking about RAM, not disk space). Apple insists that you can run System 7.1 with 2 megabytes of RAM, and you can, if you don't want to run any application that needs more than about 500K of memory to run.

If you have a Mac with System 7 and only 2 megabytes of RAM, do yourself a favor: buy more. Flip back to Chapter 14 for information on adding RAM. Even if you have 4 megabytes (or more) of RAM, you can still run into difficulties. Here are the most common.

Out of Memory Messages

When you try to run a big, fat application, you may get a message that says something like, **This big, fat application prefers 1024K of memory to run, only 768K available;** or **Not enough memory to open document.** Depending on how cranky the application is, it may ask you to quit any applications you have open, or it may ask if you want to try to run the application anyway. You can try, but you'll probably need to change the application's memory allocation.

Similarly, if you can't open a document because of memory, you'll definitely have to change the application's memory allocation. Here's how do to it:

1. Quit the application in question.

2. Click on its icon to select it.

3. Select **Get Info** from the **File** menu (or press ⌘-I).

4. You'll get the application's **Get Info** window. In the bottom right corner is the Memory Requirements box.

   ☛ The *suggested size* is what the company recommends as an optimum memory setting. You can't change it.

   ☛ *Minimum size* is the least amount of memory you want the application to have. Double-click in the text box, and enter your minimum memory allocation. Generally, it can be a little less than the suggested size. If you change it and the application won't run, increase the minimum size until it will.

☞ *Preferred size* is the amount of memory you would like the application to have (in the best of all possible worlds). You change the number the same as you did the minimum size. Don't set the Preferred size to more memory than you have. Leave your System a little elbow room. Check to see how much memory your System uses with the **About This Macintosh** command in the menu.

When you change an application's memory allocation, and you reopen the application, your Mac will try to assign it the amount of memory specified in your *preferred size* setting. If that much isn't available, it will get as close as it can to that setting, without going below the *minimum size* setting.

Check Your Cache

If you frequently get **Out of Memory** messages, you can pare down your memory usage by limiting the amount of RAM set aside as a cache with the Memory Control Panel (discussed in Chapter 11).

Even a minimum cache (32K is the smallest) will help your Mac work a little more quickly, but anything over 256K runs smack into the law of diminishing returns. The memory you assign to the cache (over 256K) won't noticeably increase your Mac's effectiveness.

You can free up a little RAM by reducing the size of the cache while still improving your Mac's performance.

Virtual Memory

In a pinch, you can fake your Mac into thinking you have more RAM than you actually do, buy turning on Virtual Memory, also in the Memory Control Panel.

If your Mac can't handle Virtual Memory (Mac Classic, SE, LC, or Mac Plus), you won't even see the option in the Memory Control Panel. Don't panic; you aren't missing much.

With Virtual Memory turned on, you can select a hard drive to use as your fake RAM. You can create as much fake RAM as you have empty room on the selected hard drive.

If you have 4 megabytes of real RAM, and 8 megabytes of free hard drive space, you can fake your Mac into thinking you have 8 megabytes of virtual memory. Why only 8, why not 12? Here's why: When you turn on virtual memory, your Mac will read in as much information as your real RAM can hold (in this example 4MB). When you want it to read in more stuff (such as another application), first your Mac will write all of the information already in RAM to the space you assigned on your hard drive. Then it dumps that memory from RAM and reads in the new stuff.

When you want to read in the old stuff again, it writes the new stuff to your hard drive, then reads the old stuff back into RAM. (Are you confused yet?)

So the total amount of RAM you have (your real RAM, plus your fake) can't total more than the amount of hard drive space you have to write it all in, because it has to be able to hold all of that information. That's also why it's a bad idea to use virtual memory to create more than double your real RAM: your Mac will spend all of its time reading and writing the data that won't fit in your real RAM. If you have 4MB of RAM, don't set virtual memory to more than 8MB, even if you have the hard disk real estate to spare.

In addition to being confusing, virtual memory will also slow down your Mac incredibly (all that reading and writing of data takes time—lots and lots of time). It's okay for infrequent, emergency use, but if you find yourself using virtual memory on a regular basis, you should bite the bullet and buy some more real RAM.

Defragmenting RAM

Like your hard drive's storage memory can get fragmented, so can your RAM. Here's the scenario:

You have 6MB of RAM (6144K). Your System takes 2MB (2048K) of RAM (because of all those PostScript fonts and funky extensions you use). You open your word processor to write a blistering letter to the editor of your favorite Mac magazine. Your word processor (MondoHuge Words version 6.1.3x) uses 3MB (3072K) of memory. When you're finished, you send the letter to your laser printer, automatically opening Print Monitor, which uses another 64K of memory.

While you wait for that letter to print, you decide to play a hand of Solitaire with a shareware game that uses 384K. While you're playing Solitaire, the printer finishes, and the Print Monitor goes away.

The phone rings. Someone wants to make an appointment with you, so you call up your planning calendar, which uses 640K of memory. Your Mac protests: **Not enough memory**.

If you do the math:

System RAM:	6144K
System:	-2048
MondoHuge:	-3072
Subtotal:	1024K
Print Monitor:	- 64K
Solitaire:	- 384
Total available:	576K

There's not enough memory left to open your 640K calendar program. Ah-ha! you say. The Print Monitor shuts down, freeing up another 64K. You should be able to open the calendar. In theory, that's right, but memory isn't like a pool where all the bits of memory float around and can get sucked up by whatever application needs them. Instead it's like— oh, let's say a loaf of French bread.

Each application cuts off a chunk to make a sandwich of a particular size. Your System software cuts a chunk and keeps it. The word processor cuts a chunk and keeps it. Print Monitor cuts a small chunk, and Solitaire cuts a small chunk.

When the Print Monitor is finished, it puts its chunk of bread back on the table, right where it took it from. There's a gap between it and the chunk left at the end. Instead of having one big chunk left to make a real sandwich, there's two little chunks left with the Solitaire program's missing chunk separating them. Neither chunk is big enough to make your calendar program's sandwich. In order to unite those two chunks, you'd have to quit the Solitaire program.

When it tosses its chunk back on the table, the three chunks come back together again to form one very big chunk (if only real bread did this). Then you can open the calendar program. (All this talk of sandwiches is making me hungry. You?)

In other words, memory is only available in chunks. When you free up chunks that aren't concurrent (right beside each other), you can only open an application that's as big as the biggest chunk available. Your RAM is fragmented. In order to open a big application, you'd have to close an application between those chunks of memory.

Here's how to avoid fragmenting your memory: If you always use a certain application (or applications), open it (them) first. Then open the applications you only use briefly or occasionally. When you close them, then you'll free up bigger blocks of memory.

> ### By the Way . . .
> If you know anything about accounting, it's like the LIFO theory: *last in, first out.* When trying to free up RAM, close the applications in reverse order of how you opened them: *last opened, first closed.*

Adding More RAM

Your best defense against these and any other RAM-related difficulties is to add more RAM. You won't regret it. Here are the Top 10 Reasons to Add More RAM:

10. No matter what anyone tells you, it is the size of your RAM that counts.

9. It's cheaper than buying a new Mac.

8. You'll actually be able to use the spelling and grammar checkers that came with your word processor.

7. Buy enough RAM, and you'll be able to keep all of your applications open all of the time.

6. Applications almost never get smaller.

5. Applications almost always get bigger.

4. You'll need lots of RAM to do all the weird and wonderful things you'll be able to do with freeware and shareware extensions and control panels.

3. You'll need it if you get into PostScript fonts and Adobe Type Manager.

2. You'll need it if you want to add a CD-ROM drive, scanner, or other funky multimedia tool (such as QuickTime). Animations and other way-cool multimedia stuff (such as big sound files) take oodles of RAM.

1. Your stress level will be reduced when you eliminate most (if not all) of those annoying out of memory messages.

Peripheral Neuropathy

Sometimes, our Macs are working fine, but all of a sudden—bam! One of the bloody accessories decides its time to blow some smoke up our shorts. There are easy ways to deal with many of the common problems that don't involve sending your peripherals out for repairs.

Eek! The Mouse!

Our mice can seem to get lazy: they don't want to move the pointer as far as we moved the mouse. There are a couple reasons that may be happening.

Don't ask me why this happens, but it does: if the mouse cable gets too snarled and tangled around itself like a phone cord, it gets cranky. Unplug it from the ADB port (while your Mac is off, naturally). Hold the plug-end at eye level while the mouse-end dangles, spins, and untangles itself. It can work wonders for a sluggish mouse.

TECHNO NERD TEACHES

In order to use more than 8MB of RAM in your Mac, you have to turn on the 32-bit addressing function in the Memory Control Panel (as discussed in Chapter 11). Otherwise, any memory over 8MB will be ignored by your Mac.

However, not all Macs can use 32-bit addressing, specifically: Mac II, IIx, IIcx, and SE/30 models. These particular Mac models can't handle it. Don't despair. You can get a hold of Mode-32, by Connectix, which will allow these older Mac models to use over 8MB of memory. You can get it for free (well, almost free) from Apple, by calling 1-800-776-2333.

The other thing you can do is clean the sucker. Turn it over on its back. There's a ring around the gray ball that locks it into place. Turn it (there is an arrow to show you what direction), and remove it. Remove the ball. Clean it with some rubbing alcohol, and set it aside.

With a cotton swab (or one of those spongy, lint-free numbers), clean off the three rollers inside the mouse. They're usually a white or clear plastic. They turn black when they're dirty: the black stuff is built-up dust, oils, and other riffraff. Just clean them.

Pop the ball back in, lock on the locking ring, and try it out. It should work much better.

Keyboard Acrobatics

Unless you cover your keyboard when its not in use, it's a prime place for crud buildup. I find an occasional blast of compressed air (the kind without those nasty chlorofluorocarbons, thank you very much) right between the keys will go a long way toward keeping the keyboard crud-free.

You can also unplug it from your Mac (while it's turned off, of course), turn it upside down, and give it a good shake. Big chunks of crud may come floating out.

If the keys begin to stick, you can carefully pry out the offending key and swab around it with an alcohol swab. That should ungunk it. Another shot of compressed air might help, too.

By the Way . . .

It is possible to open some keyboards and clean inside. I don't recommend it for anyone who's the least bit nervous about it.

If your keyboard is giving you a whole lot of grief, it might be time for a new one, or a visit to your Local Authorized Apple Dealer for a checkup.

My Printer Won't Print

As always, check the obvious first: plugged in, turned on, connected properly to your Mac. If that's all okay, open the **Chooser** on the menu. Make sure that the correct driver is selected and configured for your printer.

If you fail to find the problem there (especially for laser printers), take a long look at the document you're printing: does it have four or five fonts or a complicated graphic; or is legal-sized paper selected? It may be over-whelming your laser's memory. There may be too many things for it to cope with.

Try removing the graphic or changing the fonts to simplify the document, and print it again. Or print a basic text file of "Mary Had a Little Lamb" as a test. If it prints this time, the complicated document is to blame: remember the KISS rule (**Keep It Simple, Stupid**). You either have to learn to limit your creativity to simpler documents, or you have to buy more memory for your printer.

My Printer Prints Badly

If the problem is jagged text from a laser printer (or any printer with ATM installed), you're probably using a font that isn't built into the printer and that you don't have a printer font for in your Font folder.

Using the application you used to create the document, check to see what font is selected (Caslon Bold Italic, for example), and then look in your Font folder to make sure that the printer font is installed. If it isn't, scrounge up the disk it came on, and reinstall it. (See Chapters 15 and 16 for more information on printers and fonts.)

If you don't have the correct printer font, you'll have to live with jagged text, or switch to a font you do have a printer font for.

By the Way . . .

If it's a font used in a painting or drawing program, don't hurt yourself with all this looking. It stopped being a font when you put it in a picture. Now it's a picture of a font, and will look jagged regardless.

If the problem is icky, dark streaks across your laser printout, your printer is dirty. You can clean the rollers (after you let them cool down) with an alcohol wipe or swab, or print the Cleaning Page file that came with your printer-driver disk.

Icky, light streaks, on the other hand, mean you're probably running out of toner. Remove the toner cartridge, and rock it gently (like you had to do when you installed it). This will redistribute the toner that's left so you'll get a little more mileage out of it. Meanwhile, buy another one.

A streaky printout with a dot-matrix printer means either your ribbon is shot (it probably had a hole punched in it) or your print head is dirty. Remove the ribbon, and check it for holes; replace it if necessary. If that isn't it, try cleaning the print head with an alcohol swab, and then print a test page without the ribbon. That should clear it up.

A streaky printout from an inkjet printer means the print head is probably clogged. Try cleaning it with an alcohol swab. You may also be running low on ink.

> ## By the Way . . .
> Plain isopropyl alcohol is perfect for many technoid cleaning jobs (if you haven't noticed). I always keep a bottle of it near (and a box of swabs) at all times. Call me the Heloise of Macintosh.

Print Monitor Errors

Print Monitor is good about letting you know when things go wrong. If your printer is out of paper, it will let you know. If it doesn't have enough memory, it will ask politely before it snatches some more.

Depending on how you have the Print Monitor configured, the messages will pop up on your screen and discretely signal you from the **Application** menu, or just beep. See Chapter 15 for your configuration options.

Your best bet is to do what Print Monitor tells you to do. It usually knows best.

General Scuzziness

As I said earlier in Chapter 14, dealing with the requirements of building a functional SCSI chain is a weird and wonderful experience. The closer you come to the six SCSI device limit, the weirder it becomes. These are the rules (explained in more detail in Chapter 14, but worth repeating here):

☛ You can only add six SCSI devices to your Mac.

☛ You must set each one with a different SCSI ID number (1–6).

☛ The first (physically closest to your Mac, usually an internal hard drive) and last (the one furthest away from your Mac) items in the chain must be terminated.

☛ The total amount of SCSI cable connecting your chain cannot total more than 20–24 feet in length (unless you install a signal booster before the 20-inch mark).

☛ All of these rules are subject to change at any moment.

I know folks who followed these rules to the letter, and their SCSI chain didn't work. I've known others who didn't follow any of these rules, and their SCSI chains work fine. Go figure. My best advice, when faced with a SCSI problem, is to try anything and everything possible with your combination of devices. Either that, or at the first sign of trouble, call the technical support line for your latest SCSI device, and ask them for help.

Pick a Card: When PDS and NuBus Cards Go Flaky

Short of using the hardware diagnostic tools (usually too expensive and infrequently used to be a practical purchase for most Mac users), the simplest thing to do when an expansion card starts to get flaky is this:

Pop the hood on your Mac (if you're comfortable doing it, and bearing in mind that it may void your Mac's warranty), and check to be sure that the card is still seated firmly in its slot. Sometimes, vibrations (you pounding on the keyboard, footsteps, or traffic) accumulate to shake your cards loose.

Look to see that the bottom of the card is fully in the slot (little golden prongs, like fingers, will be exposed if it isn't). If it's loose, gently but firmly push the card back in. Be careful, cards are fragile (not that fragile, but you can break them if you push too hard or in the wrong direction).

If the idea of doing that gives you the jimjams, don't do it. Call your Local Authorized Apple Service Center and let them check it out. It's not worth the gray hair.

When All Else Fails . . .

Read the manual.

The Least You Need to Know

Things go wrong for a reason. Once you've shot a few troubles on your own, you'll begin to get a handle on what kinds of things cause what kinds of problems. It only takes a little practice.

Hopefully, this appendix will act as a primer, helping you along as you become a do-it-yourself kind of Mac trouble-shooter. Whatever troubles you encounter, keep these four thoughts in mind:

☞ Don't panic.

☞ Check the obvious—more and more things will fall into the "obvious" category as your Mac skills increase.

☞ Solutions that don't work are not failures, they're the elimination of possibilities. Troubleshooting is a process of trial and error.

☞ Call for help wherever you can, whenever you can, especially if you feel intimidated by a problem.

Speak Like a Geek: The Complete Archive

ADB Stands for Apple Desktop Bus, and is pronounced by saying each letter ("A-D-B"). The Apple Desktop Bus is the standard way of connecting mice, keyboards, and a few other peripherals to the Mac. The Desktop Bus has been standard since Apple introduced the Macintosh SE. (Before the SE, they used connectors that looked like the ones that connect your telephone cord to the wall jack—in case the question ever comes up in Trivial Pursuit or something.)

backup A spare, or emergency copy of something. You can back up your hard drive, make a backup copy of a program or data disk, or even back up a single file. While everybody should back up their data on a regular basis, the only folks who actually do it are the one's who have been traumatized by the loss of an important file.

capacity How much something holds. In many Mac-related usages, it denotes how much crap you can cram onto a diskette or hard drive.

clip art A collection of graphic images meant to be copied and pasted into other documents.

compressed A file that has been mashed down with a *file compression utility* to take up less disk space. Compressed files have to be *decompressed* (unmashed) before you can work with them.

cursor   There are a variety of cursors you will use on your Mac. One is the arrow. You control cursors with your mouse and use them to point at and select items on your Mac's screen.

desktop publishing   Literally *publishing from the top of your desk*, as opposed to having to pack up all your text and woes to send them to a typesetter and printer.

dip switches   Little teeny-tiny switches (like microscopic light switches) that you have to use a pencil-point or other teeny-tiny thing to flip, because most fingers are too big to do it. They must have been invented by a dip.

disk(ette)   The first floppies were big, 8-inch monsters made of a soft plastic that sort of flopped—well, it moved anyhow. Then came those 5.25-inch disks, favored by many DOS users. When 3.5-inch disks were introduced (because they're so small and cute), they called them *diskettes*. But you can call them disks if you want.

dither(ed)   If a person is in a dither, they're all confused. When a picture is dithered, the dots that make it up are all confused. The dots get jumbled and tinkered with so the eye is faked into seeing many more shades of gray than are really there. Dithering reduces the quality of an image by making it look blurry.

document   Just about any file you produce with an application is called a document. Your Mac calls these files "documents" to easily distinguish them from applications and folders.

dots   There are a lot of words used in computing to distinguish one kind of dot from another. In a printout, dots are just called *dots* (as in *dots per inch*) when they make up letters and lines. On your monitor, each dot is called a *pixel*, borrowed from the terminology of television design. It's a contracted form of *picture element*. In drawing, and in fonts, a dot that is part of a letter or line is called a *bit* because it takes one *bit* (the smallest unit of memory) to create and place that dot somewhere.

download(-able)   If you use a font in a document that isn't already in your laser printer's memory, the printer sends a message to your Mac asking it to send that font down. The process is called a download, or downloading, and also applies to file transfers between computers. A font that can be sent to a laser printer is called a *downloadable font.*

electronic bulletin board   These are companies and just plain folks who (when you have a *modem*) let you access a wide variety of files and information on their computer(s). Electronic Bulletin Board Services (BBSs) are usually smaller, home-grown services that charge little or nothing for you to join them.

environment   In computerese, the *environment* is much like the environment of the world at large, or your "work environment." It's the atmosphere, surroundings, and even the decor of your computer. The Macintosh environment is graphical, and is sometimes called a graphical user interface or GUI, (pronounced "GOO-ey") because it uses pictures (icons) to represent functions and operations.

ergonomics   The science of designing things to accommodate the natural shape and motion of the human body. The bridge of the Starship Enterprise is very ergonomically designed. It's from the Greek word "erg" that denotes a unit of work. Or it's a cross between "ergo" and "economics" because any product that boasts "sleek, ergonomic styling" will cost 50% more than it's non-ergonomic competitor.

export   The capability of an application to save a file in a format easily imported by another application, usually with the **Save As** command.

freeware   A special kind of software that is free for your use. Its partner is *shareware.*

GUI   Graphical user interface, pronounced "GOO-ey." It's an interface (like Mac's) that uses pictures to represent functions, rather than all typed commands.

Hayes-compatible   A term that identifies a modem that conforms to the standard set of modem commands developed by the Hayes Corporation. Hayes compatibility is fairly standard among modems. I wouldn't mess with one that isn't—it will complicate your life unnecessarily.

highlight color/highlighted   Your Mac wants to show you when you've selected an item. Icons go dark. Text, including the names of files and folders, gets washed with a color.

import The capability of an application to take a document created with one application and use it itself.

insertion point (or cursor) The vertical line that moves ahead of your typing to show you where the next thing you type will land.

jaggies The rough edges of letters and drawings that would be smooth if it weren't for the limitations of computer (and monitor) technology.

launch To start an application. It can also be called *starting* or *opening* an application or program.

modem An electronic device that allows your Mac to interact with a distant computer over phone lines.

multitasking A geeky way of saying "doing more than one thing at a time." In computing, it generally means running more than one program simultaneously.

network An assortment of computers and peripherals linked together. In its simplest terms, a network can be as small as one Mac hooked up with one laser printer via AppleTalk. At its most extreme, a network can be dozens of Macs hooked up to each other, as well as to several printers.

NuBus A high-speed slot that accepts cards that work along with your Mac's central processor to supplement its functions. The information is fed along a data path called a *bus*, like your Mac's ADB (Apple Desktop *Bus*) that feeds your Mac information from your mouse and keyboard.

on-line service These are companies and just plain folks who let you (if you have a *modem*) access a wide variety of files and information on their computer(s). *On-line service* generally refers to corporate entities, and everything you do with the service costs you some money. CompuServe, America Online, and Prodigy are on-line services.

PDS Processor Direct Slot. A slot that feeds information directly into the central processor of your Mac, rather than through a bus.

parallel printers (and/or ports) Receive bits of information in sets of eight. Most IBM compatible computers come with two parallel ports, so parallel printers are popular for them.

peripheral An add-on piece of equipment, like a printer, that's not essential to simply operate the computer—like extra options on a car, you don't need air conditioning to use the car, but it makes you more comfortable. I think the term came about back in the days when you could only add things, like hard drives, as external options that sat on your desk in the periphery of your computer. Nowadays, the term is used vaguely. An internal hard drive can be considered a peripheral, as can a keyboard and a monitor, but try to run a computer without them.

point size A font term borrowed from typesetters. One point is approximately 1/72 of an inch. Point is abbreviated pt. (as in 12-pt.).

propeller-head An adjective used to describe someone fascinated by the technical minutiae of computing (from the famous propeller beanies kids used to wear). Also known as **toy-brains**.

proprietary The property of, or specific to a particular computer or service.

SCSI It stands for Small Computer Systems Interface. It's another way of connecting peripherals to computers.

scan(ned, -ner) A scanner is a piece of hardware that converts text, photographs, or line drawings into digital information that can be used on a computer. You *scan* a page. A *scanned* image is a *scan*.

screen name Literally, the name that appears on the screen whenever you "speak" to someone else on a electronic service, such as America Online or CompuServe. Try to pick one that suits your personality.

serial printers (and/or ports) Receive bits of information one at a time.

shareware Software that you pay a fee to use (but generally a small fee) directly to the program's author. Always pay your shareware fees.

stationery pad Behaves like its real-world counterpart. A document saved as stationery, when opened in an application, appears as a new, untitled document, so the original stationery pad is never altered. This format is ideal for letterheads, or form letters, or any other kind of file of information you use frequently with only minor changes.

SYSOP(s)   Short for System Operator(s), pronounced "SIS-op." That's the propeller-head in charge of an electronic bulletin board.

technical support   Typically, it means the part of a software or hardware company devoted to answering technical question about their product. I expand the definition to include anyone I can call in a pinch—user-group members, Mac-friends, and so on—especially because many companies have added 900-numbers, pay-per-minute technical support lines.

third-party   Not the party you go to after the first two. Third party refers to a company that isn't *you* and isn't Apple. Most often, they're referred to as *third-party developers*.

32-bit Addressing   The option available on most Macs, allowing them to access and use more than 10 megabytes of RAM. You turn it on and off (if your Mac can handle it) through the Memory control panel.

version number   The (re)incarnation of the software. Version 1.0 is its debut. Version 1.2 will fix everything that should have been fixed before 1.0 was released. Version 2.0 will be its next incarnation. Version 2.1 will fix the new incarnation, and so on. When the first number changes (1.0 to 2.0), it's called a *version upgrade*, a major overhaul. 2.0 to 2.1 means its still essentially the same program, but now it works. Versions like 2.1 are sometimes called *bug fixes*.

Index

Q

GO AHEAD. PLUG YOURSELF INTO PRENTICE HALL COMPUTER PUBLISHING.

Introducing the PHCP Forum on CompuServe®

Yes, it's true. Now, you can have CompuServe access to the same professional, friendly folks who have made computers easier for years. On the PHCP Forum, you'll find additional information on the topics covered by every PHCP imprint—including Que, Sams Publishing, New Riders Publishing, Alpha Books, Brady Books, Hayden Books, and Adobe Press. In addition, you'll be able to receive technical support and disk updates for the software produced by Que Software and Paramount Interactive, a division of the Paramount Technology Group. It's a great way to supplement the best information in the business.

WHAT CAN YOU DO ON THE PHCP FORUM?

Play an important role in the publishing process—and make our books better while you make your work easier:

- Leave messages and ask questions about PHCP books and software—you're guaranteed a response within 24 hours
- Download helpful tips and software to help you get the most out of your computer
- Contact authors of your favorite PHCP books through electronic mail
- Present your own book ideas
- Keep up to date on all the latest books available from each of PHCP's exciting imprints

JOIN NOW AND GET A FREE COMPUSERVE STARTER KIT!

To receive your free CompuServe Introductory Membership, call toll-free, **1-800-848-8199** and ask for representative **#K597**. The Starter Kit Includes:

- Personal ID number and password
- $15 credit on the system
- Subscription to CompuServe Magazine

HERE'S HOW TO PLUG INTO PHCP:

Once on the CompuServe System, type any of these phrases to access the PHCP Forum:

GO PHCP   **GO BRADY**
GO QUEBOOKS   **GO HAYDEN**
GO SAMS   **GO QUESOFT**
GO NEWRIDERS   **GO PARAMOUNTINTER**
GO ALPHA

Once you're on the CompuServe Information Service, be sure to take advantage of all of CompuServe's resources. CompuServe is home to more than 1,700 products and services—plus it has over 1.5 million members worldwide. You'll find valuable online reference materials, travel and investor services, electronic mail, weather updates, leisure-time games and hassle-free shopping (no jam-packed parking lots or crowded stores).

Seek out the hundreds of other forums that populate CompuServe. Covering diverse topics such as pet care, rock music, cooking, and political issues, you're sure to find others with the same concerns as you—and expand your knowledge at the same time.